The Classic Racehorse

The
Classic Racehorse

Peter Willett

STANLEY PAUL
London Melbourne Auckland Johannesburg

Stanley Paul & Co. Ltd

An imprint of Century Hutchinson Ltd

62–65 Chandos Place, London WC2N 4NW

Century Hutchinson Australia (Pty) Ltd
89–91 Albion Street, Surry Hills, NSW 2010

Century Hutchinson New Zealand Limited
PO Box 40–086, Glenfield, Auckland 10

Century Hutchinson South Africa (Pty) Ltd
PO Box 337, Bergvlei 2012, South Africa

First published 1981
Reprinted 1982
Revised edition 1989
© Peter Willett 1981, 1989

Phototypeset in Linotron Bembo by Input Typesetting Ltd, London
Printed and bound in Great Britain by
Mackay's of Chatham PLC, Chatham, Kent

British Library Cataloguing in Publication Data
Willett, Peter
The classic racehorse
1. Race horses
I. Title
798.4'3 SF337

ISBN 0 09 146110 3

(m) 636. 102 132 w

Contents

Illustrations

Acknowledgements

Copyright photographs are acknowledged as follows: R. Anscomb, P. Bertrand Chantilly, Rex Coleman, Colour Labs International Ltd, Jose Maria Martinena, Werner Menzendorf, New York Racing Association Inc., Photoline Recoupe, Press Association Ltd, W. W. Rouch & Co., Sceptre.

Preface

'The Classic Racehorse' is a phrase lacking official definition. 'Classic' is not found in the list of Definitions in the British Rules of Racing or in the corresponding French rules, the Code des Courses. The omission is curious, because the Rules of Racing do contain the words 'Horse' – which is stated to include 'mare, gelding, colt and filly' and for the purpose of Rule 35 (concerning compulsory vaccination) includes a 'pony, mule, ass or hinny' – and 'Pattern Races' – though confining description of that category of important races somewhat unhelpfully to those which, in any particular year, appear in the Pattern Race Book published by the Authority of the Jockey Club. If we have 'Pattern Races' why do we not have the 'Classic Races', a term which entered the phraseology of the Turf in the 1880s?

This official reticence is all the harder to understand because until 1980 the Pattern Race Book included a section giving advanced notice of the dates and conditions of 'The Classic Races in England, Ireland and France' in 1981. The following year, however, this anomaly was removed by a change of term to 'Early Closing Races'. These Classic races, in the case of England, were the 1000 Guineas and the Oaks for three-year-old fillies and the 2000 Guineas, the Derby and the St Leger for three-year-old colts and fillies. So knowledge of the nature of a Classic race must be arrived at by inference and without the aid of official explanation. This might be regarded as a typical case of British pragmatism were it not for the fact that the Pattern Race Book was published jointly by the racing authorities of Great Britain and France and therefore the anomaly had the implied sanction of the logical French.

Dictionary definitions of 'classic' as 'of the highest class or rank' and 'famous through being long established' certainly help to indicate the true significance of Classic races. It is reasonable to deduce that they are races of long standing which habitually attract the best horses and are regarded as the criteria of excellence. The St Leger

11

was first run in 1776, the Oaks in 1779, the Derby in 1780, the 2000 Guineas in 1809 and the 1000 Guineas in 1814. Most of the greatest horses in British Turf history are enrolled among the winners of those races. Run an eye down the records and glorious names like Gladiateur, Ormonde, Hyperion, Tudor Minstrel, Nijinsky, Brigadier Gerard, Mill Reef, Sceptre, Pretty Polly, Petite Etoile, Dancing Brave and Reference Point leap from the page.

The English Classic races were in being before commercial interests had made a real impact on the Turf, before there was any notion of a co-ordinated programme of racing and before there was an explicit connection between individual races and the selection of stallions and mares for breeding. They are a vital part of English racing tradition, but they took root and flourished naturally, not as a result of deliberate policy, and for that reason the purposes they serve have not been given formal expression. The rationale of Classic races must be sought in countries where they have been imposed on a traditional programme: for instance in New Zealand, where long distances and poor communications between the main population centres in the early days of racing led to the proliferation of regional races with Classic titles. The rationalization scheme of 1973 created a single national series of New Zealand Classic races, heavily subsidized from the central prize money fund, with the declared purpose of identifying the best three-year-olds of each generation for the benefit of New Zealand breeders and of foreign buyers of New Zealand bloodstock.

Classic racehorses, it is fair to conclude, are those horses which not only compete, but compete with distinction, in Classic races, and embrace also those horses that show such excellent form in other important races as to warrant their assimilation with Classic horses. They are an elite among the hundreds of thousands of horses that race each year throughout the world, most of whom spring from the breed of the British thoroughbred, or are assimilated with that breed. The thoroughbred was a creature of British breeders, and is one of Britain's most remarkable gifts to the world. Other countries have developed a taste for horse racing and have flattered this British creature in the sincerest way by importing British stock and basing their own breeds of racehorse on the British model.

Nevertheless, it would be wrong to suggest that the breeding of thoroughbreds outside the British Isles has been purely imitative. Perhaps the most striking lesson to be learned from a study of the thoroughbred in a world-wide context is that many countries have contributed in smaller or greater degree to the later stages of its evolution. The differences in the types of horses bred in one country and another have resulted less from climate and environment than from contrasts in their racing programmes. Often the contrasts are epitomized in their Classic series.

For the Classic series developed in various countries have not been identical. In France, for example, no fewer than fifteen races were designated 'classiques' before the introduction of the International Pattern Race system in 1971. Those races were the Prix Robert Papin, the Prix Morny, the Prix de la Salamandre and the Grand Criterium for two-year-olds; the French 1000 Guineas, the Prix Saint Alary, the French Oaks and the Prix Vermeille for three-year-old fillies; the French 2000 Guineas, the Prix Lupin, the French Derby, the Grand Prix de Paris and the French St Leger for three-year-old colts; and the Grand Prix de Saint Cloud and the Prix de l'Arc de Triomphe for three-year-olds and upwards.

Thus the French is broader than the English concept, and 'classique' cannot be equated exactly with 'classic'. There are nuances in other important racing countries. On the other hand it is certain that the term 'classic' strikes a chord of meaning which is recognized universally. The emphasis everywhere is on excellence over middle distances at three years of age. The description of 1¼ (2000 metres) to 1½ miles (2400 metres) as the 'pure' Classic distance has wide current usage. The horse that shone solely as a two-year-old, or as a sprinter, or as a long distance performer at three years old and upwards, would nowhere be accepted as a 'Classic Racehorse'.

A definition of 'The Classic Racehorse' which was valid for many years was that used to describe the ideal racehorse in the report of the Duke of Norfolk's Committee on the Pattern of Racing in August 1965: 'The ideal racehorse has more speed than the best specialist sprinter, although he may never in fact race over a shorter distance than 7 furlongs [1400 metres], and is supreme over distances from a mile [1600 metres] to 1¾ miles [2800 metres] at three years old and upwards.'

The intention in this book has been to trace the development of the thoroughbred, first in Britain and later in other countries where racing and breeding have thrived, and to investigate the contribution that each of those countries has made to the concept of 'The Classic Racehorse' in the late twentieth century. However, the practically universal tendency to devalue stamina which gathered momentum in the last quarter of the century would require a change of the upper distance limit to 1½ miles (2400 metres) for the definition to retain its validity.

1

The Early Days of Racing and the Thoroughbred in Britain

Anyone with even the most superficial knowledge of breeds of horses in the second half of the twentieth century would correctly identify the term 'thoroughbred' with the kind of horse used for racing in the nearly fifty countries in which the sport is practised, and in most of which it flourishes. He would recognize at once, even if he were unable to describe, its salient characteristics: its graceful movements, its singular combination of strength and beauty, its concave profile, broad forehead and head tapering to the nose, its slender arched neck, sloping shoulders, short back and high croup, its delicately formed but powerful limbs – above all, its disdainful air of the aristocrat.

He would recognize these characteristics, but it is very unlikely that he, as the man-in-the-street among horse-lovers or followers of horse racing, would be able to define the term 'thoroughbred' or give an account of the extraordinarily concentrated evolution of the breed of the racehorse from parent stock existing in England between two and three centuries ago. Nor could he be blamed for his ignorance, since no official definition of the term had ever been made until 1970, when the Preface to Volume 36 of the *General Stud Book* (the genealogical records of racehorses in England and Ireland) stated that any horse claiming admission should be able to be traced at all points of its pedigree to strains already appearing in earlier volumes, these strains to be designated 'thoroughbred', or else fulfil certain other conditions which justified its assimilation with thoroughbreds. On the other hand the term had belonged to the phraseology of the Turf for at least 200 years before the English authorities gave it precise definition, and this looseness helped to make it contentious and to charge it, at times, with chauvinistic overtones. The racehorse, the so-called 'thoroughbred', evolved in England long before other countries conceived a taste for racing and began to develop breeds of their own based on the English model and on imported English stock. In some parts of the world, notably the North American and Australian continents, these imported horses were mingled with strains already in the country and claimed to be thoroughbred, but of unauthenticated origin. Were the products of these unions to be called 'thoroughbred', or 'American' or 'Australian thoroughbred', and were they to be accepted as equivalent to the genuine English article or condemned to second-class status? These questions gave rise to controversies and crises which will be examined in a later part of the book.

One of the earliest attempts to define the word 'thoroughbred' was made by William Osmer, veterinary surgeon and shoeing smith of Blenheim Street in London, who stated in his *Treatise on the Horse* as early as 1761: 'Let us suppose a case: here are two mares, both originally bred from Arabian horses, and mares, or the descendants of such, which I suppose is all that is to be understood by the term "thoroughbred".' But Osmer's assumption that the English thoroughbred horse was derived exclusively from Arabian sources was incorrect. The thoroughbred is a hybrid in the sense that it is an animal derived from genetically diverse stock, and conforms to Mendelian laws in respect of the inheritance of characters such as colour; and the original stock was certainly drawn from sources wider and more differentiated than the pure-bred horses of the desert. However, centuries of breeding based on selection for racing ability have produced a high degree of genetic uniformity for the characters affecting performance in the modern racehorse, as compared with neutral factors like colour.

The way in which the degree of genetic uniformity of the modern thoroughbred has been achieved can be inferred from analysis of the pedigree of Bahram, winner of the English Triple Crown (2000 Guineas, Derby and St Leger) in 1935. In her monumental *Thoroughbred Racing Stock* Lady Wentworth calculated that the pedigree of Bahram contained 222,281 crosses of the Unknown Arabian (sire of Old Bald Peg), 123,037 of Darcy's White Arabian, 179,105 of Darcy's Chesnut Arabian, 40,305 of the Lister Turk, 66,893 of the Helmsley Turk, 29,232 of the Godolphin Arabian, 44,079 of the Darley Arabian, 64,032 of the Byerley Turk, 112,667 of the Leedes Arabian; and if, as Lady Wentworth believed, the Morocco Barb and the Helmsley Turk were the same horse, it contained 289,174 crosses of the Morocco Barb. These figures suggest the extraordinarily potent influence of a small number of stallions of Eastern origin in founding and consolidating the breed of the 'thoroughbred'. A study of inbreeding and infertility in thoroughbred horses by Professors G. A. T. Mahon and E. P. Cunningham of the Dublin Agricultural Institute and published in a 'Report on Genetic Studies in Horses' in 1978 confirmed this idea, though placing the principal founder stallions in a different order of precedence. Mahon and Cunningham found that nearly 81 per cent of all the genes in the modern thoroughbred derive from only thirty-one original ancestors. But the most important gene contributions were those of the Godolphin Arabian (14.9 per cent), the Darley Arabian (7.5 per cent), the Curwen Bay Barb (5.6 per cent) and the Byerley Turk (4.8 per cent). The Godolphin Arabian, the Darley Arabian and the Byerley Turk are the three Eastern horses from whom all modern thoroughbreds descend in the male line, and the research of Mahon and Cunningham has supplied telling evidence of the magnitude of their influence on the breed. Nevertheless, the presence of the Curwen Bay Barb, whose male line did not persist, in the leading four indicates the error of overstressing direct lines of descent simply because they conform with the dynastic thinking of most human societies.

The result of this concentration is that the thoroughbred has a genetic uniformity which makes him a dominant influence when mated to representatives of other breeds. For all the variations of appearance in modern thoroughbreds, they are all unmistakably members of the same breed; and although there appear to be differences in class between the racing performances of the best and the worst thoroughbreds, those performances actually cover a narrow range in terms of average speed for distance run.

The formative period of the thoroughbred was in England during the century that followed the Stuart Restoration in 1660. The foundation stock were few, and the entire thoroughbred population still numbered no more than a few thousands in the middle of the nineteenth century. The history of the thoroughbred in the last 100 years has been one of astonishingly rapid expansion both in overall numbers and in geographical spread. A population explosion occurred in the second half of the nineteenth century when the breeding industries of England and Ireland, the United States, France and Australia, with others toiling enthusiastically in their wake, began to respond to the mass appeal of horse racing. A series of further explosions, interspersed with periods of relative quiescence and even recession corresponding to the ebb and flow of world economic conditions, have raised the thoroughbred population to levels which would have been inconceivable to the early breeders.

The explosions after the Second World War merged into a process of practically continuous combustion. The popularity of racing as a spectator sport, as a gambling medium, and as a source of profit, recreation and social advancement for the owners of thoroughbreds, has increased at such a rate in both the traditional horse-racing countries and in countries, like Japan, which were relative new-comers to the sport, that breeders have had a powerful incentive to increase production progressively. The demand for more horses on a world-wide scale has been insistent.

For a long time attempts to calculate thoroughbred population were largely a guessing game, and little serious work was done in the field of census. Franco Varola's figure of 223,000 for world thoroughbred population was probably a substantial underestimate at the time of its publication in the French periodical *Courses et Elevage* in March–April 1962, and was certainly left far behind by the continuous fast growth of subsequent years. It was not until Eduardo Blousson, the President of the Consejo Tecnico Ejecutivo de la Organizacion Sud Americana de Fomento del Pura Sangre de Carrera, based in Buenos Aires, began to compile and collate stat-istics of foalings from official sources in all the principal thorough-bred-producing countries in the mid–1970s that an accurate idea of the size and growth of thoroughbred population could be formed. Blousson's research showed that annual thoroughbred births in the twenty countries with more than 500 births each rose from 86,115 in 1975 to 131,596 in 1987, an increase of 53 per cent in thirteen years. However, the overall growth rate concealed some significant differences between countries. The United States and Australia out-stripped all the others in both total thoroughbred population and growth rates. The United States led the way with an increase from 25,929 to 49,894 foals, or 92.4 per cent, while Australia's annual foalings more than doubled from 10,628 to 21,443 in the period under review. New Zealand foalings also rose steeply from 3835 to 6982, an increase of 82 per cent. On the other hand foalings in some other thoroughbred-producing countries, including Great Britain and France, actually fell during the same thirteen years.

The figures for 1987 foalings indicate a thoroughbred population in the twenty countries, inclusive of yearlings, horses in training, broodmares and stallions in addition to foals, of about 600,000. Even this total takes no account of some thirty other countries in which thoroughbreds are bred, or of racehorses in retirement or of thoroughbreds used for purposes outside racing and breeding such as hunting, riding, eventing and other sporting activities.

So rapid an increase of population could hardly be achieved without some sacrifice of quality. The specialized racing ability of the thoroughbred was developed by careful selection of both sires and dams, and from the earliest days priority was given in breeding to those individuals of both sexes who had shown the most considerable aptitude on the racecourse. It was possible to apply far stricter standards of selection to stallions than to mares, because a mare produces only one foal a year – twins seldom survive to lead useful lives among thoroughbreds – but a stallion can cover many mares in a season with forty or fifty as the normal complement for a top-class stallion in modern practice. A mare averages about seven live foals in her stud career, and these are divided almost exactly between the two sexes. Thus it is necessary to retain one in every three and a half filly foals for eventual stud purposes, a proportion which restricts severely the scope for selection, simply in order to maintain the thoroughbred population, let alone increase it. An inevitable consequence of rapid population growth is that many mares that are unsound or lack racing ability, and ought to be culled, have to be retained for breeding.

The ill-effects of lax standards of selection have been reduced in some countries with high population growth rates, in particular the United States, by large scale importation of high-class stallions and mares. American wealth and the prosperity of the American racing and breeding industry has enabled American breeders to buy the best bloodstock wherever it is available in Europe, the Antipodes, South America and South Africa. This aggressive buying tended to deprive some of the exporting countries – particularly England, Ireland, France and Italy – of stock required to raise or maintain their own quality of production, but in these cases the effects were mitigated by the fact that they were not raising output at such a rapid rate as American breeders; moreover the English had been exporting steadily for a century and a half and had always managed to generate sufficient resources to uphold the reputation of the British thoroughbred. A further mitigating factor was that some of the principal stud owners in all countries practised much more stringent and discriminating methods than the majority of breeders who were anxious only to cash in on a rising market.

The result of these forces at work in the field of the thoroughbred was an inevitable decline in average standards of performance and soundness, compensated to some extent by maintenance of standards and even progress in the relatively small sector represented by breeders of wealth and discerning judgement. One of the significant developments of the second half of the twentieth century was the creation of an equine elite at one end and a much larger number of mediocrities and semi-cripples at the opposite end of the scale. The strength of the breeding industries of England, Ireland, France and New Zealand lay in the success in preserving their thoroughbred middle-classes which embodied the essential virtues of soundness, constitution and reasonable racing merit.

What were the ingredients of this breed that was to become famous all over the world as the British Thoroughbred and was to become so numerous in all the five continents in the twentieth century? And in what proportions were those ingredients mixed? These are questions to which no reliable or wholly satisfactory answer can be given. The origins of the thoroughbred are lost in the mists of antiquity, in times when authentic stud records were not kept and there was no adequate documentation, either public or private, of the breeds of horses in England.

Attempts to unravel the tangled skein of evidence have been complicated by the peculiar methods of description used by the horse owners of the seventeenth and eighteenth centuries, the formative period of the thoroughbred. The practice was to call a horse after his owner of the time, and if a horse changed hands three times, then he is liable to be found in the contemporary records under three names. An equally confusing habit was to label horses of Eastern origin 'Arabians', 'Turks' and 'Barbs' indiscriminately and irrespective of their real breeding and country of origin; and the possibilities of false identity were aggravated by the even looser and more reprehensible practice of describing animals, and particularly mares, as Arabians, Turks or Barbs merely because their sires were such. Thus Honywood's Arabian was identical with Sir J. Williams's

Turk and Sir C. Turner's White Turk; Sir Charles Sedley's Arabian was the same horse as the Compton Barb; and many mares described as Barbs or Arabians in early pedigrees were by Eastern stallions but sprang from unknown female strains.

Riding boldly over the difficulties, many historians of the Turf have shown an unjustifiable readiness to identify the principal formative influences in the thoroughbred. They have divided themselves into two schools – on the one hand those who have made it a matter of patriotic principle to stress the Englishness of the thoroughbred, and on the other hand those who have attributed the qualities of the thoroughbred almost exclusively to Eastern origins. The advocates of both points of view have pursued their claims with all the classical aids of special pleading, selecting those pieces of evidence that suit them and distorting or ignoring the rest.

Horse racing in England has an extremely long history, and races are believed to have been held at York during the Roman occupation. A remarkable feature of the whole history of racing and the thoroughbred has been the continuous intimate relationship of the north of England and even Scotland with the mainstream of events, and the fast ponies, or Galloways, bred in the northern regions seem to have provided the basic racing stock in the earliest times and through the Middle Ages. During the Middle Ages, and later, under the Tudors, there were frequent importations of animals bearing some signs of Eastern influence, though these horses derived mainly from Italy or Spain and represented crosses of Arabian and Barb with European strains. It is impossible to tell how much these imported horses influenced the horses used for racing up to the end of the sixteenth century, but it is probable that their influence was felt more in the south of England than in the traditional Galloway regions of the north. Races for Galloways, defined as animals of not more than 13 h.h. (1.32 metres), were still being run in the north at the end of the eighteenth century.

James I, the first of the Stuart kings of England, had no love of racing, but enjoyed hunting as his favourite pastime and maintained a hunting lodge at Newmarket, thus establishing a royal connection with the little Suffolk town and its heath which was to have the utmost significance for the evolution of racing and the thoroughbred in the future. In 1617, James bought a so-called Arabian from a Nottinghamshire breeder called Markham, though the horse may have been merely a son of an imported Arabian. In any case the

Markham Arabian was useless for racing and Gervase Markham, the breeder's son, expressed a poor opinion of the speed of Eastern horses generally in his prolific writing on the subject. 'For swiftness', wrote Markham, 'what nation hath brought forth that horse which hath exceeded the English? When the best Barbaries that ever were in their prime, I saw them overunne by a black Hobbie at Salisbury; yet that hobbie was more overunne by a horse called Valentine, which Valentine, neither in hunting or running was ever equalled, yet was a plainbred English horse, both by sire and dam.' The Hobbies were the racing or running horses bred in Ireland and corresponding to the Galloways. Markham also explained what he meant by the best type of English horse when he wrote: 'Him I mean that is bred under a good clime, on firm ground, in a pure temperature, is of tall stature and large proportions; his head, though not so fine as either the Barbarie's or the Turk's, yet is lean, long, and well fashioned; his crest is hie, only subject to thickness if he be stoned, but if he be gelded then it is firm and strong; his chyne is straight and broad; and all his limbs large, leane, flat, and excellently pointed. For their endurance I have seen them suffer and execute as much and more than ever I noted of any foraine creation.'

Nevertheless, Markham believed that Arabians made the best stallions, and that if Arabians were not available then Barbs – horses from the parts of North Africa now comprising Libya, Tunisia, Algeria and Morocco – were the next best.

The royal studs were the largest and best stocked in England under the Tudors and the Stuarts up to the time of the Civil War. They were situated at Hampton Court, Malmesbury, Eltham in Kent and Tutbury in Staffordshire, and were the subject of a report by the Neapolitan horsemaster Prospero d'Osma, which was commissioned by the Queen during the reign of Elizabeth I. The studs were dispersed by Cromwell after Charles I had been beheaded in 1649, but the inventory of 'Tutbury Race' has survived and shows that the stud contained 140 head including thirty-eight mares. Among the mares were two called Black Morocco, one called Young Morocco and one called Morocco, names which clearly indicated their origin. There was also a mare called The Spaniard, and there were six mares whose descriptions included the word Newcastle, suggesting that they had been obtained from or were by stallions owned by the Duke of Newcastle, one of the greatest stud owners of the time. The Newcastle mares were probably of substantially foreign extraction, as the Duke was a firm believer in the virtues of Spanish and Barb horses, saying that 'Spanish horses were like princes, and barbs like gentlemen in their kind.'

At the Restoration, the Tutbury Stud was found to have fallen into such a state of dilapidation that no attempt was made to resuscitate it, and the tracks of the dispersed stock had been covered so thoroughly that they could not be traced. No doubt many of the mares had passed into the hands of other leading breeders, and their mixed blood may be taken as typical of the strains from which the Restoration breeders set about the task of developing the racehorses for which there was a swiftly growing demand. This demand owed a great deal to the King's passion for racing. Charles II converted Newmarket, which had been a mere hunting lodge for the first of the Stuarts, into a genuine centre of the Turf with all the prestige that royal patronage, royal arbitration in racing disputes and the presence of the Court for long periods of the year were able to confer. Apart from providing an ideal natural racecourse, Newmarket had the incomparable advantage of a situation equally accessible from London and the traditional horse-breeding areas of Yorkshire. Charles II gave racing the impetus that launched the thoroughbred, and after his death his trainer-manager, the shrewd if disreputable Tregonwell Frampton, held the same post under William III, Queen Anne and the first two Georges and used his enormous experience and organizing ability to confirm the position of Newmarket as the focal point of competition between north and south. In the middle of the eighteenth century, the Jockey Club, an association of the principal owners and breeders, stepped into the breach that had followed the death of Frampton, set up its headquarters at Newmarket and ultimately fashioned the English Turf institutions that were to become the model for all other countries in which the sport of horse racing took root. Although race meetings were held all over the country, Newmarket was the sport's focal point and provided the tests by which the success of breeders was judged.

Resigning himself to the loss of the principal royal stud and its stock, Charles II commissioned James D'Arcy, the Master of the Royal Stud, to supply him with 'twelve extra-ordinary good colts' each year for a fee of £800 from his stud at Sedbury in the Bedale region of Yorkshire. Charles II himself bred few racehorses, and the researches of C. M. Prior have shown that the *General Stud Book* version of the origin of the so-called 'Royal Mares' found in many of the early pedigrees, that they were mares imported at the King's order by the Master of the Horse, was completely false. The Royal Mares were more likely to have been some of the mares used by D'Arcy to supply the King's needs, and some were descendants of the mare Grey Royal who had been in the possession of D'Arcy's grandfather as early as 1620.

J. B. Robertson, one of the most painstaking and reliable historians of the thoroughbred, concluded that few mares of Eastern or Barb origin were imported in the 100 years that followed the Restoration, and that the sources of Eastern influence during that period were mainly stallions. The *General Stud Book* listed 103 stallions that were imported or of entirely foreign pedigree. Other records, such as William Pick's *Turf Register*, suggested that about 160 stallions altogether may have been imported, though an exact count is not possible owing to the contemporary practice of naming horses after their owners. About 50 per cent of the stallions seem to have been Arabians, and 25 per cent each Turks and Barbs.

The most famous of those stallions were the Darley Arabian, the Godolphin Arabian and the Byerley Turk. All modern thoroughbreds descend from them in the male line though, as already explained, they may not have played a more vital part in the evolution of the thoroughbred than some other imported stallions whose male lines died out. The grey colour of about 3 per cent of modern thoroughbreds is traceable to two of the other early imported stallions, the Brownlow Turk and Alcock's Arabian; and what is true of a single, easily discernible character like colour may be equally true of other characters that are less apparent but more closely related to racing ability.

The earliest of the three male line progenitors of the thoroughbred was the Byerley Turk. Unlike the others, he was a spoil of war, for he was captured by Captain (later Colonel) Byerley when Buda was taken from the Turks in 1686–87. Byerley afterwards rode his Turk at the Battle of the Boyne before sending the horse to stud first at Middridge Grange in County Durham and later at Goldsborough Hall near York. According to the *General Stud Book* he covered few well-bred mares, but sired in Jigg a horse good enough to give a firm foundation to a male line which can be traced down to such powerful twentieth-century dynasties as those of The Tetrarch and Tourbillon.

The Godolphin Arabian, the last of the three, was a brown horse foaled in 1724 and remarkable for his longevity besides other qualities, for he was twenty-nine when he died at Lord Godolphin's Cambridgeshire seat, Gogmagog. A host of legends surround the career of this wonderful horse. Among the more far-fetched were that he was discovered in Paris drawing a water-cart, and that he was employed as a teaser to Hobgoblin at Gogmagog until he fought Hobgoblin for the favours of Roxana, and having won the battle, covered the mare. The Godolphin Arabian and Roxana union produced two good horses, Lath and Cade, and Cade continued the male line which has been represented by Hurry On, Precipitation and Santa Claus in England, and has exerted a potent influence in New Zealand in the twentieth century.

A less romantic but possibly more truthful account of the Godolphin Arabian is that he was derived from the Jilfan strain of the Yemen and was exported via Syria to the stud of the Bey of Tunis. This account states that he was one of four Arabian horses presented by the Bey to the King of France. Three were turned out in the forests of Brittany for the purpose of improving the wild herds that roamed there, and the fourth was sold to Edward Coke, of Longford Hall, Derbyshire. This horse was later acquired by Lord Godolphin and became known as the Godolphin Arabian.

The Darley Arabian intervened between the Byerley Turk and the Godolphin. He was foaled in 1700 and had reached the great age of thirty when he died at the Darley family seat Aldby, in East Yorkshire. A bay with a white blaze and three white feet, he was a horse of exquisite beauty and had much more surely authenticated antecedents than the other two members of the famous trio. The finest Arabians were supposed to come from Aleppo, but only Lord Oxford's Dun Arabian and the Bloody-shouldered Arabian beside the Darley Arabian are known to have been shipped from that Syrian port. Thomas Darley, described as an agent in merchandise abroad and the British Consul in Aleppo, sent the horse home as a four-year-old, explaining in a letter to his father Richard that he was 'of the most esteemed race among the Arabs both by sire and dam, and the name of the race is called Manicha.' The Darley Arabian covered few mares except those belonging to the Darley family, but his male line, by a continuous process of ramification, has become far the most numerous and, of the important male lines of the present time, the Ribot, the Crepello, the Star Kingdom, the Tudor Minstrel, the

Northern Dancer, the Nasrullah, the Royal Charger and the Raise A Native all spring from it.

Neither the Byerley Turk, the Darley Arabian nor the Godolphin Arabian ran in a race. Indeed very few of the imported Eastern horses, as far as can be ascertained from the early records, showed any racing ability, and this raises the question why so many were imported, and why they were used almost exclusively by the most discriminating breeders during the period when the foundations of the thoroughbred were being laid. The answer must surely be that English stock had been reduced to a bastard state by repeated mixtures of foreign blood, mostly representing the cross-breeds of Spain and Italy, and that Arabians and Barbs, the products of centuries of selective breeding, alone possessed the quality and the ability to breed true to type that were essential weapons in the armoury of breeders with carefully defined objectives. It was not the speed of Arabians and Barbs, for that was negligible, but their prepotency that the English breeders of the seventeenth and eighteenth centuries were trying to introduce in their stock.

Yet surprisingly enough the first truly great racehorse, Flying Childers, traced back to exclusively Eastern sources if the *General Stud Book* account of his pedigree is to be accepted as genuine. Flying Childers, bred by Mr Leonard Childers of Doncaster in 1714 but owned by the Duke of Devonshire throughout his racing and stud careers, was described as a 'surprising' horse and as 'the fleetest horse that ever ran at Newmarket, or, as generally believed, was ever bred in the world'. Few of his performances were recorded, though it is known that he beat the Duke of Bolton's Speedwell in a match over 4 miles (6400 metres) in April 1721, and the Earl of Drogheda's Chaunter in a match over 6 miles (9600 metres) in October of the following year. Flying Childers was said to have achieved some phenomenal times, but methods of timing were so primitive in the early part of the eighteenth century that no reliance can be placed on them. A better idea of his greatness is conveyed by his performance against Fox, one of the leading horses of the time, in a trial in May 1722. Fox won three King's Plates, the Ladies Plate at York and several matches including one for 2000 guineas against Lord Hillsborough's Witty gelding, yet Flying Childers gave him 1 st (6.35 kilos) and beat him by nearly 2 furlongs (400 metres) over an unspecified distance.

Flying Childers was a bay horse like his sire the Darley Arabian, and had four white feet and a splash of white on his nose. His dam Betty Leedes in the *General Stud Book* version of her pedigree was by Old Careless (by Spanker out of a Barb mare), out of Cream Cheeks by the Leedes Arabian, out of a mare by Spanker, out of the Old Morocco mare, who was Spanker's own dam. The Old Morocco mare was also known as Old Peg, and was by Lord Fairfax's Morocco Barb out of Old Bald Peg, by an Arabian out of a Barb mare. Spanker himself was by the Darcy Yellow Turk. Thus the pedigree of Flying Childers, if the *General Stud Book* is to be believed, involved very close inbreeding to Spanker, and even closer inbreeding to Spanker's dam, besides the use of stock of exclusively Eastern origin.

It is only fair to mention that C. M. Prior repudiated the *General Stud Book* version of this great horse's pedigree in his book *The Royal Studs of the Sixteenth and Seventeenth Centuries* (1935). He could not bring himself to believe that a breeder of the repute of Mr Edward Leedes, who was responsible for the production of Cream Cheeks and Betty Leedes, would have countenanced such incestuous breeding in his stud. Moreover he discovered in the stud book of Mr Cuthbert Routh, another leading breeder of the time, a different version which gave the great granddam of Flying Childers as 'a famous roan mare of Sir Marmaduke Wyvill's'. Unfortunately no pedigree of the Wyvill roan mare was appended, so it is impossible to pronounce upon the validity of the objection.

Nor does the argument that Mr Leedes would not have considered such close inbreeding as is found in the pedigrees of Betty Leedes and Cream Cheeks carry any weight. The early thoroughbred breeders had no inhibitions about inbreeding as they attempted to stamp the desired characters in their stock, and in this respect were setting an example which was followed enthusiastically by men like Robert Bakewell of Dishley who achieved revolutionary improvements in the breeds of cattle and sheep during the eighteenth century.

In the first edition of Volume I of the *General Stud Book* the granddam of Fying Childers was unnamed, and in later editions only was she called Cream Cheeks. Evidently further and corroboratory evidence had come to light, and the *Stud Book* editors noted of the pedigree of the Old Morocco mare (sometimes called Old Peg) and her breeding record that their own version agreed with details written 'on the fly-leaf of Mr Butler's copy of Mr Fairfax's "Compleat Sportsman".' Of the mating of the Old Morocco mare with her son

Spanker, J. B. Robertson stated flatly: 'I have not the slightest hesitation in accepting the Stud Book and many old pedigree versions of the alliance as correct . . .' However, Robertson·gave no explanation of this blunt assertion, and in the absence of proof the true pedigree of Flying Childers must remain a mystery.

Spanker was the best horse to run at Newmarket during the reign of Charles II and, if the *Stud Book* version of the pedigree of Betty Leedes is accepted as authentic, then Leedes must be given credit for adopting the principle of inbreeding to racing merit when he used him so intensively in his breeding plans. The mating of Betty Leedes with the imported representative of the purest Arabian strains provided a means of stamping type and quality with momentous consequences for the breed of the racehorse. The career of Flying Childers was one of the most significant milestones on the road of thoroughbred progress.

2

The Evolution of the Thoroughbred in the Eighteenth and Nineteenth Centuries

Flying Childers was sent to the Duke of Devonshire's stud at Chatsworth, in Derbyshire, where he remained until his death in 1741 at the age of twenty-seven. William Pick made this note of him: 'He was not only particularized as a racer, but allowed by breeders to be a very valuable stallion, though he covered only a few mares except the Duke of Devonshire's.' At first sight this seems to indicate a culpable neglect by breeders, but the remoteness of Chatsworth from the main centres of horse breeding in Yorkshire was their justification. The later practice of sending mares long distances to be covered by stallions, however eminent, was not then established.

Flying Childers did not found an enduring male line, but, despite this failure, was not without a lasting influence on the evolution of the thoroughbred. His son Snip was an indifferent racehorse, but according to Pick, 'his high blood, justness of shape and fine appearance recommended him to breeders as a promising stallion'. Snip seized his opportunity and sired Snap, who was one of the best racers of his time, and helped to perpetuate the influence of Flying Childers by becoming the maternal grandsire of the Derby winners Saltram and Sir Peter Teazle (otherwise known simply as Sir Peter), and appearing three times close up in the pedigrees of the Derby winners Whalebone, Whisker and Phantom and twice close up in the pedigree of the Derby winner Pope. Breeders at the end of the eighteenth century had a saying: 'Snap for speed and Matchem for truth and daylight.'

It was left to Flying Childers's own brother Bartlett's Childers to found a permanent branch of the male line of the Darley Arabian. Named after his owner, of Nuttle Court near Masham in Yorkshire, Bartlett's Childers was useless for racing because he was a blood-

29

vessel breaker and his frequent nosebleeds made it impossible for him to be trained. Unlike his famous brother, Bartlett's Childers was accessible to the Yorkshire breeders and was used extensively at stud. He sired many good horses, of whom the one that really counted was Squirt, a winner of races at Newmarket, Epsom, Stamford, Winchester and Salisbury. Squirt had a narrow escape when he was in Sir Harry Harpur's stud; he was ordered to be shot because he was crippled by laminitis, but, as he was being led out by the stallion man Miles Thistlewaite to the dog kennel, Sir Harry's stud groom pleaded successfully for his life. This reprieve had fateful consequences for the evolution of the thoroughbred, for Squirt afterwards became the sire of Marske, who in his turn was the sire of Eclipse.

Marske was bred by Mr John Hutton, who lived at the village of that name near Richmond in Yorkshire, and as a foal was swapped for a chestnut Arabian belonging to William, Duke of Cumberland. Marske won the Jockey Club Plate over the Round Course of 3 miles 6 furlongs and 93 yards (6085 metres) at Newmarket, and won a match and received one walk-over, but was not a high-class racehorse and was beaten in the other three races in which he ran. Fortunately the Duke decided to give him his chance in his stud in Windsor Forest. In 1763 he mated him with Spiletta, a daughter of Regulus that he had bought from Sir Robert Eden. The result of this union was a chestnut colt who was given the name of Eclipse after the great eclipse that occurred in the year of his birth.

The Duke died in 1765, and all his bloodstock were sold by Mr Richard Tattersall, the founder of the auctioneering firm which still operates the principal English thoroughbred sales at Newmarket. Marske, considered to be a bad stallion, was sold for a small sum and spent the next season covering country mares in Dorset at a fee of ½ guinea. He was then bought by Mr William Wildman, a Smithfield meat salesman, for 20 guineas, to the delight of his owner who considered that he was well rid of the horse. Wildman, however, knew what he was doing. Later he sold Marske to Lord Abingdon for 1000 guineas, and before his death at the age of twenty-nine the horse had spent several seasons at Rycot in Oxfordshire covering mares at 100 guineas, an exceptionally high fee for those days.

The reason for Wildman's purchase of Marske was that he had bought Eclipse for 75 guineas at Cumberland's dispersal sale and must already have been aware of the horse's brilliant promise. Eclipse and Marske were two of the finest bloodstock bargains of all time, for Eclipse was to follow Flying Childers and become the second truly great racehorse of thoroughbred history. Wildman sold a half share in Eclipse to Dennis O'Kelly – an adventurer who lived by his wits and rose to the rank of colonel in the Westminster Regiment of the Middlesex Militia – for 650 guineas after his second victory, and the remaining half share to O'Kelly for 1100 guineas when the horse was six. Before he died in 1788, a year earlier than Eclipse, O'Kelly reckoned that the horse had earned him £25,000 in stud fees alone, quite apart from the large amounts gained in stakes and wagers.

Eclipse made his first appearance on a racecourse in the Nobleman and Gentleman's Plate, run in three 4-mile (6400-metre) heats at Epsom, as a five-year-old in 1769. In heat races a horse was not required to run again if he could 'distance' his opponents, that is beat them by 240 yards (219 metres) or more, in one of the first two heats. Before the second heat O'Kelly bet that he could place the first three horses and, when called upon to do so, uttered the phrase than has gained an indelible place in the annals of the Turf: 'Eclipse first, and the rest nowhere' – a forecast that was proved correct when Eclipse distanced his four opponents. It was a breathtaking performance, because the horses were all together after 3 miles (4800 metres), but Eclipse then came right away from the others despite his rider John Oakley restraining him with all the strength at his command. Eclipse was never beaten, and when he was taken out of training in October 1770, had won ten races and received six walk-overs. He was credited with eleven King's Plates, 4-mile (6400-metre) races in which he had to carry 12 st (75 kilos).

The dark chestnut colour of Eclipse was set off by a white blaze and a white stocking on his off-hind leg. He was a big horse by the standard of his time, standing 15.3 h.h. (1.6 metres), and had the peculiarity that the highest point of his quarters was about 1 inch (2.54 centimetres) higher than his withers. He had great length from hip to hock, a short and powerful forearm, and long, sloping shoulders. These physical qualities gave him his tremendous stride and, allied to his fiery and aggressive temperament, made him the most efficient galloping machine produced up to that time.

The exceptional size of Eclipse is suggested by the fact that Gimcrack, another famous horse of the same era, stood only

14.0¼ h. h. (1.43 metres). Gimcrack who, like Eclipse, was owned by Wildman for part of his career, was amazingly tough and was the first British racehorse to raid France where, as a six-year-old in 1766, he won a match over 22½ miles (36,000 metres) within the hour. His prowess is commemorated by the Gimcrack Stakes, one of the most important two-year-old races run, at York in August, and by the 'Anciente Fraternite of York Gimcracks' whose annual dinner, held at York racecourse, is one of the most celebrated social gatherings of the racing year.

Gimcrack was a grandson of the Godolphin Arabian, but his influence was transmitted mainly by his son Medley as a broodmare sire in North America. The perpetuation of the Godolphin Arabian male line in the second half of the eighteenth century depended on Matchem, just as the male line of the Byerley Truk depended on King Herod and his son Highflyer during the same period. Matchem, by the Godolphin Arabian's son Cade, was foaled in 1748 and earned the reputation of being 'an excellent honest horse', though he was not invincible by any means and was beaten twice in the Jockey Club Plate. He became a leading stallion in the north of England and his stud fee, which began at five guineas, was increased progressively until it was ten times that amount at the height of his fame.

The Duke of Cumberland, the victor of Culloden, made one of the most momentous contributions to the development of the British thoroughbred when he bred Eclipse, but had made a contribution of equal importance by breeding Herod (as King Herod is more generally called), sixteen years earlier. He bred Herod by sending the mare Cypron, whom he had purchased from Sir William St Quintin, to the Byerley Turk's great grandson Tartar. Herod was a first-class racehorse, winning two matches for 1000 guineas at Ascot and Newmarket in which he beat Tinker and Antinous respectively. William Pick provided an admirably succinct account of him when he wrote: 'King Herod was a remarkable fine horse, with uncommon power, and allowed to be one of the best horses this kingdom ever produced, and as a stallion second to none, being sire of a larger number of racers, stallions and broodmares than any other horse either before or since his time.'

Highflyer was bred by Sir Charles Bunbury, the first dictator of the Turf – he was to be followed by Lord George Bentinck and Admiral Rous in the nineteenth century – in 1774, and was afterwards owned by Lord Bolingbroke and Mr Richard Tattersall.

Highflyer made his first public appearance as a three-year-old in a 100 guineas sweepstakes over a course of 2 miles (3200 metres) at Newmarket, and won the race despite being 'much out of condition'. He won seven more races before he was sold to Tattersall in May 1779, and gained four more successes that year and then retired to stud. His last victory was in the King's Purse of 100 guineas run in 3-mile (4800-metre) heats at Lichfield. The Turf historian James Christie Whyte appended the information about his final performance that he was 'lame and much out of condition, notwithstanding which he won easy'.

Highflyer retired unbeaten and went to stud at Ely. He was an excellent stallion and enabled Tattersall to build an elegant mansion, named Highflyer Hall, out of the fortune that he accumulated from his stud fees. When Highflyer died in 1793, Tattersall caused to be inscribed on his gravestone: 'Here lieth the perfect and beautiful symmetry of the much lamented Highflyer, by whom and his wonderful offspring the celebrated Tattersall acquired a noble fortune, but was not ashamed to acknowledge it.'

The dominance of the four great sires who played vital parts in the evolution of the thoroughbred in the second half of the eighteenth century is reflected in the statistical records. The progeny even of Matchem, the least successful of the four, amassed £151,000 in stakes. The progeny of Eclipse won 862 races and £158,000, those of Herod 1042 races and £201,500, and those of Highflyer 1108 races and £170,000. Although the stud careers of the four horses did not overlap to a considerable extent – the years 1783 to 1786 were the only ones in which all four were represented by winners on the Turf – and only Herod (1758–80) and Eclipse (1764–89) were contemporaneous in any significant degree, they outshone the best of their rivals in a manner that has seldom been equalled in any racehorse-breeding country.

The stud careers of these great forefathers of the modern thoroughbred, particularly those of Herod, Eclipse and Highflyer, took place against a background of revolutionary change on the Turf. They all raced in the days when horses were allowed plenty of time to reach physical maturity and were mostly not expected to race until they were four years old, but were then set to carry big weights over long distances in races decided in three heats. By the end of the century all this had changed and, although some of the old tests of strength and endurance survived a good deal longer, a

33

recognizably modern pattern of racing with the emphasis on speed and early maturity had been instituted.

The practice of racing two-year-olds began and grew rapidly in the last quarter of the eighteenth century. In 1786 the seal of official approval of racing horses of this age was fixed by the institution at Newmarket of the July Stakes of 50 guineas each, colts to carry 8 st 2 lb (51 kilos) and fillies 8 st (50 kilos), with the condition that the progeny of Eclipse and Highflyer were to carry 3 lb (1¼ kilos) extra, a singular tribute to the superiority of those two sires. The race, which was won by Bullfinch in a field of seven, has remained one of the most important two-year-old races right down to the present day. Within the next few years there were isolated instances of racing yearlings, but happily the pursuit of precocity to this outrageous length did not become general and was soon suppressed. Although racing was taking place on ninety courses at this time and the role of the Jockey Club was purely advisory, the example of Newmarket was invariably followed in essential matters.

Another significant innovation about the same time was the Handicap, a type of race in which the weights to be carried by the horses are allotted by a specially appointed official for the purpose of equalizing their chances. These races were essential if racing was ever to become popular entertainment with attractive betting possibilities for the masses. The first important handicap, the Oatlands Stakes of 100 guineas each, was run at Ascot in 1791 and brought out a field of nineteen. The range of weights, from 9 st 10 lb (61 kilos) to 5 st 3 lb (32½ kilos), indicates the kind of burden that was considered reasonable for a thoroughbred to bear in the last decade of the eighteenth century. It is notable that whereas the top weight was almost identical with the top weight imposed in English handicaps in the middle of the twentieth century, the bottom weight was nearly 2 st (12.5 kilos) less.

But the most important of all the developments at the end of the eighteenth century was the advent of the Classic races, those supreme tests which were to establish for nearly two centuries the ideal type of the thoroughbred for breeders to aim at – the horse capable of excelling over distances from 1 mile (1600 metres) to 1¾ miles (2800 metres) at three years of age. The St Leger, the longest of the five Classic races, dates from 1776 and is run over 1 mile 6 furlongs and 132 yards (2973 metres) at Doncaster in September. The Oaks, founded in 1779, is the next oldest, followed by the

Derby, which was first run a year later. They are both run over 1½ miles (2400 metres) at Epsom, usually in the first week of June. The 1 mile (1600 metres) Classic races, the 1000 Guineas and the 2000 Guineas, both run at Newmarket at the end of April, are of more recent institution, as they were first run in 1814 and 1809 respectively.

The 1000 Guineas and the Oaks are confined to fillies, while the other three races are open to both colts and fillies, with weight allowances for fillies. In practice, however, few fillies run in the 2000 Guineas, the Oaks and the St Leger, and only six fillies – Eleanor, Blink Bonny, Shotover, Signoretta, Tagalie and Fifinella – have won the Derby. It is appropriate that Sir Charles Bunbury should have owned and bred the first Derby winner Diomed and Eleanor, the first of the select band of fillies to win both the Derby and the Oaks in 1801; for this mildest of dictators was largely responsible for cultivating the powers of the Jockey Club and guiding the changes that revolutionized the British pattern of racing and helped to shape the ultimate form of the British thoroughbred, with all its virtues and its limitations.

Moreover the initiative for the foundation of the Epsom Classic races came mainly from Sir Charles, and the first Derby was the result of a dinner table discussion between Sir Charles and the twelfth Earl of Derby at the latter's Epsom residence, the Oaks.

The greatness of the 'Big Four' stallions of the second half of the eighteenth century lay in their adaptability and the fact that they transmitted to their progeny the qualities necessary for success in the new circumstances in which there was a premium on speed and precocity. Matchem and Herod were past their prime (although Matchem lived to the great age of thirty-three) by the time the earliest three Classic races were well established; nevertheless Matchem was the sire of the Oaks winner Teetotum and the St Leger winner Hollandaise, and Herod sired three of the first five Oaks winners in Bridget, Faith and Maid of the Oaks, besides the St Leger winner Phenomenon. Eclipse and Highflyer, on the other hand, each sired three winners of the Derby, as Eclipse was responsible for Young Eclipse (1781), Saltram (1783) and Sergeant (1784), and Highflyer for Noble (1786), Sir Peter (1787) and Skyscraper (1789).

But the most significant aspect of the stud achievements of Eclipse and Highflyer, and of Highflyer's sire Herod, was not that they were able to sire winners of the newly instituted Classic races over

1½ miles (2400 metres), but that their joint influence was the mainspring of this epoch-making phase of thoroughbred progress. The progeny of Eclipse tended to be speedy, light-fleshed, temperamental and precocious. The breeders of the time had a saying: 'The Eclipses were speedy and jady, and the Herods hard and stout' (stout in this context meaning stout-hearted). Herod himself was a blood-vessel breaker, and some of his offspring inherited the same affliction, though happily Highflyer and Highflyer's best son Sir Peter were free from it. Thus the qualities of Eclipse on the one hand and of Herod and Highflyer on the other were complementary and it was from this cross, endlessly repeated, that the middle distance Classic thoroughbred largely sprang.

The value of the Eclipse-Herod cross was demonstrated time after time in the breeding of the Derby winners in the late eighteenth and early nineteenth centuries. Sergeant was by Eclipse out of Herod's daughter Aspasia, and Skyscraper, the winner five years later, was an example of this successful cross in reverse, because he was by Highflyer out of the Eclipse mare Everlasting. John Bull, the 1792 Derby winner, was by Herod's son Fortitude out of Xantippe by Eclipse; the 1795 winner Spread Eagle was by Volunteer by Eclipse out of a Highflyer mare; the 1799 winner Archduke was by Sir Peter (by Highflyer) out of Horatia by Eclipse; and Champion, the next year's winner, was by Eclipse's son Pot–8–os out of Huncamunca by Highflyer.

The supreme model of the Eclipse-Herod cross was Waxy, who won the Derby for Sir Ferdinando Poole in 1793. He was by Pot–8-os out of Maria by Herod. Although he was a bay whereas Eclipse was a chestnut, he had his grandsire's white stocking on his off-hind-leg, and was a horse of superb quality, with a beautifully chiselled concave profile of the Arab type. His greatest asset as a sire was that he passed on this quality to most of his progeny. 'The Druid', the famous nineteenth-century writer on racing and hunting topics, called him 'the modern ace of trumps in the Stud Book', and he was principal agent in perpetuating the male line of Eclipse. Other branches of the line sprang from Eclipse's sons Joe Andrews and King Fergus. The next link in the chain was Dick Andrews in the case of Joe Andrews and Hambletonian in the case of King Fergus, and both Dick Andrews and Hambletonian were out of Highflyer mares.

Waxy became the keystone of the phenomenal success of the third and fourth Dukes of Grafton, who won no fewer than twenty-six Classic races between 1802 and 1831. The Dukes actually owned Waxy for the last ten years of his long life, which ended at Newmarket in 1818, when he had reached the age of twenty-eight. The third Duke was one of the oddest of English eccentrics but his faith in the Eclipse-Herod cross made his stud at Euston Hall - near Thetford in Norfolk and less than 20 miles (32 kilometres) from Newmarket – the most powerful in England in the first quarter of the nineteenth century. All the four Grafton Derby winners were results of the cross, though the first, the 1802 winner Tyrant, was not by Waxy, but by Waxy's sire Pot–8–os out of Sea-Fowl by Herod's son Woodpecker; the remaining three were all by Waxy and depended on an intensification of the influence of Herod, since Pope, the winner in 1809, was out of the Highflyer mare (Prunella), and Whalebone and Whisker, victorious in 1810 and 1815 respectively, were out of Prunella's daughter Penelope. Whalebone became one of the strongest pillars of the *Stud Book* and the male line ancestor of the 'Emperor of Stallions' Stockwell and of those two founders of powerful modern Classic dynasties, Teddy and Blandford.

Nor was the efficacy of this particular form of the Eclipse-Herod cross confined to the stud of the Dukes of Grafton, for Web, a sister of Whisker and Whalebone, was the foundation of the great stud which the fifth Earl of Jersey, one of the most thrusting fast riders to hounds of his day, began to build up at Middleton Stoney in Oxfordshire towards the end of the first decade of the nineteenth century. Web, a year younger than Whalebone, was nothing like as good as her two famous brothers on the racecourse and won only two small races, but proved a real treasure of a broodmare after Jersey bought her. She was the dam of Middleton, who won the Derby for Jersey in 1825, and should have been the dam of another Derby winner if her son Glenartney had not been pulled by his jockey Harry Edwards at Epsom two years later in order to allow Jersey's other runner Mameluke to win.

The family which Web founded at Middleton Stoney quickly ramified and produced several branches that bore Classic winners. Her daughter Fillagree, a filly of no special distinction on the racecourse, bred a Classic winner before she did herself, as Fillagree's daughter Cobweb won the 1000 Guineas and the Oaks in 1824. Fillagree later bred the 1000 Guineas winner Charlotte West and the 2000 Guineas winner Riddlesworth. Two other daughters of

Fillagree attested her extraordinary merit as a broodmare by their own deeds at stud. One, an unnamed mare by Phantom (and so a full sister of Cobweb), bred the 2000 Guineas winner Ibrahim and the Oaks winner The Princess; the other, Joanna, became the grand-dam of the Derby winner The Cossack.

Cobweb herself equalled the achievement of her dam by the rare feat of producing three Classic winners. One of these was Bay Middleton, who threatened to become unmanageable early in his three-year-old season and was brought under control only by the fine horsemanship of Jem Robinson, 'the safest rider of his day'. It is on such factors that momentous events on the Turf have often depended and Bay Middleton, thanks to Robinson, was not dismissed as a rogue, but was described instead as a 'fine, slashing, clean-limbed, high-couraged colt' who was not beaten in any of his six races and had the 2000 Guineas and the Derby among his successes. Cobweb's other Classic-winning offspring were Clementina and Achmet, who scored in the 1000 Guineas and the 2000 Guineas respectively.

Trampoline, the other daughter of Web besides Fillagree to make a name for herself as a broodmare, was the dam of the 2000 Guineas winner, Glencoe. The family did not die out, and Clementina was the ancestress in the direct female line of Royal Palace, the winner of the 2000 Guineas and the Derby in 1967 and one of the best horses bred in England in the 1960s. Yet the Derby victory of The Cossack marked the end of the period of dominance of the Classic scene by the Eclipse-Herod cross and by the family of Prunella and Penelope. The Cossack's triumph was gained in 1847 and brought the story almost to the middle of the nineteenth century, by which time these elements permeated Classic pedigrees and had proved the making of the British thoroughbred as an animal capable of excelling over 1½ miles (2400 metres) at three years of age.

Bay Middleton stood 16.1½ h. h. (1.66 metres) when he won the Derby, 2½ inches (0.07 metre) taller than Eclipse, a big horse in his own day, had been when he was racing nearly seventy years earlier. The thoroughbred had come a long way from his ancestors of the desert. The Darley Arabian had stood 15 h. h. (1.52 metres), and many of the imported Eastern horses, and many of the leading English racehorses of the eighteenth century had been smaller. By the middle of the nineteenth century the thoroughbred was, on an average, about 6 inches (0.15 metres) taller than his forefathers of a century and a half earlier. The changes were not restricted to size, as generations of selective breeding in conditions of favourable environment and feeding had wrought a physical transformation with striking increases in scope, speed and length of stride.

The differences between modern Arab horses and thoroughbred can be marked. Some thoroughbreds, like Djebel and many of his descendants, resemble Arabians closely in concavity of profile, prominence of eye and delicacy of appearance, but others, the majority, are coarser in outline. All thoroughbreds show certain contrasts with Arabians and of these the most significant is in length and slope of shoulder, the physical character which gives the thoroughbred his sweeping stride and permits maximum development of speed.

Admiral Rous, the third and last of the dictators of the British Turf – the second dictator, Lord George Bentinck, played a leading part in exposing the scandal of Running Rein's 1844 Derby and bred, but did not own, Surplice, who won the Derby four years later – summed up the state of the thoroughbred in the preface to his book *On the Laws and Practice of Horse Racing*, published in 1850. The Admiral erred in his assertion that 'the English race-horse boasts of a pure descent from the Arabian', but gave vivid expression to his conviction that the thoroughbred of his own day was vastly superior to his Arabian ancestors when he wrote: 'It is generally believed by the most learned of men of the Turf that a first class English racehorse would give 6 st (37½ kilos) to the best Arabian that can be found, for any distance under 10 miles (16 kilometres). The clearest proof of the improvement that has taken place in the English racehorse is the fact that no first or second cross from the imported Arab, with the exception of one mare by the Wellesley Arabian [Fair Ellen], is good enough to win a £50 plate in the present day.' He gave his opinion that this improvement had been continuous and that Flying Childers, Highflyer and Eclipse might not have been good enough to win the lowest class races of his own times.

Rous's view that thoroughbreds were infinitely superior to Arabians as racehorses was confirmed some years later, when a number of Arabians had been imported with the object of refreshing the thoroughbred stock with fresh infusions from the original source. In May 1885 a moderate four-year-old thoroughbred called Iambic was matched against Asil, the best Arabian of the day, over the last

3 miles (4800 metres) of the Beacon course at Newmarket; and Iambic, conceding 4 st 7 lb (28 kilos) to his rival, beat Asil by twenty lengths. Two years earlier Iambic had met St Simon, one of the greatest thoroughbreds of all time, in the Prince of Wales's Nursery over 1 mile (1600 metres) at Doncaster, and St Simon, giving 2 st 7 lb (15½ kilos) to his rival, beat him in a canter by eight lengths. In the late nineteenth century the superiority of the best thoroughbreds to the best Arabians could not be measured in terms of weight.

By the middle of the nineteenth century, at the time when Rous's perpetual presidency of the Jockey Club was about to begin, the thoroughbred was fully established as an independent breed incapable of improvement, as a racing animal, by crossing with other breeds. Instead the thoroughbred had achieved a sufficient degree of genetic uniformity to dominate in crossing experiments, and had already been used to improve or to help in the development of other breeds, like the trotters of the United States and France. The progress of the previous two centuries was the result of methods which reflected the ideas of scientific stock breeding that were current among enlightened farmers and landowners. Careful selection for a single quality or combination of qualities in previously unselected stock can lead to dramatic improvement for a number of generations, especially in a favourable environment. This is what had occurred in the case of the thoroughbred, and the process had been accelerated by the astute repetition by leading breeders of the successful Eclipse-Herod cross. But before very long the pace of progress is bound to slow down as the genetic material begins to approach its optimum arrangement. By the time that Admiral Rous was at the height of his power and influence, the scope for further evolution of the thoroughbred along lines so far followed was considerably reduced. Future progress was to be harder and slower, and in the century following the publication of *On the Laws and Practice of Horse Racing* periods of rapid change in the capabilities of the thoroughbred have resulted mostly from changes, in Great Britain and elsewhere, in the pattern of racing which have opened up new avenues of selection for a limited number of equine generations.

3

The Later Evolution of the British Thoroughbred

The sport of horse racing had grown rapidly in Britain during the half century before Admiral Rous wrote his booklet and became the supreme authority on all Turf matters. In 1802, when eighty-three courses were in use, a total of 536 horses ran, of whom thirty-one (5.8 per cent) were two-year-olds and 117 (21.8 per cent) were three-year-olds. Twenty years later 106 courses were in use and 988 horses ran, of whom 112 (11.3 per cent) were two-year-olds and 285 (28.8 per cent) were three-year-olds; and by 1849, the year before the publication of *On The Laws and Practice of Horse Racing*, the number of courses had risen to 109 and the individual runners to 1,315, of whom 264 (20.8 per cent) were two-year-olds and 419 (31.9 per cent) were three-year-olds. Rous computed that there were about 200 stallions and 1100 mares, with annual foal production of about 830, at stud in the mid-nineteenth century. With regard to this output of the breeding industry Rous commented: 'There are generally three in the first class of racehorses, seven in the second class; and they descend gradually in the scale to the amount of 480, one half of whom never catch the judge's eye; the remainder are either not trained or are found unworthy at an early period'.

The significance of the figures lies not only in the growth of horse racing as a whole but in the progressive emphasis on precocity. The proportion of two-year-old runners increased nearly fourfold, and the proportion of two-year-old and three-year-old runners combined from a quarter to a half, between 1802 and 1849. Nor did the proportion of two-year-old runners then level off, as by 1870 807 (31 per cent) of the 2569 runners were two-year-olds. The trend towards ever-increasing precocity was reflected in the weight-for-age scales published by Rous in 1850 and 1866. In the first version

41

of these scales, which assessed the amounts of weight necessary to equalize the chances of average thoroughbreds of different ages over various distances at monthly intervals throughout the season, Rous estimated that a four-year-old ought to give 37 lb (16.7 kilos) to a two-year-old over 6 furlongs (1200 metres) in October, but only sixteen years later he had reduced the amount to 34 lb (15.4 kilos).

Many critics of racing thought that the pursuit of precocity had gone too far. *The Times*, which missed no opportunity of thundering against the abuses of the Turf, referred to 'the monstrous development of two-year-old races'. Within the Jockey Club the party of reform found a champion in Sir Joseph Hawley, who won the Derby with Teddington, Beadsman, Musjid and Blue Gown. In 1869 Hawley, convinced that the racing of immature animals had become excessive, proposed severe restrictions of two-year-old racing of which the most controversial were the following:

1. That no two-year-old should be permitted to run earlier in the season than 1 July.

2. That no money should be added from the funds of the Jockey Club to any race for which two-year-olds might be entered.

Admiral Rous opposed the Hawley proposals implacably and, as usual in any controversy in which he engaged, his views prevailed. The Hawley reforms were whittled down to a ban on two-year-old racing before 1 May, but even this compromise solution was quietly dropped after a few years. From 1873 two-year-olds have been permitted to run from the beginning of the season in March, and this early two-year-old racing has been an integral part of the whole English racing system, in contrast to some other important thoroughbred producing countries like France and Italy, where few concessions are made to the precociously speedy animal.

Hawley, saturnine and ungracious, was not the man to influence his fellow members of the Jockey Club; nor did the clothes of a reformer fit him particularly well, because he was alleged to be one of the heaviest bettors of the age. In debate he was no match for the extrovert Rous, whose characteristic blend of bluster and common sense was irresistible. Moreover there was a strong vested interest in the early racing of two-year-olds, and Rous, while deploring the trend towards extreme precocity in the thoroughbred, was adamant in his opinion that it was impossible to put the clock back. He explained the position lucidly when he wrote: 'It is much to be regretted that the old system of not training horses till their powers are fully developed is abolished. The great expense of training induced horse-owners to bring forward all the important sweepstakes at two years old and three years old; and with the exception of a few cups and the Port Stakes at Newmarket, and country handicaps, there is very little business for horses after four years old. Yearlings are often tried in October and December, to ascertain if they are sufficiently promising to be entered for the two year old stakes which close in the Houghton and on the 1st January. Many two year olds are trained to the highest point of perfection in the month of May; consequently few horses retain their racing powers after five years of age. This system unfortunately cannot now be altered.' And on another occasion the Admiral stated: 'It is preposterous to suppose that at this date of progress we should reverse previous experience, and decline all the advantages of early maturity, in order to encourage the production of late offspring.'

Rous probably exaggerated the lack of opportunity for older horses in 1850. When he wrote the passage quoted the great weight-for-age long distance 'Cup' races – the Ascot Gold Cup and the Goodwood and Doncaster Cups – were already established and regularly contested by top-class horses, as were those famous Newmarket handicaps the Cesarewitch and the Cambridgeshire, which certainly could not be dismissed in the contemptuous term 'country handicaps'. Nevertheless, his argument that the trend towards increasing precocity was a matter of inexorable economic logic was incontrovertible. Even when popular meetings like Sandown Park and Newbury, depending on gate-money for their existence, sprang up later in the nineteenth and early in the twentieth centuries, little encouragement was given to older horses as such, for precedence was given to two-year-olds, three-year-olds and handicaps. Although the Eclipse Stakes, the celebrated Sandown Park prestige-bearing race over 10 furlongs (2000 metres), was won by the six-year-old Bendigo on the occasion of its inaugural running in 1886, thereafter it was confined to three- and four-year-olds until the age limit was relaxed in the 1960s.

If Rous regretted, but refused to oppose, the growing emphasis on precocity in the British thoroughbred, he was also equivocal in his attitude to handicaps. He earned the reputation of being the first great handicapper and spent a large proportion of his racing life calculating the weights that different horses ought to carry for the purpose of equalizing their chances but, as an idealist in all matters of the thoroughbred, he could not bring himself to approve of these races which, as he himself said, are 'boons to bad horses with no other prospects of success'. His words were paraphrased in the report of the Committee on the Pattern of Racing under the chairmanship of the Duke of Norfolk in 1965, which stated: 'Handicaps must be regarded as a necessary evil because they put a premium on mediocrity'. In some other countries, notably the United States and Australia, valuable handicaps have been accepted as indispensable to the pattern of racing, and no horse is regarded as a true champion until he has succeeded in giving weight and a beating to other good horses in some of the prestige-bearing handicaps. The most important handicaps never attained this status in England, where the proliferation of small handicaps has enabled bad horses too often to pay their way at the expense of better horses who just lacked the class to carve out careers for themselves in the principal weight-for-age races.

Two grave faults which persisted in the British pattern of racing until a determined effort was made to correct them in the late 1960s contributed to the discomfiture of British thoroughbreds in competition with foreign-bred rivals at various times in the last 100 years. The first was the concentration on precocious speed at the expense of absolute speed in the fully mature racehorse; the second was the too easy tolerance of mediocrity and its active encouragement through the provision of an excessive number of handicaps. The French and the Americans have avoided these pitfalls, the French by placing almost exclusive emphasis on excellence over the Classic middle distances and the Americans by mitigating the cultivation of precocity by submitting mature horses to the most searching tests of speed. The victory of the French horse Gladiateur in the English Triple Crown races (2000 Guineas, Derby and St Leger) in 1865 revealed the ability of French horses to challenge successfully in the Classic field in which English ascendancy had been taken for granted, and the American invasion at the turn of the century exposed the vulnerability of the British thoroughbred in the realm of pure speed.

Nevertheless, despite the flaws in her pattern of racing which were reflected in her thoroughbred standards, Great Britain continued to be the prime source of high-class bloodstock for all countries that were trying to build up their racing and breeding industries. Between the mid-nineteenth century and the outbreak of the First World War great racehorses like St Simon, Isonomy, Ormonde and the fillies Sceptre and Pretty Polly, and great sires like Stockwell, Hermit and St Simon were produced. It may be worth mentioning parenthetically that American and Australian critics would have appreciated Isonomy specially, because his reputation depended to no small extent on his magnificent weight-carrying performances in hotly contested handicaps; a small horse standing only 15.2 h.h. (1.57 metres), he won the Cambridgeshire with a ridiculously low weight as a three-year-old, and in the next two years won the Ebor Handicap with 9 st 8 lb (60 kilos) and the Manchester Cup with 9 st 12 lb (61½ kilos) besides winning the Ascot Gold Cup twice, in 1879 and 1880.

Although the attitude of Admiral Rous to handicaps in general was censorious, the most famous of his handicapping feats, concerning the Great Match between the Flying Dutchman and Voltigeur at York in May 1851, had a romantic connection with some of the most momentous events in Turf history which followed later in the century. The Flying Dutchman, who was destined to found one of the most enduring male lines in France, won the Derby and the St Leger in 1849, and Voltigeur the same two Classic races the next year. They met for the first time in the Doncaster Cup two days after Voltigeur had won the St Leger, and Voltigeur won by half a length. Many observers declined to accept the result as conclusive, and during the winter arrangements were made for what was to be regarded as a decisive test at handicap weights to be allotted by Rous. According to the legend, Rous deliberated for weeks before announcing his decision that The Flying Dutchman should concede 8½ lb (3.8 kilos) to Voltigeur; the truth was more commonplace, as 8½ lb was the amount that Rous had decreed a five-year-old should give a four-year-old over 2 miles (3200 metres) in May when he had published his weight-for-age scale the previous year – a fair enough solution to the problem since two dual Classic winners were involved. The match, which aroused as much public interest as most races for the Derby, resulted in a victory for The Flying Dutchman by a margin curiously described as 'a short length'.

Twenty years later Voltigeur's son Vedette was mated with The Flying Dutchman's daughter Flying Duchess by Mr Taylor Sharpe of Baumber Park in Lincolnshire. The produce of this mating, Galopin, was bought for 520 guineas by Prince Batthyany, a Hungarian who spent much of his life in England, was elected a member of the Jockey Club and was a lavish patron of racing. Galopin, a handsome horse gifted with tremendous speed, won the 1875 Derby comfortably and then sired a horse even better than himself in St Simon. Probably because his dam St Angela had a disappointing breeding record, St Simon was entered only for the 2000 Guineas. Even this solitary Classic engagement was cancelled, according to the rules in force at the time, on the death of his breeder Batthyany from heart failure on the steps of the Jockey Club luncheon room at Newmarket in the spring of the colt's two-year-old season. At the Batthyany dispersal sale the wealthy young Duke of Portland bought St Simon for 1600 guineas, a marvellous bargain because St Simon, despite his lack of Classic opportunities, became one of the greatest racehorses and stallions of all time. St Simon was never extended, let alone beaten, in any of his races, and he had that aptitude, possessed only by the most brilliant horses, of producing at will a sudden burst of speed that left even top-class opponents reeling within a few strides. His finest public performance was, as a three-year-old in 1884, to beat the bad-tempered but otherwise admirable Tristan by twenty lengths in the Ascot Gold Cup. Tristan had won the Gold Cup the previous year, had been second to the American horse Foxhall in the Grand Prix de Paris in 1881, and gave further proof of his class by winning the Hardwicke Stakes at Royal Ascot three times. However, the reputation of St Simon as one of the Turf's true 'greats' rests most firmly on the opinions of those in a position to know most about him, his trainer Mat Dawson and Fred Archer who rode him in most of his races. Dawson tried St Simon as a two-year-old with Harvester, who was to deadheat with St Gatien in the Derby, and Busybody, who was to win the Oaks the next year, and St Simon outpaced them as if they were selling platers. Dawson trained six winners of the Derby and one winner of the Grand Prix, but used to say as an old man: 'I have trained only one smashing good horse in my life - St Simon'. Archer was also the regular partner of the superlatively good Ormonde, winner of the Triple Crown and only two years younger than St Simon, and was convinced that St Simon was the better of the pair. Close observers spoke of his 'electricity' and said that he moved 'as if made of elastic'.

46

It was this 'electricity', and his perfect action, that St Simon was able to transmit to many of his progeny and so become one of the great stallions of thoroughbred history. The Duke of Portland remarked that the stock of Galopin and St Simon were more nearly robots than any he had known before or since, and the Turf historian Sir Theodore Cook summed up succinctly when he wrote that St Simon and his progeny set the pattern by which trainers were wont to judge horses for many years.

St Simon was leading sire of winners nine times, which was more times than any stallion since the 1787 Derby winner Sir Peter, who headed the list ten times. This achievement of St Simon has not been equalled in the twentieth century; and he was leading sire twice more than Stockwell (who was dubbed 'the Emperor of Stallions' in his own time), and Hermit, who both preceded him as great sires in the second half of the nineteenth century. But the pre-eminence of St Simon, ten of whose sons and daughters won seventeen Classic races, was not fundamentally a matter of statistics. Each of his rivals for the title of best sire in the Victorian era carried the genes for a serious constitutional defect. Stockwell's dam Pocahontas was a roarer and although Stockwell himself, who won the 2000 Guineas and the St Leger, was clean-winded, he transmitted the taint to some of his offspring and descendants, notably his great grandson Ormonde. Hermit, who won the snow-ruined Derby of 1867 with a sensational late burst, was a blood-vessel breaker and many of his progeny inherited his vascular weakness. By contrast St Simon was an absolutely sound horse in every respect and, although the 'electricity' made him and many of his progeny irritable and impatient, his influence on the breed was wholly beneficial.

Galopin, St Simon and St Simon's sons dominated the list of winning sires for a quarter of a century. Galopin did not approach the greatness of St Simon as a stallion and statistically speaking was inferior to Stockwell and Hermit, but was leading sire of winners three times, in 1888, 1889 and 1898. St Simon reached the top in 1890, when his first runners were three-year-olds, and remained there for the next six years. Then there was an interval in which his fortunes receded, but he returned to the top of the list in 1900 and 1901. Persimmon, the best of St Simon's sons and winner of the Derby, the St Leger and the Ascot Gold Cup, was leading sire four times between 1902 and 1912. St Simon's son St Frusquin, winner of the 2000 Guineas, ranked first in 1903 and 1907, and another son of St Simon, Desmond, was leading sire in 1913. Two other St Simon horses, William the Third and Chaucer, were second in the list of winning sires in 1914 and 1916 respectively. Most of these sires also exerted a powerful influence on later generations through their daughters; Galopin, St Simon, Persimmon, William the Third, St Frusquin and Chaucer headed the list of sires of dams of winners on sixteen occasions altogether. Sons and grandsons of St Simon transferred his influence to most of the other principal racehorse-breeding countries, notably Rabelais, Prince Palatine and St Bris in France.

Inevitably the influence of St Simon as a single ingredient in pedigrees was diluted as generation succeeded generation, but it was reconstituted and made extremely effective in many cases through inbreeding. Thus Hyperion, Nearco and Ribot, three of the best racehorses and most potent sires of the twentieth century, were all inbred to St Simon in various degrees. Hyperion was bred in 1930 by the seventeenth Earl of Derby, the direct lineal descendant of the founder of the Epsom Classic race of the same title. The rotund and genial Earl, who was also prominent in public and political life, was one of the most popular owner-breeders ever to tread the turf and, through his stud-produce Hyperion and the brothers Fairway and Pharos, exerted an influence on the thoroughbred all over the world which has seldom been surpassed. The chestnut Hyperion, a son of the First World War Triple Crown winner Gainsborough and the top-class staying mare Selene, was one of the most sweet-tempered and also one of the smallest horses to gain the highest honours since the early days of the thoroughbred, for he stood no more than 15.1 h.h. (1.56 metres) when he won the Derby in 1933, but he made up for his lack of size by absolutely perfect conformation and sweeping action at the gallop which expressed the graceful movements of the thoroughbred in their most exquisitely developed form. His Derby victory was gained in record time although he had the race won a long way from the finish, and he went on to win the St Leger with equal ease. With Nearco he dominated Classic breeding in England in the middle years of the twentieth century. He was the leading sire of winners in England six times, the highest total achieved by any stallion since St Simon. His son Aureole, bred by King George VI and owned as a racehorse and stallion by Queen Elizabeth II, became the most successful English Classic sire of the next generation, and many of Hyperion's sons, like Heliopolis,

Khaled and Alibhai in the United States, carried his influence abroad in very potent form.

Hyperion had St Simon in the third and fourth generations of his pedigree, because Gainsborough's dam Rosedrop was by one of St Simon's sons, St Frusquin, and Selene was by another of St Simon's sons, Chaucer. The influence of St Simon was still more concentrated in the pedigree of Nearco, as St Simon was duplicated in the third and fourth generations of Nearco's sire Pharos and in the second and third generations of Nearco's maternal grandsire Havresac II. Bred by the Italian genius Federico Tesio in 1935, Nearco won all his fourteen races including the Grand Prix de Paris, and spent his entire stud career in England where he headed the list of winning sires twice. Like Hyperion, he had a world-wide influence, particularly through his gifted but temperamental son Nasrullah, who was leading sire once in England and five times in the United States, and Nearctic, who was exported in utero to Canada.

Ribot, the last of the great horses bred by Tesio, was unbeaten in sixteen races and had two victories in the Prix de l'Arc de Triomphe and one victory in the King George VI and Queen Elizabeth Stakes to his credit. Foaled in 1952, he was one of the world's foremost Classic stallions until he died at the age of twenty. This invincible and masterful horse had an even stronger concentration of the influence of St Simon in his pedigree than Nearco; if the pedigree of Ribot is divided into four quarters represented by his grandparents Bellini, Tofanella, El Greco and Barbara Burrini, then each quarter has a stallion inbred to St Simon, namely Havresac II, Apelle, Pharos and Papyrus – and St Simon is repeated no fewer than thirteen times in the pedigree of Ribot as a whole.

If Pharos, the leading sire in 1931, was inbred to St Simon, so of course was his brother Fairway, the winner of the St Leger in 1928 and the leading sire of winners four times between 1936 and 1944. Blandford, who could be regarded as the most successful Classic sire of the period between the two World Wars since he got the Derby winners Trigo, Blenheim, Windsor Lad and Bahram and was leading sire three times, had St Simon only once in his pedigree but had three crosses of St Simon's sire Galopin. Moreover Blandford sired the best of all his progeny, the Triple Crown winner Bahram, when mated with a mare, Friar's Daughter, in whose pedigree St Simon appeared three times in the first four generations. There was a strong concentration of the influence of St Simon in Bahram, and an even stronger concentration of the influence of Galopin.

Phalaris, the most potent Classic sire of the inter-war period apart from Blandford, had St Simon only once in his pedigree. But his sons, the full brothers Fairway and Pharos who were the principal means of perpetuating and spreading his influence, had St Simon's son Chaucer as their maternal grandsire and so were inbred to the patriarch of Welbeck in the third and fourth generations. Indeed most of the high-class progeny of Phalaris were got from Chaucer mares, and most of the high-class products of Chaucer mares were by Phalaris. It has been claimed that the Phalaris-Chaucer 'nick' (a natural affinity between two separate strains) was one of the most potent in the evolution of the thoroughbred and comparable to the Eclipse-Herod 'nick' of an earlier period.

Neither Phalaris, nor Chaucer, nor Scapa Flow, the dam of Fairway and Pharos, was a top-class racehorse. Scapa Flow was beaten once in a selling race, and Phalaris and Chaucer were regarded merely as good handicappers during their racing days, when Phalaris had definite limitations of stamina. The fact that they were both owned by Lord Derby, the most successful and extensive breeder of the day, meant that they were given chances at stud that they would probably not have obtained otherwise, and also that they tended to be used jointly in mating plans. It was no coincidence that Fairway and Pharos were bred by Derby, and it is fair to assume that the duplication of St Simon in their pedigrees sparked off the electricity that enabled them to transcend their parents and grandparents.

Other important elements in the development of the British thoroughbred in the first half of the twentieth century were stock imported from the United States and the most extraordinary freak in racing history, The Tetrarch. The circumstances of a strong flow of American horses into the British Isles in the last decade of the nineteenth and first decade of the twentieth century, and the stopping of that influx by the so-called 'Jersey Act' of 1913, are described in a later chapter. It is only necessary to state in this context that the importation of the stallion Americus and the fillies Rhoda B and Sibola had a profound effect on the modern thoroughbred not only in England but in many other countries. Sibola became the great granddam of Nearco, Rhoda B was the dam of the Derby winner

Orby, and Americus was the sire of Americus Girl, a mare whose pervasive influence would be difficult to exaggerate.

Although Orby, a grandson of Ormonde, failed to found an enduring Classic male line, he was the origin of one of the most potent of the specialized sprinting lines, and the line's distinctive qualities of pure speed and precocity may be attributed in a large degree to Rhoda B. This line has been consolidated by inbreeding, and Gold Bridge, the acme of its massive physical type and of its sprinting excellence, had Orby twice in the third generation of his pedigree. Lacking further consolidation, this sprint dynasty had passed into irreversible decline by the final quarter of the century, and had been replaced by a new sprint dynasty founded by Tudor Minstrel.

The existence of The Tetrarch was owed to the ambition of one

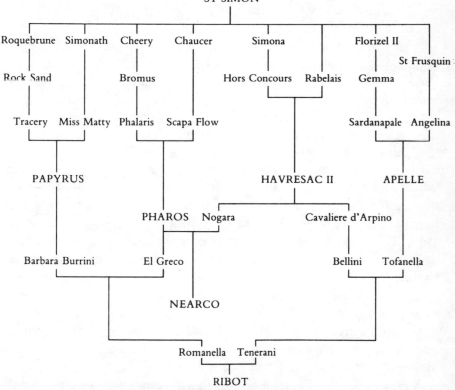

man, Mr Edward Kennedy of the Straffan Station Stud in County Kildare, to revive the waning fortunes of the once dominant Herod male line. To this end he bought in 1909 the French five-year-old Roi Hérode. That Herod was ten generations back in the pedigree and that Roi Hérode was a stayer of only second-grade ability who had been beaten in the Doncaster Cup did not deter the enthusiastic Kennedy. Roi Hérode at least had the recommendation of a superb pedigree, because his sire Le Samaritain had won the French St Leger and his dam Roxelane had won the French Oaks. In 1910 providence took a hand in shaping the destinies of the Turf and making Kennedy's dream come true. Kennedy had kept him in training in the hope of winning the Chester Cup, but Roi Hérode broke down in the course of his preparation and had to be sent to stud. It was far too late in the season to get many mares for him, but fortunately Kennedy had the thirteen-year-old Vahren, a shy breeder who was due to foal late, at home and put her to Roi Hérode when she had produced her foal by John o'Gaunt or Symington. The result of this fortuitous union was The Tetrarch.

In no respect was The Tetrarch quite as other horses are. In colour he was a kind of elephant grey with white and lime patches of various shapes and sizes, as if someone had splashed him with a brush dipped in a bucket of whitewash. He was nicknamed 'the Rocking Horse' and 'the Spotted Wonder'. When Atty Persse, who trained at Chattis Hill near the Wiltshire Village of Stockbridge, tried him for the first time in April of his two-year-old season he discovered that the strange-looking colt was a phenomenon; and when Persse, who specialized in teaching two-year-olds their job so thoroughly that they could show their form first time out, produced him in public at Newmarket in the middle of that month, he won as he liked by four lengths. The only time that he was in the slightest danger of defeat was in the National Breeders Produce Stakes at Sandown Park in July, when he was left at the start and Steve Donoghue managed to push him to the front only in the last few strides to win by a neck. The Sandown Park race was then one of the most important two-year-old races, and his six other races included important events like the Woodcote Stakes at Epsom, the Coventry Stakes at Ascot and the Champagne Stakes at Doncaster.

A rapped joint in September of his two-year-old season, followed by further leg trouble the next spring, prevented him from ever running again after the Champagne Stakes. The unanswerable question is whether a horse with such blinding speed could have stayed well enough to win the Derby. Persse was convinced that he would have stayed 1½ miles (2400 metres) in the best company. 'I honestly don't think he would ever have been beaten at any distance. He was a freak and there will never be another like him,' said the trainer. Persse attributed his amazing speed to his mechanical perfection, for The Tetrarch, despite his bizarre colour marking, was a magnificent speciment of the thoroughbred.

Persse's opinion of his stamina received some confirmation from the fact that The Tetrarch sired the St Leger winners Caligula, Polemarch and Salmon Trout. On the other hand these were far from vintage Classic winners, and the influence of The Tetrarch was transmitted to later generations mainly by his fast sons Tetratema and Stefan the Great and by his brilliant daughter Mumtaz Mahal. Unfortunately his fertility was poor; he was completely sterile for ten years before his death in 1935 and he got only 130 foals in the whole of his stud career.

A quarter of a century after his death exceptionally fast horses like the 2000 Guineas winner Pall Mall and the 1000 Guineas winner Caergwrle, who carried strong concentrations of his blood, continued to bear witness to his influence. However, The Tetrarch had his most profound and far-reaching influence on the evolution of the thoroughbred when the hereditary factors which he transmitted were combined with those derived from the American-bred Americus. In 1920 The Tetrarch was mated to Lady Josephine, a very fast mare who had won the Coventry Stakes the year after The Tetrarch had done so. Lady Josephine was by the sprinter Sundridge out of Americus Girl by Americus. The product of the mating was a grey filly who was bought by George Lambton, Lord Derby's trainer and one of the shrewdest judges of a yearling, for 9100 guineas at the Doncaster Sales. Lambton was acting for the Aga Khan, who was then laying the foundations of the stud and stable that were to make him one of the world's leading breeders. This filly was given the name Mumtaz Mahal. Her speed was such that she was nicknamed 'The Flying Filly', and her sheer class enabled her to finish third in the 1000 Guineas in 1924 although she had no pretensions to stay a mile properly. Mumtaz Mahal more than any other mare helped the Aga Khan to gain his pre-eminent position among breeders, and her descendants include a galaxy of celebrities like

Mahmoud, whose time for the 1936 Derby is still a record, the great sire Nasrullah, Abernant, Royal Charger, Kalamoun, the wonderful filly Petite Etoile who won the 1000 Guineas and the Oaks in 1959, and the ill-fated Derby winner of 1981, Shergar.

Another daughter of Lady Josephine, namely Lady Juror who rather incongruously was by the stayer Son-in-Law, bred Fair Trial when she was mated with Fairway. A top-class miler himself, Fair Trial became one of the most potent influences for speed in the modern thoroughbred.

These were the factors, shaped and directed by the pattern of racing, that made the British thoroughbred in the first half of the twentieth century; and this British thoroughbred emerged in 1945 from five years of isolation to face international competition of unprecedentedly fierce intensity. The result was a disaster. Foreign-bred horses, mostly from France but reinforced by the products of the United States and Italy, moved in to sweep the board in many of the English Classic and other prestige-bearing races. The first onslaught was led by the powerful French owner-breeder Marcel Boussac, who had great stayers like Caracalla II, Marsyas II and Arbar as the spearhead, but once the myth of English superiority had been dispelled other owners were not slow to seize the opportunity to plunder the richest English prizes.

There had been intimations of a serious foreign challenge between the two World Wars when fast French horses like Sir Gallahad III, Epinard, Rodosto and Le Ksar had demonstrated their prowess on English courses. In 1938 a French-bred horse, Bois Roussel, inflicted the indignity of defeat on his British-bred opponents in the Derby, though the impact of his victory was mitigated by the fact that he was owned by an Englishman, Mr Peter Beatty, and prepared by the English master trainer of Classic horses Fred Darling. Nobody in England was disposed to read any tragic implications into the isolated reverses, and breeders as a whole entered the Second World War in a mood of mild euphoria as far as a threat to the supremacy of the British thoroughbred was concerned. This mood was induced by the fact that in 1939 the 2000 Guineas and Derby – the St Leger was cancelled on account of the outbreak of war – were won by a British horse of indisputable excellence, namely Blue Peter.

Memories of Blue Peter made the shock of the post-war defeats all the more cruel. These defeats multiplied at such a rate that by 1965, when twenty post-war seasons had been completed, thirty of the 100 Classic races had been won by horses bred abroad. Foreign successes had been on a similar scale in the most important weight-for-age races apart from the Classics; for example there had been six victories for foreign-bred horses in the Eclipse Stakes, nine in the Champion Stakes and ten in the Ascot Gold Cup. No less than forty-two of these fifty-five victories had been gained by horses bred in France, mainly because France was the nearest country with the high quality thoroughbreds to take advantage of English weakness.

What had gone so wrong that the English, the creators of the thoroughbred, were losing their own principal tests of racing merit to foreign rivals at the rate of nearly one in three? To some extent the traumatic condition could be explained as a self-inflicted wound resulting from the 'Jersey Act' of 1913. The English had cut themselves off deliberately from a source of progress by denying thoroughbred status to some of the world's fastest horses and, as related in a later chapter, the imperative need to reverse this suicidal policy was acknowledged by the repeal of 1949.

Nevertheless, it would be superficial to attribute the humiliations of the British thoroughbred after 1945 entirely to the 'Jersey Act'. A variety of contributory causes had been at work and shared the responsibility. These included the pattern of racing, the methods of selection of breeding stock adopted by many breeders, the export of top-class stallions and the fragmented state of the breeding industry.

The pattern of racing had changed little since the days of Admiral Rous. The introduction of races of 1¼ miles (2000 metres) or more in which horses above the age of three might run - like the Coronation Cup, the Hardwicke Stakes, the Eclipse Stakes, the Jockey Club Stakes and the Champion Stakes – had modified but had certainly not arrested the trend to bring forward all the important sweepstakes at two and three years of age which Rous had noted 100 years earlier. The longer races for older horses were not rich enough or numerous enough to distract the majority of breeders from the preoccupation with precocious speed. There was the paradox that while the Derby was regarded as the greatest English race and the horse capable of staying 1½ miles (2400 metres) was enshrined as the ideal British thoroughbred a substantial share of the resources of the breeding industry was directed to producing animals capable of winning over 5 and 6 furlongs (1000 and 1200 metres) between March and June as two-year-olds, with no prospect of ever staying more than a mile.

This dichotomy was reflected in the combined breeding industry of Great Britain and Ireland. In 1949 the joint industry produced less than 5000 live foals, and of these about 1000 were purpose-bred for National Hunt racing; of the flat-bred foals approximately one-third were bred primarily for precocious speed, so that of the total annual foal crop only about 2700 were bred with the expectation of staying 1½ miles at three years old.

Thus all that was required was a short swing of the pendulum, the existence of a handful of exceptional sires and mares, the application of slightly stricter or more inspired standards of selection and stud management in France, in order to convey an entirely disproportionate impression of superiority at the winning post of important races. Indeed it was in the middle and long distance races that most of the English reverses occurred. In two-year-old races, sprints and races up to 1 mile the products of England and Ireland were generally able to hold their own, and maintain superiority in many cases.

It is impossible to assess the extent to which the competitive position of the English and Irish breeding industry as a producer of Classic horses was compromised by the export of top-class stallions like the Derby winners Blenheim, Mahmoud and Bahram by the Aga Khan during the Second World War and Nasrullah – bred by the Aga Khan but owned by Mr Joe McGrath's Brownstown Stud before he was exported – in 1950. They all, with the exception of the luckless Bahram, became influential sires in the United States. The effects of losses of top-class stallions on this scale must have been grave, but these losses alone cannot be held responsible for the crushing reverses suffered by British bloodstock after the Second World War. They must have been compounded by misjudgements and errors of selection, and some of these may be traced to another dichotomy, which is that between owner-breeders and commercial breeders. The commercial breeders, whose main effort was directed to supplying the foal and yearling markets, accounted for a share of total thoroughbred production which had been rising steadily since the middle of the nineteenth century and finally reached as much as 70 per cent.

Some of these commercial breeders have made a vital contribution to the progress of the British thoroughbred and have produced stock of the highest class at various times. One of the first of these commercial breeders to make an impact on the Classic scene was William Blenkiron, a Yorkshireman who built up a flourishing hosiery and haberdashery business in London and invested some of the profits by founding the Middle Park Stud, at Eltham in Kent, about the middle of the century. The annual sales of the yearlings at the Middle Park Stud, which at one time comprised more than 120 mares, were one of the features of the racing season until the laying of a new railway line, which cut through the paddocks, forced the closure of the stud in 1882. Many top-class horses, including the Triple Crown winner Gladiateur and the Derby and St Leger winner Blair Athol, stood at Middle Park; and the produce of the stud included the Derby winners Caractacus and Hermit, sold as yearlings for 150 guineas and 1000 guineas respectively.

The first William Blenkiron died in 1871, but his son continued the stud on the same vast scale until its dispersal eleven years later. Six years before his death the elder Blenkiron donated £1000 to the Jockey Club to endow a two-year-old race over 6 furlongs (1200 metres) at Newmarket in October. The Middle Park Plate, or the Group I William Hill Middle Park Stakes as it became a century later, was one of the first sponsored races and has always stood out, as the original sponsor intended it should, as an incentive to yearling buyers to seek the precociously speedy kind of horses he was trying to breed.

There is bound to be a subtle difference in emphasis between the aims of the commercial breeder and the aims of the owner-breeder of racehorses. The criterion of success for the commercial breeder is the prices his yearlings realize in the sale-ring, whereas the criterion of success for the owner-breeder is the number, value and importance of the races that his horses win. In the long run the commercial breeder is unlikely to obtain good prices for his yearlings unless his products win their fair share of races, but fashions in bloodstock are capricious, and it is by toeing the fashionable line, and by his showmanship, that the commercial breeder makes his profits.

The great aristocratic owner-breeders – like Lord Falmouth and the Dukes of Westminster and Portland in the nineteenth century and Lords Derby, Astor and Rosebery in the period between the two World Wars – played the chief parts in sustaining the reputation of the British thoroughbred as a Classic performer. Yet taxation, death duties and economic factors generally gradually eroded the position of the once powerful private studs to a point at which few of them were still operating and fewer still were capable of producing top-class horses with any regularity. It was not until the last quarter of the century that owner-breeders made a come-back through an injection of wealth from an entirely fresh source.

The consolation for breeders in England and Ireland in the dark days that followed the Second World War was that the British thoroughbred had not lost his speed. The essential asset of the racehorse is the ability to cover the distance between two given points in the quickest possible time, and what was required in the next quarter of a century was the restoration of the ability to keep up that speed long enough to win the most important races over middle and long distances in conditions of the toughest international competition. The Aga Khan, who had bred the pre-war Derby winners Mahmoud and Bahram and bred the 1952 Derby winner Tulyar in Ireland, put the point succinctly when he wrote in an article in *The Times*: 'Breeding for speed has made the British Thoroughbred, and the ultimate remedy [for the failures of the time] must be more and more speed.' He was convinced that any attempt to down-grade speed would defeat its object and reverse the process by which the British thoroughbred had become the ancestor of racehorses all over the world, not least in France. He concluded the article: 'I have only one piece of advice to offer – be careful when you throw out the water from the tub; do not let the baby fall as well. And that baby is speed.'

The defeats of British thoroughbreds by foreign-bred horses after 1945 could be a shock therapy only for the outlook and modes of thought of British breeders. The remedy for the failings of the British thoroughbred, which involved the blending of speed with sufficient staying power to produce a type of animal capable of facing world-class opposition successfully over middle and long distances, was bound to be a long-term process. Mindful of the necessity to retrieve the situation, breeders eagerly set about the task of finding the right material in spite of the fact that the impoverished state of English racing, with prize money rising at a much slower rate than in competing countries like France and the United States, made it easier to export than to import high-class bloodstock. A few excellent horses of good stamina and sound constitution like Chanteur II, who sired the Derby winner Pinza, were imported, and efforts were made to exploit to the full the assets of home-bred Classic stallions like Crepello, a Derby winner endowed with a sprinter's speed, and Aureole. The Turf authorities gave active support to these efforts, appointing two committees to inquire into the problem. The first of these, the Duke of Norfolk's Committee on the Pattern of Racing, was given the responsibility of examining the general programme of races with special attention to the top-class horses of all ages and the improvement of the thoroughbred. The recommendations of this committee, and those of its successor Lord Porchester's Flat Race Pattern Committee, have been examined in a later part of the book (Chapter 13). In the present context it will suffice to say that the Norfolk Committee set up the goal for breeders by defining 'the ideal racehorse as one with more speed than the best specialist sprinter . . . and supreme over distances from 1 to 1¾ miles at three years old and upwards': and proclaimed the duty of the Turf authorities to assist breeders to attain that goal by ensuring that 'a series of races over the right distances and at the right time of the year are available to test the best horses of all ages.'

Thus the Norfolk Committee assigned to the Jockey Club a more paternalistic role in race planning than anything previously contemplated. Nor was the Senior Steward of the day, Major-General Sir Randle Feilden, slow to act on this advice.

The Norfolk Committee reported in 1965 and was followed two years later by the appointment of the Porchester Committee, whose brief was to produce detailed plans for implementing the recommendations of the Norfolk Committee. The outcome was the first officially inspired 'Pattern of Racing' designed to achieve a proper balance between speed and stamina and to provide incentives for breeders to produce horses capable of upholding the prestige of the British thoroughbred.

Unfortunately the Pattern, for all the good intentions, could not provide a complete cure for the dispersion of effort and resources which was a grave source of weakness in the British breeding industry. The overall British racing programme calls for such disparate performance types as precociously speedy two-year-olds and sprinters, milers, Classic middle distance horses, stayers and steeplechasers. None of the other principal racing countries attempts to cover such a wide range of performance.

The official Pattern received the blessing and the necessary financial support of the Levy Board, the body with the statutory duty of raising money from betting for the benefit of horse racing, on an ascending scale. In 1988 grants to Pattern races accounted for £1,047,450 of the total of £7,710,750 allocated to flat racing in the Levy Board Prize Money Scheme.

The heat of foreign competition had been turned down, albeit temporarily, before these measures could begin to have any effect. Huge increases in prize money for races in France had made raids on English races much less attractive. Conversely, French races became more attractive to English owners, and from the mid–1960s English trained horses began to race in France in increasing numbers. As an indication of the different levels of prize money in the two countries, the Benson Committee of Inquiry into the Racing Industry in 1968 quoted the earnings of thirteen English-trained horses who had won races in France the previous year. By August they had won a total of fourteen races in France worth the equivalent of £52,350. The same horses had won twenty races altogether in Great Britain, worth a total of only £18,276.

Many English owners adopted the practice of having some at least of their horses trained in France in order to take advantage of the high prize money, and many French owners began to buy horses in England and Ireland. As early as 1965 horses bred in England and Ireland won races worth more than £350,000 during the flat season in France. They made practically a clean sweep of the few valuable sprint races, did well in two-year-old and 1-mile (1600-metre) races and had one first-class middle distance representative in the filly Aunt Edith. Four years later the total had risen to more than £850,000 with representatives of English and Irish breeding playing leading roles in every department from speedy two-year-olds to extreme stayers.

The two-fold revival of the fortunes of British and Irish-bred horses (less French competititon in England and more success for British and Irish-bred horses in France) was accelerated by a decline of some of the principal French studs. One of the worst affected was that of Marcel Boussac, whose dominance came to an abrupt end in the 1950s, leaving a vacuum which British, Irish and American-bred horses were able to exploit.

The most significant aspect of the increased success of British and Irish thoroughbreds in the late 1960s was the evidence of middle distance prowess, the category in which the previous weakness had been most pronounced. The Prix de l'Arc de Triomphe, the most valuable international race in Europe run over 1½ miles (2400 metres) at Longchamp in October, was won by the Irish-bred horses Vaguely Noble, Levmoss, Rheingold and Star Appeal in the 1960s and 1970s, while the British-bred horses Aunt Edith and Pleben chimed in with victories in the Prix Vermeille and the Grand Prix de Paris, two of the most important French three-year-old races, during the same two decades.

The 'Arc' victories stressed the progress of Ireland as a racehorse breeding country. So far in this account of the evolution of the thoroughbred Great Britain and Ireland have been treated as a single unit. The breeding industries of the two countries have indeed always been closely linked however the political winds may have blown. They share one set of breeding records, the *General Stud Book*, and the Irish mares, formerly segregated in a section of their own, have been included in the main body of the work since 1905 at the request of Irish breeders. Nevertheless, the two industries have set divergent courses since Irish independence, and the differences have become increasingly apparent in the second half of the twentieth century as Irish breeding, with positive fiscal incentives and the status of a major national industry, has grown towards quantitative parity and qualitative superiority in relation to British breeding. By the late 1970s Irish-bred horses were not only winning more important races than home-bred horses in the traditional British market, but were outshining British-bred horses in Europe. For these reasons it is possible to do justice to the evolution of the Classic racehorse in Ireland only by describing it in a separate part of the book (Chapter 5).

Evidence of the progress of the Irish breeding industry was found not only in quality but in quantity. In 1971 Irish production of thoroughbred foals, at 2834, trailed the British figure of 4342, but then began to creep up and finally took the lead in 1984 with 4642 compared with the British figure of 4542 foals.

No single adverse factor could be held responsible for this British decline. The division of the industry into more or less rigid compartments is a flaw, but hardly a decisive flaw because it applied equally to Irish breeding. Loss of national wealth, high taxation and lack of fiscal incentives have certainly been prime causes, leading to the dispersal of large studs, a low level of investment in quality bloodstock and the sale for export to richer countries of choice mares and potential stallions. In the late 1970s the large majority of British breeders owned only one mare each. The small breeder could not hope to compete successfully or consistently as bloodstock values soared ahead of the general rate of inflation.

If British breeding was at a low ebb in the late 1970s, a revolution was at hand. The quadrupling of the price of oil and the consequent world recession in the middle of the decade put colossal wealth in the hands of the oil producers of the Persian Gulf, and before long the attractions of bloodstock as an investment medium for some of that wealth became apparent. Initially the impact of Arab investment was mainly on the principal yearling sales of North America and Europe, but in the 1980s many of the leading Arab owners began to build up large-scale breeding operations in Britain and Ireland. The Al Maktoum family of Dubai and Khaled Abdullah of Saudi Arabia were the leaders of an Arab invasion which swept up a high proportion of the best stud land in the British Isles, particularly in the favoured Newmarket area.

The lavish Arab expenditure at the yearling sales, though bringing home the lesson from time to time that top prices and athletic ability are not invariably linked, soon began to secure horses whose racing prowess made them potential high-class stallions. The first wave included Khaled Abdullah's 2000 Guineas winner Known Fact and Prix de l'Arc de Triomphe winner Rainbow Quest, who both opened their stud careers at his Juddmonte Farm in Berkshire: the same owner's Rousillon, the best European miler as a four-year-old in 1985, who went to the National Stud: and yet another Khaled Abdullah-owned champion, the General Accident 2000 Guineas, Coral Eclipse Stakes, King George VI and Queen Elizabeth Diamond Stakes and Trusthouse Forte Prix de l'Arc de Triomphe winner Dancing Brave, who joined the Irish Sweeps Derby winner Shareef Dancer at the Maktoum family's flagship stud, Dalham Hall, at Newmarket. The leading Arabs were equally assiduous in acquiring mares of similar quality, and in 1985 Sheikh Mohammed became the first of the Arabs to win a British Classic race with a horse of his own breeding when Oh So Sharp carried off the 1000 Guineas and proceeded to add further Classic victories in the Gold Seal Oaks and the Holsten Pils St Leger.

By the late 1980s the Arabs had built up breeding empires so vast that they dwarfed all other stud operations in the British Isles, both past and contemporary. By 1988 Darley Stud Management, the company name covering Sheikh Mohammed Al Maktoum's racing and breeding interests, embraced seven studs (Aston Upthorpe, Dalham Hall, Derisley Wood, Hadrian and Rutland Studs in Britain and Kildangan and Woodpark Studs in Ireland) and a total of 430 mares, of which no fewer than 86 had racing records bearing that hallmark of class, Pattern race victory.

The colossal Arab investment revolutionized the British thoroughbred industry. For most of the years since the Second World War it had been underfunded and had declined relentlessly as a large number of the best stallions and mares were sold for export and not replaced by imports of similar quality. Most of the high quality exports had gone to the United States, helping to raise the standard of the American Thoroughbred to unprecedented heights. What the Arabs did for British breeding – as Robert Sangster and his associates had done for Irish breeding – was to reverse this process by aggressive purchasing of the choicest Kentucky-bred yearlings, racing them in Europe and retaining for stud duty those of either sex that had passed the racecourse test with honours.

The Arabs did more than raise the quality of the thoroughbred population of Britain. They also worked wonders for employment in the racing and breeding industry, and brought prosperity to many ancillary professions and trades like auctioneers, bloodstock agents, veterinary practices, horse transport firms, saddlers, corn merchants, builders and suppliers of sophisticated equipment, who helped to realize their ambitions to modernize and raise their stud and stable amenities to the highest possible level of perfection, regardless of expense. The rebuilt stable blocks at Dalham Hall Stud were designed to last five hundred years. The Arabs were generous sponsors of races, particularly Pattern races. Nevertheless, the Arab impact on British racing and breeding failed to win universal approval, because one of its effects was to polarize the industry. The Arabs might be responsible for the presence of more high-class thoroughbreds in Britain than there had been since the 1930s, and they might have made British racing the most competitive in the world, but owners and breeders with limited financial resources saw these developments in a less favourable light. Small breeders could not afford to patronize the highly priced stallions promoted by the Arabs, and the cheap horses owned by small owners could not compete with the aristocratically bred and expensively bought Arab-owned horses which sought easy pickings on courses throughout the land. Consequently prices at the lower end of the yearling market tended to be depressed, bringing further distress to small breeders. Some substance was given to the contention that small owners and breeders were being squeezed out by the fact that the five Al Maktoum brothers and Khaled Abdullah alone won a total of 232 races with an aggregate value of £2,294,999 in 1987, thus accounting for 9.2% of all the races and 10.9% of the prize money on offer in Britain – and they were only the most prominent of a host of free-spending Arab owners.

There were strong counter-arguments: that in racing and breeding operations as vast as those mounted by the Arabs culling was inevit-able, giving British breeders the opportunity to acquire choicely bred bloodstock at reasonable cost: and that Arab concentration on the upper section of the yearling market forced their competitors to spend their money available for yearling purchases on the less obvi-ously favoured individuals, thus supporting the middle market. The critics were unconvinced, and the arguments remained finely bal-anced. Nobody denied that there was an enlarged core of top-class bloodstock in Britain, but the sharp divisions between the most highly capitalized and the less well-endowed sections meant that there was an underlying malaise in the breeding industry.

A reduced number of British owner-breeders continued to hold their own in the production of Classic horses. For example the decade to 1987 was studded with the Derby victories of Lord Hal-ifax's Shirley Heights, Sir Michael Sobell's Troy, Mr Eric Moller's Teenoso, Lord Howard de Walden's Slip Anchor and Mr Louis Freedman's Reference Point, although Sir Michael Sobell's stud was located in Ireland. Shirley Heights and Reference Point were both by Mill Reef, and Slip Anchor was by Shirley Heights. The presence of the 1971 Derby winner Mill Reef at the National Stud at Newmar-ket was the strongest buttress of quality breeding throughout his career as a stallion, which came to an end with his early death in 1986. The Mill Reef era had run parallel with the period of growing Arab investment, and made its own vital contribution to the resurgence of British bloodstock.

4

Stud Books

There can be no organized horse racing or betting on horse races, nor can there be any regular trade in racehorses, unless records of the results of races are kept and published. The man who sets his own horse to run against other horses in a race, the man who wishes to back a horse to win a race, the man who wishes to buy a horse to race – all need to be able to refer to the past performances of the horse concerned in order to assess his merit in relation to the merit of other horses.

There can be no organized breeding of racehorses, or improvement of the breeds of racehorses, unless there are reliable records of the pedigrees and of the matings of stallions and mares. The breeder needs to know and match the physical characteristics and the temperaments of the animals he uses, but he has an equally imperative need to have some knowledge of the ancestors of those animals, their characteristics and their racing form, for at least two or three generations back.

Thus the development of the thoroughbred from the original stock in Great Britain depended on two kinds of documentary aid – records of race results and breeding records – applied in conjunction. In the early days these records were rudimentary. The *London Gazette* of 12–15 February 1679 contained the advertisement: 'Mr John Nelson doth keep a Register at the Groom Porter's Office in Newmarket of all such horse matches . . . as any person therein concerned hath or shall desire him to Register . . .' Nelson's *Register* was probably not even the first to be kept, but it is certain that its foundation was swiftly followed by others, though continuous and complete records of the principal matches and horse races that have survived down to the present day did not begin until nearly half a century later. In the eighteenth century the *Calendars* of Heber, Pond and Cheney provided the authentic records of race results which are the source material of British Turf history.

Inevitably the early breeding records tended to be less comprehensive. Racehorses in the seventeenth and eighteenth centuries were mostly bred, it is true, in the Bedale district of Yorkshire, but there was no accepted uniform method of recording matings and pedigrees, no central registry, and no system of preserving the stud records of stallions and mares for posterity. Nor was there any means available of correlating racing and breeding performance and, so far as the latter was concerned, everything depended on the whim, the industry and the sense of orderly documentation of the individual breeder.

The haphazard was the rule until late in the eighteenth century, when British racing and breeding found the man, or rather the family with the will and the ability to provide the documentary services that racing urgently required. James Weatherby, the son of a Northumberland solicitor, obtained an official post in racing when he was appointed by the Jockey Club at Newmarket in 1770 as Keeper of the Match Book in succession to William Tuting, and consolidated his position soon afterwards when he succeeded Thomas Fawconer as Secretary to the Jockey Club. Tuting and Fawconer had been publishing a *Sporting Calendar*, giving the results of all races, thus continuing the earlier work of Heber, Pond and Cheney; and James Weatherby, once he had ousted them from their official posts, was able to take over the publication of the *Calendar*. James Weatherby's *Calendar* appeared in 1773, and the *Calendar* has been published by him, his heirs and descendants ever since. The *Calendar* was the property of the Weatherbys for nearly 130 years and, although it was then purchased by the Jockey Club, the Weatherby family firm, which formed the permanent civil service of the Turf government, continued to publish this official organ of racing.

James Weatherby the First did not die until 1793, and *An Introduction to a General Stud Book* was published by James Weatherby two years earlier. Some doubt, however, used to surround the identity of the compiler and editor of that historic volume. Eric Rickman tried to elucidate the mystery when he wrote in his book *Come Racing with Me*: 'The impression is possible, on the face of it, that the James Weatherby to whose diligence and enterprise are due this and some succeeding volumes of a unique and scrupulously guarded register of pure blood, was old James. He was still active and was continuing to publish his Racing Calendar. But it was his nephew, the second James, who started the General Stud Book, after most careful and discriminating research among old racing records and private stud books.' Other researchers have suggested that the compiler of the *Stud Book* was not a Weatherby at all, and that the initial connection of the Weatherby family with the *General Stud Book* was mainly entrepreneurial.

Whoever the originator of the *General Stud Book* may have been, he seems to have had few private stud books to assist him, owing to the unsystematic methods of the early racehorse breeders; and he was forced to depend on Cheney's and Heber's *Calendars* of races past from 1727, on the histories of William Pick, on old sale catalogues and on his own inquiries as the principal sources of information concerning the pedigrees of racehorses before his own day. He was confronted by grave difficulties, and was candid enough to confess that his work might not be entirely free from error, but subsequent research and such private stud books of the eighteenth century as have come to light have, on the whole, provided striking testimony to his accuracy. Once founded, this record of pedigrees was never allowed to lapse, for the *General Stud Book* has remained the property of the Weatherbys down to the present day and has been kept up to date by the periodic publication of fresh volumes.

In this way the Weatherbys put the racing and breeding community eternally in their debt by supplying the twin documentary aids needed for improving the racehorse. As the great Italian breeder Federico Tesio wrote in his book *Breeding the Racehorse* published in 1958: 'These two books, the *Racing Calendar* and the *Stud Book*, form the most imposing and dependable source of information the world has ever known. The former makes it possible to check the performance record of every horse. The latter provides a sure means of tracing back his complete ancestry over a period of more than 150 years.'

James Weatherby's method of compiling a stud book was to list the mares in alphabetical order, append a short pedigree of each mare for the purpose of identification, and account for her produce year by year, giving details of colour, sex and name of sire. The introductory volume of 1791 was followed by further editions in 1793, 1800 and 1803, and the final publication of Volume 1 in 1808, to which the earlier editions were merely preliminaries. Volume 2 was published in 1822, Volume 3 in 1832, Volume 4 in 1836 and Volume 5 in 1845. Volume 6 was published in 1849, and from that time down to Volume 40 in 1985 new volumes have appeared regularly at four yearly intervals. From Volume 20 in 1905, Irish mares, formerly placed in a separate section, have been included in the main body of the *Stud Book* at the request of Irish breeders, and cannot be differentiated from mares located in England.

James Weatherby declared that the purpose of his *General Stud Book* was to correct the 'increasing evil of false and inaccurate pedigrees'. No doubt many genuine mistakes were made, but the lack of any reliable means of identification of horses in the second half of the eighteenth century must have given all too much scope for genuine mistakes of identity and for fraudulent horse dealing. Weatherby claimed, with justice, that his *Stud Book* contained 'a greater mass of authentic information respecting the pedigrees of horses than has ever been collected before'. The word 'horses', in the context, clearly meant racehorses, and Weatherby's claim suggested that no principle of discrimination governed admission to the *Stud Book*. The object was merely to provide the pedigrees and means of identifying as many racehorses as possible. Jean Romanet, later director-general of the French racing authority, the Société d'Encouragement, remarked in an article in 1948 that the *General Stud Book* in its original form was simply a 'registry of citizenship'.

The editor did not use the word 'thoroughbred' in Volume 1, but implied its existence by using its opposite 'half-bred' to describe horses that could not be admitted. For example he noted of the Young Marske mare bred by Sir John Webb: 'In 1806 missed to Sir Peter, having previously bred 14 foals; those unnoticed here [there were three of them] were by half-bred stallions.' The reverse of 'half-bred' must be 'thoroughbred', and the exclusion of the progeny of half-bred stallions implied that thoroughbreds only were admissible.

It was recorded in the 1814 Supplement to the *Stud Book* that the Crop mare had in 1810 a filly by a horse 'not thoroughbred'. The word thoroughbred was mentioned again in Volume 2 published in 1822, though the term was still not defined.

Copenhagen, the Duke of Wellington's charger at the battle of Waterloo, was by Meteor, and the pedigree of his dam Lady Catherine was given as 'got by John Bull, her dam by the Rutland Arabian, out of a hunting mare not thoroughbred'. Apparently this was a warlike equine family, because Lady Catherine had been ridden by General Grosvenor at the siege of Copenhagen when she was in foal and actually carrying the Duke's future charger.

Copenhagen was not only a war-horse. He was also a racehorse of respectable ability and ran ten times in 1811, winning a match at Newmarket and a sweepstakes at Huntingdon. Deference to a national hero may have helped to secure Copenhagen's original admission, but respect neither for the Duke nor for his own useful racing form sufficed to keep Copenhagen in the *General Stud Book*, for his name was expunged from succeeding editions.

It seems that what Weatherby had in mind as the condition for eligibility for the *Stud Book* was direct descent from a small number of original mares, less than 100, who were regarded as the foundation stock of the thoroughbred. The pedigrees of these mares could be traced back no further, and had their productive careers mostly in the second half of the seventeenth century.

The matings of these mares and their offspring and descendants, with the Eastern stallions and their offspring and descendants who were imported during a period of approximately a century following the Stuart Restoration, formed the breed which Weatherby accepted as thoroughbred and eligible for his *Stud Book*. This interpretation is corroborated by a later editor, who stated in the Advertisement to Volume 14 'that a recent importation of Arabians from the best Desert strains will, it is hoped, when the increase of size has been gained by training, feeding and acclimatization, give a valuable new line of blood from the original source of the English thoroughbred'.

It may be noted in passing that this hope was to be disappointed, for events proved that the genetic pool from which successful racehorses could be bred was already filled and, as Admiral Rous pointed out so trenchantly, the Arabians were so inferior as racehorses that they could not be assimilated with the thoroughbreds of the nineteenth century. Two centuries of selective breeding in a favourable environment had set an unbridgeable gulf between the English racehorse and his desert ancestors.

The seeds of future controversy concerning admission to the *General Stud Book* were sown in the earliest days by James Weatherby's somewhat equivocal and inexplicit attitude. On the other hand the aim he set himself was to produce a stud book for a purely domestic sport and incipient breeding industry, and he could not have foreseen the complexities that would follow the spread of racing and the exportation of English thoroughbred stock to many other countries. Nor would the controversies about the admission to the *General Stud Book* which have raged from time to time have been avoided unless Weatherby had opted uncompromisingly for a 'registry of citizenship', with its attendant risks of mistaken identity, from the beginning.

The complexities gradually became apparent as other countries built up their own breeding industries. At first the *Stud Book* editors were not worried. The preface to Volume 2 noted that attempts were being made in a number of foreign countries to establish breeds of horses on the English plan, together with a more careful selection of stallions and broodmares than was the practice in England. Foreign breeders were confident that their improved methods would enable them soon to produce better horses than the English, who would be compelled to send abroad for sound, if not for speedy horses. In view of later developments this was an extraordinarily percipient comment, but the editor summed up complacently and in a somewhat patronizing tone: 'The hint about soundness may be worth attention, but for the rest, with the advantages this country already possesses, and so long as horse-racing continues to be followed up with spirit by her men of rank and opulence, there can be little to apprehend.'

Gladiateur shattered that illusion by winning the 2000 Guineas, the Derby and the St Leger – the so-called 'Triple Crown' – in 1865. The myth of English supremacy was destroyed, and the English breeders and *Stud Book* authorities were forced to realize that at least one other country, France, was producing some racehorses as good as their own; and where one country had succeeded other countries were likely to follow. During the second half of the nineteenth century the English trade in racehorses ceased to be one-way, and imports of mares became increasingly numerous, not only from France, but also other countries like Australia and the United States where the racehorse population was considerable.

The *General Stud Book* editors first took official notice of the changed situation in the preface to Volume 18 published in 1897. The preface stated: 'The importation of a number of horses and mares bred in the United States of America and in Australia, a few of which will remain at studs in this country, may have some effect on the stock bred here, but the pedigrees of these horses, though accepted in the Stud Books of their own country, cannot in all cases be traced back to the thoroughbred stock exported from England, from which they all claim to be and from which, no doubt, they mainly are descended; these animals are, therefore, in those cases, marked with reference to their own Stud Books.'

Clearly the editors were in a quandary – a quandary which could not have been foreseen when the *General Stud Book* was first compiled a century earlier. The preface to Volume 18 was obviously composed in a spirit of compromise and procrastination, but the solution of the problem of entry to the *General Stud Book* which it embodied was quickly revealed as unsatisfactory when American and Australian horses continued to be imported in increasing numbers. Weatherbys thought it advisable to refer the question to the Stewards of the Jockey Club, as the supreme authority in all matters relating to the Turf, and as a result framed the first qualifying test for admission to the *General Stud Book*, to which all imported horses and mares included in Volume 19 had been submitted. The qualification was that 'any animal claiming admission should be able to prove satisfactorily some eight or nine crosses of pure blood, to trace back for at least a century, and to show such performances of its immediate family on the Turf as to warrant the belief in the purity of its blood'.

Unfortunately the qualifying clause of Volume 19 was soon overtaken by the pace of events. In the first decade of the twentieth century anti-betting legislation threatened to kill racing in the United States. There was panic selling of racehorses in that country, and the bottom fell out of the bloodstock market there. In England, breeders had nightmares of the market being flooded by imported American horses of dubious origin. These fears were reflected in more stringent qualifications for admission to Volume 20, and the preface stated that no horse or mare could be admitted unless it could be traced to a strain already accepted in the earlier volumes of the *Book*. But this was a regulation that could satisfy nobody. It represented a panic reaction to panic American selling, and its ambiguities became all too obvious to the *Stud Book* authorities who had to apply it. At the Jockey Club Meeting in the spring of 1913, Lord Jersey, the Senior Steward of the previous year, put the case for making the regulations even stricter and more precise. His motion was passed by the Club and acted on by Weatherbys, who inserted the following rule for admission in Volume 22, published the same year: 'No horse or mare can, after this date, be considered as eligible for admission unless it can be traced without flaw on both sire's and dam's side of its pedigree to horses and mares themselves already accepted in the earlier volumes of this Book.'

This was the so-called 'Jersey Act' which at once provoked intense resentment abroad, particularly among Americans whose predicament had inspired it, and eventually became notorious at home and threatened to reduce the British breeding industry to second-class status before its repeal thirty-six years later. If the *General Stud Book* came nearest to being a 'registry of citizenship' in 1897 it was converted into what Jean Romanet has called 'a veritable *Almanach de Gotha*' by the 'Jersey Act'. Yet for a long time English breeders and Turf authorities were perfectly happy about the consequences of this exclusiveness. In his book *The History of the Racing Calendar and Stud Book*, published in 1926, C. M. Prior referred to the 'Jersey Act' in these adulatory terms: 'It is unnecessary to add that the action of Messrs Weatherby and the Stewards of the Jockey Club met with the hearty approval of all breeders of any standing both at home and abroad, it being universally agreed to be of paramount importance that the pages of the *Stud Book* should be zealously safeguarded, and that every precaution should be taken to preserve the high character of the book in its entirety. Thus from henceforth the *General Stud Book* is hermetically closed to all but those animals to whose admission there could be no possible objection.' Prior was oblivious to American feelings on the subject, and his comments ignored the inconsistent aspects of the 'Jersey Act', which was not retroactive and so allowed animals of untraced pedigree imported and admitted to the *General Stud Book* before 1913 to remain, though animals of similar pedigree were excluded after that date.

The Americans saw the 'Jersey Act' as an unscrupulous measure designed to protect the English export trade in thoroughbreds and to deny outlets to American bloodstock by stigmatizing them as half-bred. The main reason why the majority of American horses were barred was the high incidence of Lexington in their pedigrees. A great racehorse and greater sire, Lexington was champion sire in the United States no fewer than sixteen times. He was the subject of a brief note in Volume 10 of the *General Stud Book*, published in 1865, which read: 'Lexington, a bay horse, foaled in 1850, by Boston, out of Umpire's dam.' This did not legitimatize him under the 'Jersey Act' as, although he descended from the first Derby winner Diomed in the male line, he was of doubtful origin on his dam's side.

The advocates of the 'Jersey Act' should have been shaken in their complacency by the victory of the half-bred Durbar II in the Derby of 1914. Durbar II was by St Simon's son Rabelais, but his dam Armenia had Lexington in her pedigree. However, it was not until after the Second World War, when the British thoroughbred was exposed to international competition after more than five years of isolation, that the disastrous long-term results of the 'Act' were appreciated at last. French horses began to invade England in unprecedented numbers and carried all before them in many of the Classic and other prestige races. Many of these French invaders were by Tourbillon and his son Djebel, and Tourbillon's dam Durban was by Durbar II. The crisis came in 1948, when two of the five Classic races, the 2000 Guineas and the St Leger, were won by half-bred horses, My Babu and Black Tarquin. It was clear that the *General Stud Book*, with its existing rules of admission, was in imminent danger of being totally discredited. A record of the pedigrees of racehorses was both ridiculous and useless, devoid even of academic interest, if the breed it embraced was to be overrun repeatedly by horses deliberately excluded from it. This was the principle of an *Almanach de Gotha*, of purity of blood, projected into the farthest realms of fantasy. As early as July 1948, Weatherbys referred to the Stewards of the Jockey Club the question whether steps should be taken to broaden the scope of the *General Stud Book* so as to allow for out-crossings with strains then ineligible. The Stewards appointed a committee to report on the point and the committee's recommendation was that changes were required. As a result the preface to Volume 31, published the next year, announced the repeal and stipulated: 'Any animal claiming admission from now onwards must be able to prove satisfactorily some eight or nine crosses of pure blood, to trace back for at least a century, and to show such performances of its immediate family on the Turf as to warrant the belief in the purity of its blood.'

This was a return to the conditions of 1901. By a stroke of the pen the stigma of illegitimacy had been removed from the large majority of American horses and those of their descendants who had been accepted in other countries, particularly France. The change came just in time. Within fifteen years of the repeal of the 'Jersey Act' the Derby had been won by four horses – Galcador, Never Say

Die, Larkspur and Relko – and the St Leger also by four horses – Never Say Die again, Aurelius, Hethersett and Ragusa – who would have been excluded. The *General Stud Book* could not have survived such shocks as a credible record of top-class racehorse pedigrees.

Paradoxically, the *Almanach de Gotha* principle could not have been maintained as long as it was but for the period of comparative liberalism before the imposition of the 'Jersey Act'. Some of the American strains imported during that period became pillars of the British thoroughbred between 1913 and 1949. Probably the most influential of these American horses were Americus, imported as a three-year-old in 1895, Rhoda B, imported as a yearling in 1896, and Sibola, imported as a yearling in 1897. All were admitted to the *General Stud Book*, yet all had Lexington in their pedigrees and would have been barred if they had claimed admission after 1913. Indeed Americus was inbred to Lexington, as he was by Emperor of Norfolk (by Norfolk, by Lexington) out of Clara C, by Glenelg, out of The Nun by Lexington.

Americus, a good sprinter himself, sired Americus Girl, the ancestress in the female line of many of the most brilliant horses of the twentieth century from Mumtaz Mahal to Petite Etoile, and the ancestress also of stallions like Fair Trial and Nasrullah who were potent sources of top-class speed not only in England but in every country where the racehorse is bred. Rhoda B was the dam of Orby, who won the Derby and founded the most successful specialist sprinting line of the first three-quarters of the twentieth century. Sibola won the 1000 Guineas and was second in the Oaks herself, and became the great granddam of the great Italian horse Nearco, who went to stud in England and had a profound and widespread influence on the modern thoroughbred. In Nasrullah, champion sire once in England and five times in the United States, the strains derived from Sibola and Americus were united, as he was by Nearco and traced his descent from Americus Girl in the female line.

Despite the euphoria that reigned among breeders and *Stud Book* authorities in England during the 1920s and 1930s, the fact that the British thoroughbred depended heavily on descendants of Lexington for its competitiveness in the international field invalidated the basic assumptions of the 'Jersey Act'. Nothing betrayed the elements of farce and anomaly in the 'Act' more clearly than the pedigree of Diapason, the winner of the Goodwood Stakes in 1925. Diapason was inbred to Hanover in the fourth generation. Hanover was ineligible for the *General Stud Book* because his sire Hindoo was out of a Lexington mare. Yet one of the appearances of Hanover in the pedigree of Diapason was in a legitimate guise, as he was the sire of Rhoda B, whose son Orby was Diapason's grandsire; the other appearance was in an illegitimate guise as the maternal grandsire of Sir Martin who was in turn the maternal grandsire of Diapason, because Sir Martin, the unsuccessful favourite for the 1909 Derby, was imported from America after the introduction of the anomalous conditions of Volume 19. Diapason was excluded from the *General Stud Book* on account of Sir Martin. Absurdity and inconsistency could hardly go further.

Other countries had their problems in the creation and development of their own stud books, but none so acute as those of the publishers in England where the racehorse had been evolved from original stock of poorly authenticated pedigree and had later formed the foundation stock of racehorses in all other countries where the sport took root. Other countries were able to start with the simple proposition that animals inscribed in the *General Stud Book* were thoroughbreds and *ipso facto* acceptable for their own stud books. In the course of time complications appeared and required solution, and in the cases of France and the United States these problems had repercussions in the widening field of international racing.

The French Stud Book was founded in 1833 by royal decree. Unlike the *General Stud Book*, which has always been the property of a private firm, the French Stud Book was a creation of the Government and, before and after the abolition of the monarchy, was kept by the Ministry of Agriculture. It succeeded an earlier work compiled under royal patronage by Thomas Bryon, one of the founding fathers of French racing and later 'Keeper of the Archives' to the Société d'Encouragement. A Commission under Duc Decaze was charged with the duty of formulating the stud book rules and sifting claims for admission. As a result of a recommendation of the Commission, the Government adopted the following rule for admission: 'The only horses that shall be recognized as being of pure breed, and admitted as such for inscription, are pure-blooded English horses . . .' These horses could have been bred in England and imported, or bred in France. Thus the original French Stud Book rules had strong *Almanach de Gotha* overtones, though there was some later relaxation to permit the entry of thoroughbreds foaled in other countries on presentation of certificates of identity issued by the competent authorities of the countries of origin.

In the first decade of the twentieth century the French authorities, no less than the English, became alarmed at the prospect of a flood of imports of American racehorses of dubious pedigree. In 1913 the Government introduced its own version of the 'Jersey Act', which read: 'From 15 March 1913, a foreign-born horse shall not be inscribed in the French Stud Book as being thoroughbred unless its absolutely pure lineage can be proved for seven consecutive generations, and unless its ancestors, at some period, may be traced in either the English or the French Stud Book, on both the paternal and maternal sides.' Nevertheless, this was not so severe as the 'Jersey Act', because practically it permitted the registration in the French Stud Book of horses having a flaw in the eighth generation or beyond. As Romanet commented, it demanded not absolute purity, but relative purity.

Armenia, the dam of Durbar II, was imported into France from America before the restrictive measures of 1913, and was inscribed in the French Stud Book. Thus Durbar II and his descendants, though barred from the *General Stud Book*, were eligible for the French Stud Book, and Durbar's daughter Durban, as we have seen, became a principal source of the superiority of French Classic horses after the Second World War, and of the discomfiture of British thoroughbreds at the same time. The absurdity of this situation is indicated not only by the prowess of Durbar II himself, but by the fact that his granddam Urania was a marvellously tough and talented mare who won thirty-five of her eighty-seven races. On any 'registry of citizenship' principle, Urania and her descendants should have been made welcome in the pages of any stud book.

The American Stud Book was founded much later than the English and French books, for Colonel Sanders D. Bruce did not begin to publish it in weekly instalments of the magazine *Turf, Field and Farm* until 1865. These instalments were collected in the first volume of the American Stud Book published three years later. Bruce also published the succeeding volumes until he was bought out by the New York Jockey Club, who took over with the publication of Volume 7 in 1898. In his preface to the first volume Bruce stated: 'Without wishing to take the responsibility of fixing a standard for the blood-stock of the United States, the general custom has been followed of calling those thoroughbreds that have an uncontaminated pedigree for five generations. Some of our most distinguished families on the American Turf cannot be traced this far, and they have been embodied in this work, their claims being recognized by everyone familiar with the subject; and their exclusion would have wrought manifest injustice.' He developed his idea of what a stud book ought to be in Volume 2, when he explained that it was essential to give the pedigrees of distinguished racehorses as far as they were known, because after five thoroughbred crosses their descendants would qualify as thoroughbreds and therefore their antecedents must be preserved. The essence of his liberal theme was contained in the passage: 'The reputation they [the distinguished racehorses] acquired gave them importance in the sporting world. Though not up to the standard, they were bought and sold, and even run, as thoroughbreds. How, then, in the face of these facts, is posterity to be enlightened unless their true pedigrees are given, and the reader undeceived as to their correct genealogy?'

This was an exceptional statement of the 'registry of citizenship' conception. Unfortunately Bruce's practice was not equal to his lofty principles. In an article published in the *Thoroughbred Record* of Lexington, Kentucky, in March 1927, and reproduced in *The Bloodstock Breeders Review* the following year, John Hervey wrote of Bruce: 'In compiling the Stud Book, in giving to our official genealogies the forms into which they have crystallised as authentic, he did, in various, if not numerous, instances, high-handed and unwarranted things which the facts, the evidence and the testimony extant, stamp as indefensible.' According to Hervey, Bruce was chronically short of funds and was dependent on the patronage of leading breeders to publish his work. This financial dependence compelled him to accept pedigrees that were palpably false. 'He shovelled into the Stud Book pedigrees so impossible as to be nothing less than absurd, and this gave to outrageous fiction the official stamp of veracity.'

Doubts about the accuracy of the early volumes of the American Stud Book were at least a partial justification of the restrictive measures imposed in England and France, and absolve the stud book authorities of those countries of the charge of being motivated by chauvinism and cupidity.

The 'registry of citizenship' principle did not survive without modification in the United States. When the Jockey Club assumed responsibility for the American Stud Book they ruled that horses were eligible only if they had five uncontaminated thoroughbred crosses, or authentically traced to animals recorded in the first six volumes of the American Stud Book, or in a recognized stud book of another country. Nevertheless, this was a great deal more liberal than the English and French regulations. American breeders were able to adopt an eclectic policy, drawing freely on the most successful racing strains developed abroad, particularly in the advanced breeding countries, England and France. While the racehorse population of Great Britain and France existed in comparative isolation between 1913 and 1949, American thoroughbred standards were able to make continuous progress by unrestricted experiments in the blending of American, English and French bloodlines.

Thus a paradoxical situation came about in which the breeders most intent on destroying the 'Jersey Act', the Americans, derived the greatest benefit from its application, while the breeders most intent on defending the 'Jersey Act', the English, suffered most.

The repeal of the 'Jersey Act' was the first step towards the rationalization of stud book policies. Further steps could lead in time to the creation of a fully international stud book in which the horses accepted as thoroughbred in different countries would be fully interchangeable. This international stud book would bring at least two substantial benefits to breeders everywhere, by simplifying documentation and the tracing of pedigrees and by facilitating the mingling of strains successfully developed and acclimatized in various countries – a mingling which the experience of the twentieth century suggests is the most fruitful source of improvement of the racehorse. Secondary benefits would include the publication of breeding statistics as appendices to the annual supplements, since statistics of the earnings of sires' progeny, etc., compiled on a purely national basis are bound to be incomplete and largely irrelevant in an age of increasing internationalization of racing and breeding.

The principal condition for the creation of an international stud book was seen as the introduction of uniform, and fraud- and mistake-proof, methods of registration and identification of horses in the participating countries. The authorities in England and France had achieved a close similarity of method, but elsewhere the rapid growth of racehorse population and a more casual approach to the problem had left standards of documentation below the required degree of perfection. Weatherbys led the world in applying computer methods to stud book work. The prospect of the eventual spread of computerization to the stud books of other countries bore with it the possibility of increasing international co-operation in the exchange of information on all pedigree matters, and brought the goal of an international stud book significantly closer.

These developments were accompanied by, and in some respects sprang from, a realization that stud books were vital to the prosperity of the world-wide breeding industry, but that notions of an *Almanach de Gotha*, of purity of blood, were outmoded and unacceptable. Properly regulated stud books were needed to fulfil James Weatherby's original purpose of ensuring against false and inaccurate pedigrees, and of providing fool- and fraud-proof means of identification; they were required to give breeders the data for making sensible mating plans; and they must be safeguarded by rational rules of admission in order to prevent the introduction of undesirable genes into the breed through the use of untested stock.

It was clear that the conditions for entry restored in Volume 31 of the *General Stud Book* in 1949 did not fully meet modern requirements. They contained several anomalies; the phrase 'purity of blood' was unscientific, since genes, not blood, transfer hereditary factors from one generation to the next; the words 'to trace back for at least a century' were both redundant and based on a misapprehension, since the numbers of generations alone is significant in heredity; and the phrase 'eight or nine crosses of pure blood' was imprecise and liable to be misconstrued. Accordingly the conditions were revised and the new version was included in the Preface to Volume 36, due in 1969 but finally published in February of the following year. The new conditions, which answered all the objections to the old, were as follows:

Any horse claiming admission to the *General Stud Book* should be able: 1. To be traced at all points of its pedigree to strains already appearing in pedigrees in earlier volumes of the *General Stud Book*, these strains to be designated 'thoroughbred'. Or: 2. To prove satisfactorily eight 'thoroughbred' crosses consecutively including the cross of which it is the progeny and to show such performances on the Turf in all sections of its pedigree as to warrant its assimilation with 'thoroughbreds'.

By 1970 stud books seemed to be set firmly on the path of evolution in an international context. Yet the basic dilemma – thoroughbred or half-bred, to admit or to exclude – was still unsolved even on the British domestic front. Although controversy about the conditions for entry in the *General Stud Book* has sprung mainly from international causes, there always have been racehorse families in the British Isles which have not been traced to original sources accepted in the earlier volumes and have therefore been excluded. The problem is compounded by the fact that the British Rules of Racing, in contrast to the rules in force in other important racing countries, permit non-thoroughbred horses to compete on equal terms in all races. The evolution of some of these families was traced in the '*H-B*' *Stud Book* compiled by Miss F. M. Prior. This provided them with documentation, though of an unofficial kind, which could help to qualify them, in due course of generations and if their members continued to show satisfactory racing form, for admission to the *General Stud Book*. The first volume of the '*H-B*' *Stud Book* was published in 1914, but its threatened demise after the publication of Volume 8 in 1972, together with the need for official documentation of non-thoroughbred horses in order to meet the stringent requirements of international racing, forced the Jockey Club and Weatherbys to step in and introduce a 'Register of Non-Thoroughbred Broodmares' two years later. The register would maintain the breeding records of non-thoroughbreds to *General Stud Book* standards, and the properly documented produce of registered non-thoroughbred mares alone would have the right to race in Britain. It was evident that these official records would not only rectify an anomaly but make graduation of non-thoroughbreds to the *General Stud Book* much easier than it had been when their pedigrees lacked official authenticity.

The majority of the successful half-bred families, like the Reynoldstown family, have specialized in the production of jumpers. However a small number of families, of which the Solerina and the Verdict families are the most famous, have established themselves as sources of good flat racehorses over several generations, and history was made on 31 March 1969 when Peter Weatherby, the senior partner of the firm, announced that Lavant, a great granddaughter of Verdict, and her progeny were to be admitted to Volume 36 of the *General Stud Book* to be published in 1970. The admission of Lavant followed intensive lobbying and representations by the Council of the Thoroughbred Breeders Association.

In making this announcement Weatherby referred to the right reserved by his firm to decide what horses or mares could be admitted to or excluded from the *Stud Book*. He continued: 'We have in the past generally used this right to exclude animals. On this occasion we feel that Lavant and her progeny are a strain which should be assimilated with thoroughbred strains and have decided to admit Lavant and her produce, among whom is So Blessed, to the *General Stud Book.*'

The mention of So Blessed indicated one of the vital factors on which the claims of Lavant hinged, because he had been one of the fastest two-year-olds of 1967, when he won the Cornwallis Stakes at Ascot, and one of the leading sprinters the next year, when he won the July Cup. Another of Lavant's offspring, Lucasland, had won the July Cup two years earlier, when she had been a strong claimant for the title of champion sprinter. The offspring of Lavant had won eighteen races and more than £28,000 in stakes up to the time of Weatherby's decision to admit her. Nor had the racing prowess of the family been restricted to the generation of Lavant's produce. Lavant herself was a winner, as was her dam Firle. Versicle, the dam of Firle, won six races worth £5216 and Verdict won eight races including the Cambridgeshire and the Coronation Cup. Indeed Verdict, after whom the family was rightly named in Prior's *'H-B' Stud Book*, set the family firmly on the road to fame by breeding six winners of £30,658 including Quashed, who triumphed in the Oaks and the Ascot Gold Cup, and Thankerton, who was third in the 2000 Guineas and the Derby.

Counting Verdict herself, her ancestresses and descendants, the family has been represented by ten mares in the direct female line of whom eight were winners and the remaining two were not trained. Its achievements may be summarized by stating that it has bred the winners of the Oaks, the Ascot Gold Cup, the Coronation Cup, the July Cup, the Ribblesdale, the Jersey and the Diadem Stakes, the Cambridgeshire, the Ebor Handicap, two Goodwood and two Stewards Cups; and it has bred two colts who have been placed in the Derby, Curzon and Thankerton. Not many female lines in the *General Stud Book* can boast a better record, and the continued exclusion of Lavant and her progeny would have been in absolute contravention of Romanet's conception of a 'registry of citizenship'.

Indeed closer scrutiny of the Verdict family and its fight for recognition reveals the ludicrous and untenable situations to which legalistic adherence to the conditions for entry to the *General Stud Book* may lead. We have seen that Lavant and her family satisfied the condition as to racing form. Lavant could also prove no fewer than ten crosses with thoroughbred stallions in her direct female ancestry, and the last mare of dubious origin in the female line was the mare by Perion foaled in about 1837. Perion had been second in the Derby five years earlier, and was by the Derby winner Whisker. However, the first seven of these thoroughbred crosses were invalidated because the sequence was then broken by Verdict's sire Shogun, who was debarred from the *General Stud Book* because his seventh dam was a mare of untraced origin by Roseden foaled about 1812. Thus the only two animals in the pedigree of Lavant who did not belong to accepted thoroughbred strains were foaled a century and a quarter and a century and a half before the admission of Lavant to the *General Stud Book*, and the condition introduced in 1949 and retained for twenty years that the pedigree must be traced back for at least a hundred years was more than fulfilled.

Only two of the 2048 ancestors in the first eleven generations of the pedigree of Lavant had origins that were dubious according to the standards stipulated by the *Stud Book* authorities, and they were both foaled at least 130 years before her admission. That her admission, and the admission of other members of her family, had been delayed so long may be regarded as the result of an almost bigoted adherence to the principles of an equine *Almanach de Gotha*, in view of the other factors involved which supported the family's claim. The study of genetics has tended to minimize the importance of distant ancestors, and the influence of the mares of Perion and Roseden must be negligible in the case of Lavant and her offspring. In Peter Weatherby's phrase, Lavant has truly been assimilated with thoroughbred strains.

The prolonged exclusion of Lavant seems all the more illogical since the first compiler of the *General Stud Book* had not felt able to guarantee his volume as 'perfectly free from error'; nor could any general collection of pedigrees at the end of the eighteenth century have been flawless, since there had been no widely practised or systematic method of recording the pedigrees of racehorses before James Weatherby got to work. It is quite possible in fact that the mares by Perion and Roseden were bred from stock tracing without flaw to animals included, or worthy of inclusion, in Volume 1 of the *General Stud Book*.

The Lavant family, or more properly the Verdict family, would no doubt have gained admission to the pages of the *General Stud Book* a couple of generations sooner but for the mating of Finale with the half-bred Shogun which resulted in Verdict. The process of qualifying approved by the *Stud Book* authorities resembled the game of snakes and ladders; the family derived from the Perion mare had climbed the rungs of the ladder laboriously for seven generations and was in sight of the goal when it trod on the head of the half-bred snake represented by Shogun and slid precipitately to the starting point of the game in a single catastrophic movement.

The snakes and ladders concept of qualification for thoroughbred status is based on a scientific fallacy, for it involves the false assumption that inherited characteristics are transmitted from generation to generation mainly in the direct female line, and that any flaw introduced into that mainstream of heredity leaves a stain that can be erased only by the long passage of time. This is in conflict with the fact that the offspring receives half its complement of genes from each of its parents. 'Lines' as such, whether male or female, can retain their potency only if the individuals in each generation are mated with the luck or judgement to preserve an effective genetic make-up.

Having exercised the right to admit in the case of Lavant in Volume 36, Weatherbys continued the process of liberalization in Volume 37 by admitting 63 mares and their produce which had formerly been considered non-Thoroughbred. The foreword to the latter volume stated that 'these mares now have the necessary crosses of thoroughbred blood and performances in all sections of their pedigrees to justify the designation "Thoroughbred" '. These newly admitted mares included members of two of Prior's most celebrated 'H-B' families, the Arab Maid family and the Solerina family.

The former ban on Lavant and her forebears sprang from an official conception of a stud book which was the opposite of a 'registry of citizenship'. Kasimerz Bobinski, the compiler of the invaluable *Family Tables of Racehorses* and the possessor of an unrivalled knowledge of racehorse pedigrees all over the world, wrote a paper advocating amendments to the conditions governing admission to the *General Stud Book* shortly before his death in 1969, in which he stated: 'If a horse or a mare has shown sufficient racing ability to be considered a valuable asset for breeding, it is because it is thought, rightly or wrongly, that it will transmit its racing merit to its progeny. If a breeder sends a mare to a successful stallion it is because he hopes to breed an animal capable of winning races. He is not interested in the influence of that stallion in later generations, even in the second, let alone the eighth. the same applies to a horse not in the GSB if it has shown sufficient merit on the racecourse. The rules governing admission to the Stud Book should give every opportunity, unfettered, to as many animals of potential breeding value as possible. To thrust back to the eighth, seventh or even fourth generation the possible beneficial influence of an outstanding animal defeats the object of the exercise.'

In his eagerness to discredit regulations which irked him Bobinski may have overstated the case. It is certainly not true that all breeders are interested only in the immediate offspring of a mating. To cite but a single instance, Sir Noel Murless and his wife accumulated the influence of The Tetrarch for two generations until they had four crosses of that paragon of speed in the mare Caerphilly, and then applied the complete outcross of the Tetrarch-free Crepello and bred the 1000 Guineas winner Caergwrle. Commercial breeders supplying the yearling market neither need nor can afford to take the long view, but many private breeders are more far-sighted than Bobinski was prepared to allow.

Few breeders and students of breeding share Bobinski's extreme views. Elsewhere in the paper quoted he wrote: 'I am in favour of radical changes in the structure of the GSB, and of liberalising the rules of entry to such an extent that any animal of above average racing ability could be used for breeding without handicapping his owner financially.' The principle of a 'registry of citizenship' could not be more unequivocally stated, but liberalization of this degree involved dropping the very safeguards that stud books were originally intended to provide. The 1969 conditions probably represented the utmost that could reasonably be conceded to the Bobinski conception of a stud book.

5

The Thoroughbred in Ireland

Deeply though the British and Irish peoples have been divided on political, religious and national issues for long periods, they have been united in the last three centuries by the bond of a common love of racing and the thoroughbred. Indeed the history of racing and breeding in Ireland, as in England, stretches back to days much earlier than the foundation of the breed of the thoroughbred in the second half of the seventeenth century. Horse racing in Ireland is of ancient origin, and the Irish had a native breed of small running horses, the Hobby, corresponding to the Galloway breed of Scotland and England, long before there was any thought of improvement through the importation of stallions and mares from the Middle East.

This parallel can be extended a stage further because each country possessed a similar natural centre for racing and breeding – the Curragh of Kildare in Ireland and Newmarket Heath in England. These are open grassy plains ideal for racing, and are surrounded by pastures rich in limestone which are equally suited to breeding racehorses. The Curragh and Newmarket Heath have been two of the world's most favoured, and have become two of the world's most famous, regions in the context of the thoroughbred. Moreover close resemblances have been preserved between the racing systems practised and the types of racehorses produced in the two countries.

The principal natural assets of Ireland have been a mild climate, plentiful rainfall and lush grasslands, providing perfect conditions for horse breeding. Although the landed classes of England and Ireland had a sporting link in their shared passion for racing and fox hunting during the formative period of thoroughbred evolution, Irish enthusiasm for horses was not confined to this narrow social base. As Charles Haughey, later Prime Minister of Ireland but then Minister of Agriculture and Fisheries, remarked in his opening address to the Survey Team appointed for the Horse Breeding Industry in 1965:

Traditionally, the horse has been a part of the Irish way of life. In many parts of the world, the name of Ireland is known only through the reputation of her horses and the prestige of Ireland is closely linked with the quality of the horses we send out to all parts of the world.

Horse sports of various kinds are widely practised, and an understanding of and affection for horses are instinctive in the majority of Irishmen. Moreover the breeding of racehorses is regarded not as a separate, exotic activity, but as a branch of general farming worthy of encouragement by the Government. Given this set of propitious factors, it is no wonder that Ireland has been able to assume great importance as a source of racehorses and breeding stock. In the last quarter of the twentieth century Ireland, with a relatively small thoroughbred population, stands out as one of the world's leading producers of quality thoroughbreds.

The civil and religious turmoil with which Ireland was afflicted in the late seventeenth century and the first quarter of the eighteenth century, taken in conjunction with the comparative poverty and the geographical separation of the country, meant that Ireland did not participate in the importation of Eastern stallions and mares which sparked off the evolution of the thoroughbred. The thoroughbred was an essentially English creation. Irish racing and breeding began to increase after 1730. By the early years of the nineteenth century race meetings were being held on twenty-two Irish courses, with five annual meetings at the Curragh. In 1813 sixteen King's Plates, the officially sponsored races intended to encourage the breeding of horses capable of carrying big weights over long distances, were run in Ireland, only six fewer than in England. In the same year about 400 individual horses ran on Irish courses, and forty stallions were advertised to stand at studs in Ireland.

It is clear, however, that many of those Irish stallions covered mostly non-thoroughbred mares. In Volume 3 of the *General Stud Book* published in 1832 the Irish mares were segregated in a section of their own and there were only 113 of them, less than one-tenth of the number of mares accounted for in Britain. On the other hand Irish-bred horses were beginning to show the mettle of their pasture.

Bob Booty was one of the first Irish-bred horses to race successfully in England and make his name afterwards as a stallion. He was owned by Denis Bowes Daly, a friend of the Prince Regent who invited Daly to bring him over to run at Brighton in 1808. Bob Booty, then four years old, was second in two races at Brighton, and suffered two further defeats at nearby Lewes. But he did not return home empty-handed, as he concluded his expedition by winning the King's Plates, run in 4-mile (6400-metre) heats, at Warwick and Lichfield. The next year he won the Kildare Stakes, then one of the most important races in Ireland, and a King's Plate at the Curragh before retiring to stud there.

The main contribution of Bob Booty to the progress of the Irish thoroughbred was to sire Guiccioli, who was referred to disparagingly early in her life as 'a cat of a thing' but turned the tables on her critics by becoming a great broodmare and producing the two top-class racehorses Birdcatcher and Faugh-a-Ballagh. They were both by Sir Hercules, bred in the North of Ireland by Lord Langford. Sir Hercules was unbeaten as a two-year-old in Ireland, and was sent to England as a three-year-old in 1829 to win races at York, Doncaster and Newmarket and finish third in the St Leger.

Sir Hercules, whose black coat was flecked with white hairs, was retired as a stallion to the Brownstown Stud at the Curragh then owned by George Knox, a native of County Mayo. Brownstown is the oldest Irish stud, with a continuous history going back to the last quarter of the eighteenth century when Tom Tug (known as Rover at the time he won ten races in England) stood there. Brownstown has changed hands many times. It became the property of the McGrath family in 1940, and under their ownership was the source of such top-class performers as the Derby winner Arctic Prince, the Irish Derby winners Panaslipper and Weaver's Hall, the French Oaks winner Sweet Mimosa and the great and versatile Levmoss, winner of the Prix du Cadran, the Ascot Gold Cup and the Prix de l'Arc de Triomphe in the same season.

It is appropriate that the stud which was to figure in the main stream of Classic breeding for so long should have produced the first Irish horse destined to have an enduring influence on the breeding of Classic horses. Sir Hercules sired The Corsair, winner of the 2000 Guineas in 1839, and Coronation, winner of the Derby two years later. But it was Birdcatcher who, through his sons Oxford and

The Baron, founded two male lines that were still prominent in Classic breeding a century and a half later.

Birdcatcher, foaled in 1833, was a chestnut with a white blaze and stocking half way up his near hind leg. His coat was flecked with white hairs like that of his sire. He was sold to William Disney, of neighbouring Lark Lodge, when he was weaned, but went down with such a serious attack of flu as a yearling that his life was despaired of. He was turned out in a paddock to die, and the fact that he survived may be attributed to his own strong constitution rather than the drastic treatment of placing two powerful blisters on his ribs. The illness retarded his development, and he ran only once as a two-year-old, finishing unplaced in the Paget Stakes at the Curragh October meeting won by Sir Hercules's daughter Caroline. He matured rapidly during the winter and on his reappearance at the Curragh April meeting won the Madrid Stakes from eight opponents. That performance established him as one of the leading Irish three-year-olds. His best performance was given in the Peel Cup at the Curragh October meeting. The field of three included the formidable six-year-old Freney, who had carried 10 st 4 lb (65 kilos) and conceded at least 29 lb (13 kilos) to each of his nine opponents when winning the important Northumberland Handicap a month earlier. Birdcatcher took charge of his jockey 'English' Edwards soon after the start of the 1¾-mile (2800-metre) race and ran clean away to win by 500 yards (457 metres). Edwards was unable to pull him up, and he galloped out of control down the steep back road to Newbridge before he stopped of his own accord opposite the cavalry barracks. In spite of being jarred and exhausted, Birdcatcher was saddled again for the Mulgrave Handicap the next day, but was unplaced behind another son of Sir Hercules, Langford.

Not surprisingly Birdcatcher, although he did win three races as a four-year-old, was never the same again. Happily his headstrong behaviour in the Peel Cup did not prejudice his prospects as a stallion. His stud career was divided between the Curragh, Newmarket, Yorkshire and Warwickshire. His location made no difference. He lived to the age of twenty-seven, and wherever he was, the results were excellent. He was leading sire of winners in Great Britain in 1855 and 1856. His progeny included the Derby winner Daniel O'Rourke, and Oaks winner Songstress, the 1000 Guineas winners Habena and Manganese, and the St Leger winners Knight of St George, Warlock and The Baron.

As remarkable as Birdcatcher's ability to sire Classic winners was his consistency as a stallion. He figured in the top twenty sires of winners fifteen times, and in four of those years his progeny won more races than the progeny of any other stallion. In 1853, when he was fourth in the list of sires of winners, he was responsible for no fewer than forty-one individual winners of seventy-one races. In the second of his championship years he had thirty-seven individual winners of eighty races.

So genuinely prepotent a stallion was likely to have at least one son capable of continuing the dynasty. In fact he had two, The Baron and Oxford, though of this pair only the former was bred in Ireland. The Baron, foaled in 1842, was bred by George Watts, an English-born vet practising at Jockey Hall, Dublin. His dam Echidna also was bred by Watts, but had such an ugly head that he had tried to sell her, without success, when she was a three-year-old. The Baron did not run as a two-year-old, but as a three-year-old won three good races in Ireland, the Madrid, the Kirwan and the Waterford Stakes, before being sent to run in the Liverpool St Leger in July, in which he ran deplorably. According to 'The Druid', the great Malton trainer John Scott examined The Baron closely at Liverpool and observed that 'he was as fat as a bull, and had barshoes and fearfully festered soles, and had been made twice the savage he was by muzzles'. Scott approached Watts and told him that he thought he could win the St Leger with him. Watts agreed to send The Baron to Malton and Scott was as good as his word, though he commented that The Baron 'took more work than I ever gave a horse in my life, and required more management'. For good measure The Baron went on to win the Cesarewitch, but was unplaced under a penalty in the Cambridgeshire.

The Baron had three seasons at William Theobald's stud at Stockwell, now in South London. He was so poorly patronized that he was then sold to go to France, but he left behind Stockwell, winner of the 2000 Guineas and St Leger, the outstanding three-year-old of 1852 and afterwards dubbed 'The Emperor of Stallions'. Stockwell was the male line ancestor of Phalaris, the most potent factor in the Classic breeding of the second half of the twentieth century.

Oxford, foaled in 1857, had nothing like the racing class of Birdcatcher's other important son The Baron. Oxford did not win until he was four, although he ran the subsequent Derby winner

Thormanby to a neck in the Mostyn Stakes at Chester as a two-year-old. When he opened his winning account Oxford did so appropriately in the City Members Plate over 1¼ miles (2000 metres) at Oxford and went on to win the mile (1600 metres) Chesterfield Handicap at York. This was not the kind of form calculated to secure good opportunities at stud, and the highest place he ever attained in the list of sires of winners was seventh. Nevertheless, he was the male ancestor of Blandford, the best Classic stallion in England or Ireland in the period between the two world wars, and still a factor in Classic breeding half a century later.

Faugh-a-Ballagh, the eight years younger brother of Birdcatcher, became the first Irish-bred winner of a Classic race when he was successful in the 1844 St Leger. He was an extremely high-class horse that autumn, for he went on to win the Grand Duke Michael Stakes, the precursor of the Champion Stakes, and the Cesarewitch and to finish second to the year older Evenus in the Cambridgeshire. He was a fairly successful stallion in England, standing in Staffordshire. His son Leamington, a useful racehorse, became an influential sire in North America. But his triumph as a stallion came after his exportation to France in 1855. His daughter Fille de l'Air won both the Oaks and the Prix de Diane, the corresponding race in France, in 1864, and was the only filly to achieve that double until Pawneese 112 years later.

Another great Irish horse of the first half of the nineteenth century was Harkaway, bred at Sheepbridge in County Down in 1834. Harkaway, a light chestnut with a huge white blaze, was so coarsely made that he was described as more like a 'carthorse than a racer', but he had magnificent action. Tom Ferguson, who bred and owned him, was an irascible man, but his roughness of tongue and manner was redeemed partially by his intense pride in his great horse. His faith in Harkaway was such that he was always prepared to push him to the furthest limits of his ability and endurance. Even as a two-year-old, Harkaway beat the good three-year-old Langford in the Constantine Stakes over a mile (1600 metres) at the Curragh and the following June he beat Birdcatcher into second place in the Northumberland Handicap on the same course. He beat Birdcatcher again in the Wellington Stakes at the Curragh three months later, and on that occasion Birdcatcher was unplaced.

Harkaway raided England as a four-year-old and five-year-old and won three races on each of these expeditions. He demonstrated his class and versatility by winning English races over distances ranging from the 1¼ miles (2000 metres) of the Stand Cup at Chester to the 4 miles (6400 metres) of the His Majesty's Plate at Doncaster. However, his finest performances were his two victories in the Goodwood Cup.

Ferguson's pride in Harkaway overreached itself when the horse went to stud at the Curragh in 1840. His fee was set at 100 guineas. The highest fee charged for any stallion advertised to stand in England that year was 30 guineas, and that was the fee for the Derby winner Bay Middleton and the St Leger winner Touchstone. Consequently Harkaway covered only three mares. The next year he stood at Newmarket for 30 guineas, and then returned to the Curragh at the realistic fee of 10 guineas.

Harkaway did not fulfil his owner's expectations as a sire. His highest place in the list of sires of winners was seventh in 1849, and he was eighth six years later. His best son was King Tom, who was second to Andover (by Bay Middleton) in the 1854 Derby. King Tom ensured that Harkaway has a permanent place in breeding records by siring the Derby winner Kingcraft and St Angela, the dam of St Simon.

Although these good horses were bred in Ireland during the first half of the nineteenth century, many foreigners regarded them as flukes, were unimpressed with the general quality of Irish thorough-breds and regarded Ireland mainly as a source of hunters. As late as 1890 the French writer 'S. F. Touchstone' inserted this derogatory paragraph in his book *History of Celebrated English and French Thorough-Bred Stallions*:

Birdcatcher is one of the few horses that the Emerald Isle has real reason to be proud of. In Ireland, notwithstanding its glorious pasturelands, breeders rarely care to pay high prices for their stallions, and have never been very particular as to the mares that were served. Then again, apart from the financial question, corn and forage were never of first-rate quality, and this is a point about which the breeder cannot be too particular. It is easy, therefore, to understand the general inferiority of Irish produce; at the same time Birdcatcher, Harkaway, Chanticleer and Faugh-a-Ballagh are sufficient proofs that great things can be done . . . if trainers and others will but give themselves the trouble.

The deeds of Birdcatcher, Harkaway and Faugh-a-Ballagh have been noted. Chanticleer, the fourth of Touchstone's quartet of high-class Irish horses, had been an excellent stayer of the same type as Harkaway, and went to England to win the Northumberland Plate at Newcastle, the Goodwood Stakes and the Doncaster Cup as a five-year-old in 1848. He was a son of Birdcatcher, and proved his own worth as a stallion by siring Sunbeam, the winner of the St Leger in 1858.

Touchstone's criticism of the Irish thoroughbred was ill-timed. The Irish horses Barcaldine, Bendigo and Kilwarlin had shown outstanding ability during the previous decade, and only seven years after his book was published Galtee More, bred at the Knockaney Stud in County Limerick and named after the highest point of the Galtee mountains in adjacent County Tipperary, won the English Triple Crown of the 2000 Guineas, the Derby and the St Leger. Galtee More spent his racing career in England, where he was trained by Sam Darling at Beckhampton. He was certainly a horse of supreme ability, and was beaten in only two of his thirteen races – in the second of his five races as a two-year-old and in the last of his eight races as a three-year-old, which was the Cambridgeshire in which he gave a fine performance to be fifth under top weight.

Galtee More was followed five years later by his half-brother Ard Patrick, who won the Derby and as a four-year-old beat the brilliant filly Sceptre and that year's Triple Crown winner Rock Sand in one of the most dramatic races ever staged for the Eclipse Stakes. Unfortunately neither Galtee More nor Ard Patrick was given the chance to reinforce the top-class bloodstock resources of his native country. Galtee More was sold to Russia and Ard Patrick to Germany for the identical sum of £20,000.

Galtee More and Ard Patrick were bred by John Gubbins, an enthusiastic fox-hunting man and intrepid horseman whose activities at his Knockaney and Bruree Studs symbolized the efforts that were being made to raise the quality of Irish breeding in the last quarter of the nineteenth century. Gubbins's greatest stroke was the purchase of Kendal as a two-year-old from the Duke of Westminster for 3000 guineas. Kendal had been one of the best two-year-olds of 1885, when he won six of his eight races, including the July Stakes at Newmarket, and beat Ormonde in a trial before the subsequent Triple Crown winner made his racecourse debut.

In 1893, the year that Galtee More was conceived, Gubbins sold Kendal to the Bruntwood Stud in Cheshire, but replaced him at Knockaney with St Florian, a son of St Simon who had run several good races in top-class company before winning the valuable Duke of York Stakes at Kempton. Gubbins proceeded to mate Morganette, the dam of Galtee More, regularly with St Florian, and in the fourth year this mating was consummated the produce was Ard Patrick.

The opening of Leopardstown, a park course situated in beautiful countryside at the foot of Three Rock mountain close to the outskirts of Dublin, in 1888 acted as a strong stimulus to racing and breeding in Ireland. Two years later the Leopardstown Grand Prize, for two-year-olds and upwards over 5 furlongs (1000 metres) was introduced as the first £1000 race ever run in Ireland, and had a popular result when the locally trained two-year-old Eyrefield, the even money favourite, beat the English three-year-old John Morgan by three lengths. Better prize money encouraged investment in bloodstock, and by the turn of the century the Knockaney Stud was matched by other top-class breeding establishments like Eustace Loder's Eyrefield and Old Connell studs and William Hall-Walker's Tully Stud.

One of the shrewdest investments was that of Sir Henry Greer, who bought Gallinule as a five-year-old in 1889 and installed him as a stallion at the Brownstown Stud. Gallinule, bred in Lincolnshire, was one of the fastest English two-year-olds of 1886, when his four victories included the National Breeders Produce Stakes. Harsh treatment by the handicappers frustrated his attempts to win races during the next two seasons, and his racing career was terminated by a tendency to break blood vessels. He became a marvellously successful stallion, heading the list of sires of winners for the three seasons 1903 to 1905, and figuring in the top twenty sires no fewer than nineteen times.

Gallinule was a vital element in the triumph of Eustace Loder. He was the sire of Loder's Pretty Polly, one of the most brilliant fillies in Turf history and winner of the 1000 Guineas, the Oaks and the St Leger in 1904. Two years later Loder's breeding had a dual Classic success when Spearmint won the Derby and the Grand Prix de Paris.

Hall-Walker was an enthusiastic student of astrology and designed the boxes at Tully so that his horses could have a view of the sky and the stars. He combined an eccentric belief that their horoscopes were an important factor in arranging the matings for his mares with the level-headed astuteness of a knowledgeable and practical breeder. Between 1900 and the First World War he bred the 2000 Guineas and Derby winner Minoru (leased to King Edward VII), the 1000 Guineas and Oaks winner Cherry Lass, the 1000 Guineas winner Witch Elm, and the St Leger winners Prince Palatine and Night Hawk.

Hall-Walker (later Lord Wavertree) did far more than raise the status of Irish breeding during his tenure of the Tully Stud. He conferred lasting benefits of inestimable importance on all breeding in both England and Ireland when in 1915 he gave all his bloodstock to the British Government on the condition that the Government purchased his properties at Tully and at Russley Park in Wiltshire at an independent valuation. Thus for £65,625 the Government obtained not only two first-class stud farms but priceless bloodstock including forty-three mares from some of the choicest strains in the British Isles. The Tully property became the British National Stud, with Sir Henry Greer as its first Director, until the Second World War. The British interests and stock were then moved to England, and Tully was handed over to the Irish Government. Tully became the Irish National Stud and a corner-stone of Irish stud-farming policy in the second half of the twentieth century.

The improvement of the quality of Irish thoroughbreds in the second half of the twentieth century was accompanied by a corresponding increase in their quantity, both in absolute terms and in relation to the thoroughbred population of England, Scotland and Wales. By the time that Volume 19 of the *General Stud Book*, the last in which the Irish mares were segregated, was published in 1901 the Irish section comprised more than 1400 mares, nearly a quarter of the total. The relative numerical strength of the Irish breeding industry continued to increase in the second half of the twentieth century, and by the 1980's Ireland was producing more thoroughbred foals than Britain.

Early in the twentieth century Irish breeders were gaining a position as important suppliers to the growing English commercial market for yearlings. Irish yearlings became features of the sales conducted annually by the auctioneering firm Tattersalls at Newmarket and Doncaster. The Irish contribution to the Doncaster St Leger Yearling Sales was especially prominent and in 1913, the last year before the outbreak of the First World War, seventy-four of the 321 sold there came from Irish studs. Nor did the Irish yearlings suffer by comparison with the English. The previous year Edward

Kennedy of the Straffan Station Stud in County Kildare had submitted a curiously marked grey colt by Roi Hérode out of Vahren who was knocked down to Dermot McCalmont for 1300 guineas. This colt was The Tetrarch, who became a byword for speed not only through his own brilliant performances as a two-year-old but through his profound influence on the modern thoroughbred.

The advent of the Aga Khan (1877–1957) after the First World War gave a fresh impetus to high-class breeding in Ireland. His interest in the subject had been fired by conversations with William Hall-Walker during a visit to Tully as early as 1904, but it was not until 1921 that he began to lay the foundations of one of the world's greatest racing and breeding empires by judicious purchases of yearling fillies. He established breeding operations in Ireland and France and appointed Sir Henry Greer, who continued as Director of the National Stud, as his first stud manager in Ireland. At one time he had as many as five Irish studs though later, when his grandson had succeeded to control of the whole vast enterprise, breeding operations were concentrated at the Ballymany and Sheshoon Studs at the Curragh. What counted was not the number of studs but the quality of their output, and during his own lifetime the founder of this empire bred the Triple Crown winner Bahram, the Derby and St Leger winner Tulyar, the Oaks winners Udaipur and Masaka and scores of other top-class horses, including the brilliant 2000 Guineas winner Palestine, at his studs in Ireland.

Blandford, the sire of Bahram and Udaipur, was one of the prime assets of Irish breeding during the 1920s and the early 1930s. He was bred at the National Stud at Tully and retired to the Cloghran Stud near Dublin when his racing career was cut short by a leg injury as a three-year-old. He became the foremost Classic sire of the period between the two world wars and had the Derby winners Trigo, Blenheim and Windsor Lad, besides Bahram, among his progeny.

Blandford spent his last two years before his death in 1935 in England. The reason for his transfer was the imposition of a 40 per cent *ad valorem* tax on bloodstock imported from Ireland imposed by the British Government in retaliation for the Irish Free State's repudiation of the Land Annuities and other debts. The tax was a setback to the Irish breeding industry. In a rhetorical outburst one breeder wrote to the *Irish Field*:

What are we going to do with our surplus horses? Give them away? No. Produce more? No. Stop production? Yes. But think of the cost such a course will be to Ireland, the Ireland of the future. It is so easy to destroy and so difficult to rebuild.

Fortunately the tax was rescinded in 1937 before the Irish breeding industry had suffered many of the baneful long term consequences that had been feared. The period since the Second World War has been one of almost uninterrupted progress for Irish breeding. This progress was initiated by the establishment by law of a Racing Board to take over the conduct of racing while leaving disciplinary matters and the rules of racing in the hands of the Turf Club whose authority had previously been absolute. The Racing Board was to take over the operations and profits of the Tote and also draw funds from a levy on on-course bookmaking. The duty of the Board was to distribute the funds so derived for the benefit of racing. The most important result of the Racing Board's activities was substantial and progressive increases in prize money which have been reflected in improved demand for racehorses and have stimulated investment in bloodstock from both domestic and foreign sources. However, the fact that the industry received no revenue from off-course bookmaking was a constant irritant. In the late 1980s the Board, under the chairmanship of the go-ahead business man Michael Smurfit, brought strong pressure to bear on the Government to release funds from off-course bookmaking for much-needed modernization of Irish racecourses.

Increased prize money was the essential foundation upon which Irish trainers of genius like Paddy Prendergast at the Curragh and Vincent O'Brien in Tipperary were able to build. Their success in not only attracting wealthy owners from abroad but also in winning many of the most coveted races in the European programme focused attention on Ireland as a leading thoroughbred country.

The Survey Team of 1965 acknowledged, a little grudgingly, that the Irish National Stud provided 'a reasonable service to small breeders'. The Irish National Stud Company was formed in 1945 for the purpose of helping Irish breeders by standing high-class stallions at a reasonable fee to mate with approved mares selected by ballot. In 1980 the stud owned ten stallions, half of them stationed at Tully and the rest boarded out at studs in County Limerick and County Meath. In 1988 the stud owned seven flat race stallions, mostly intended for breeding precociously fast horses, and the successful National Hunt stallion Crash Course.

Thus the Irish National Stud was not concerned primarily with the production of Classic horses, though it did breed Tap On Wood, the winner of the 2000 Guineas in 1979 from one of its own small band of mares and by its own stallion Sallust. During the 1970s the Irish National Stud had broadened the scope of its assistance to the breeding industry under the inspired management of Michael Osborne, a veterinary surgeon who combined vision with a firm grasp of practical detail. The measures adopted during his regime included the investigation of improved methods of stabling, feeding and managing thoroughbreds, the organization of stud management training courses, the control of a foster mother service, the promotion of equine research and the establishment of a museum and a tourist service to enhance appreciation of the Irish horse. Osborne was succeeded as manager by John Clarke, who continued to develop the stud as an important asset of the bloodstock industry.

The Survey Team expressed the opinion that the functions of the Irish National Stud should be extended further, and that it should help to overcome the shortage of top-class stallions in the country by always standing at least one prestige stallion. To implement this recommendation would have necessitated the expenditure of huge sums of money on the escalating world market, and the stud adhered steadfastly to a policy of owning good stallions whose services could be offered at a fee which the bulk of Irish breeders could afford.

In practice private enterprise was able to take up a good deal of the slack in respect of the shortage of top-class stallions which the Survey Team had identified. A fiscal incentive to investment in stallions had been introduced by the terms of the Finance Act of 1939 under which earnings from stallions standing on a farm were included in the Schedule B assessment on the land. But this incentive was mild in comparison with the new deal for breeders of the 1970s which freed income from stallion shares and nominations from the burden of tax.

Incentives cannot be fully effective unless there are the men with drive and skill to exploit them. The quality of Irish bloodstock owed its striking improvement in the 1970s largely to the expert judgement and commercial acumen of the controllers of vast breeding enterprises like the Airlie-Grangewilliam-Simmonstown group of studs owned by Captain Tim Rogers and the Coolmore-Castle

Hyde group of studs of which John Magnier was managing director and in which his father-in-law Vincent O'Brien and the leading international owner and breeder Robert Sangster had substantial interests.

The Airlie group stood Petingo and Habitat, two of the best European stallions in the 1970s, Habitat continuing to be a leading sire of fast horses for most of the next decade also. However, Tim Rogers died on New Year's Day, 1984, after a long fight against leukaemia, and although his widow Sonia carried on and kept the Airlie group in the front rank of Irish breeding the leadership passed to Coolmore. By 1988 the Coolmore empire embraced a total of thirteen studs, six of them within a few miles of the small Tipperary town of Fethard, with seventeen high-class stallions dedicated to breeding for the flat and four designated specialist National Hunt stallions. The importance of Coolmore in the national economy had been recognized by the appointment of John Magnier to the Irish Senate, just as Vincent O'Brien's contribution as trainer and breeder received recognition by an Honorary Doctorate of Law at University College Dublin.

The mainspring of the Coolmore advance had been the invasion of the North American yearling market in the late 1970s by the football pools tycoon Robert Sangster and his associates. Their buying policy was based on two premises: firstly that the North American thoroughbred industry, underpinned by a supremely great stallion in Northern Dancer, was producing the best racehorses in the world; and secondly, that by applying the most stringent standards of pedigree and conformation to the selection process it was possible to buy numbers of yearlings at the principal sales, notably the Keeneland July Sales, that would include sufficient colts of Classic racing ability to ensure the profitability of the enterprise even though capital outlays of millions of dollars were required. A cardinal element in the policy was that the colts chosen must have stallion pedigrees – that is, pedigrees of such high class at all points that they would appeal strongly to the owners of the best mares and therefore command top prices for shares and nominations.

The buying team was headed by Vincent O'Brien himself, acknowledged to be one of the world's most discriminating judges of yearlings. Spectacular success was achieved, and in the 1980s the implementation of the policy landed the Derby winners The Minstrel and Golden Fleece, the French Derby winner Caerleon, the

2000 Guineas and Irish Derby winner El Gran Señor, the 2000 Guineas winner Lomond and Sadler's Wells, who was second in the French Derby but won the Airlie/Coolmore Irish 2000 Guineas, the Coral Eclipse Stakes and the Phoenix Champion Stakes – all sons or grandsons of Northern Dancer. Although some of these Classic winners and other high-class winners obtained through the policy went to stud in the United States, the O'Brien and Magnier connection brought Lomond, Caerleon and Sadler's Wells to Coolmore with results seen to be instantly successful for the quality of Irish breeding when they began to have runners in the late 1980s.

For several years the Sangster operations dominated this particular field, but then the going began to become progressively tougher as the Arabs burst into the same market deploying even greater financial resources. However, the Coolmore empire was so well established that it was able to continue to recruit stallions of the highest class like the proven sire Ahonoora, purchased from the Irish National Stud, the British Classic winners Commanche Run and Don't Forget Me, and the Breeders Cup Mile winner Last Tycoon.

The quality of Irish breeding was also boosted by the development of the Aga Khan's private stud operations. By the late 1980s their numerical strength had risen to more than 220 mares distributed between his two Irish (Ballymany and Sheshoon) and two French (Saint Crespin and Bonneval) studs, and the superb class of their produce was emphasized by the fact that they supplied their owner with a total of ten victories in the Derby, the French Derby and the Irish Derby between 1979 and 1988. His winners of the Derby at Epsom were Shergar (1981), Shahrastani (1986) and Kahyasi (1988), and the glow of this triumphal progress was dimmed only by the kidnapping and disappearance of Shergar after only one season, which had had encouraging results, at the Ballymany Stud. The theft and presumed killing of Shergar had tragi-comic overtones as a result of the circumstances of the police enquiry into the unsolved crime.

The success of the Aga Khan as a Classic breeder sprang partly from the continued vitality of thoroughbred families founded by fillies, for example Mumtaz Mahal and Qurrat Al Ain, purchased by his grandfather when he was setting up as a breeder in the 1920s, and partly from judicious additions to the band of mares by large scale package deals. These deals included the purchases of the bloodstock previously owned by the leading French owner-breeders

Marcel Boussac and François Dupré. The Aga Khan's private studs, together with the smaller scale operation of the Ballymacoll Stud of Sir Michael Sobell and his son-in-law Lord Weinstock, complemented the operations of Coolmore, Airlie and other commercial studs to consolidate the status of Ireland as a major producer of Classic thoroughbreds; while in the late 1980s the progress of Irish quality breeding was receiving a fresh impetus from the growing involvement of the Al Maktoum family as described in the chapter on the Later Evolution of the British Thoroughbred (q.v.).

In 1979 the Airlie and Coolmore stud enterprises combined to sponsor the Irish 2000 Guineas and Goffs, the leading Irish bloodstock sales company, sponsored the Irish 1000 Guineas. The Irish Derby had been sponsored by the Irish Hospitals Sweepstakes as the Irish Sweeps Derby since 1962, and the Irish Oaks had been sponsored by Guinness since the following year. As a result Ireland had for the first time a properly endowed Classic programme in keeping with its status as a leading producer of quality thoroughbreds. Nor was sponsorship confined to the Classic races. In 1976, according to the comprehensive *Economic Analysis of the Irish Racing and Bloodstock Industry* by Michael MacCormac of University College, Dublin, total sponsorship of Irish flat races amounted to no more than £121,360; but the appointment of a sponsorship committee by the Stewards of the Irish Turf Club led to a massive upsurge of sponsorship in the 1980s, particularly at the Curragh and at the metropolitan racecourses Phoenix Park and Leopardstown, not only by industrial firms but also by stud owners among whom the idea spread rapidly that sponsorship of a race was an indispensable promotional expense and essential in order to keep up with the Joneses.

Despite its increased prosperity Ireland remained a small, mainly pastoral and agricultural country. Inevitably its home market for thoroughbreds was restricted, and the Irish breeding industry was largely export orientated. *An Analysis of the Irish Racing and Breeding Industry*, issued by the leading sales company Goffs in 1982, estimated foreign earnings of nearly £9 million from stallion fees, mares boarding fees and keep charges. However, the viability of the industry depended mainly on its ability to sell a high proportion of its produce to foreign buyers. In 1975 a new sales complex was opened by Goffs at Kill, 15 miles (24 kilometres) south-west of Dublin, and in 1988 Goffs' rivals, the English sales company Tattersalls, began to trade at another new sales complex adjacent to the famous Irish

Grand National course, Fairyhouse, in County Meath. These ventures, with their absolutely modern facilities, were powerful factors in the promotion of the Irish Thoroughbred as an international commodity. At the same time many Irish breeders preferred to sell at least part of their output at the main English sales – the Doncaster St Leger, the Highflyer and the October Sales for yearlings, and the Newmarket December Sales for foals and breeding stock – where their horses were aimed directly at the English buyers who were their best customers, and where the international market in thoroughbreds had world-wide prestige.

Irish-bred thoroughbreds made their mark in the racing countries of every continent – not least in the country whose thoroughbred population excelled all others in quality and quantity, that is the United States. Few horses, apart from Northern Dancer in the 1970s and 1980s, have had a more profound influence on top-class American breeding than Nasrullah, bred by the Aga Khan in County Kildare in 1940, and Turn-To, bred by Major E. R. Miville and Mrs G. L. Hastings in the same county eleven years later. Turn-To was by Royal Charger, then standing at the Irish National Stud. After a brilliant racing career cut short by a bowed tendon in the March of his three-year-old season, Turn-To became one of the best American stallions of his time. A feature of his achievement was that he was a sire of sires, as his sons Hail To Reason, Sir Gaylord and First Landing all followed in his distinguished footsteps. The two first-named sired winners of the Derby at Epsom, Hail To Reason being responsible for Roberto and Sir Gaylord for Sir Ivor; First Landing sired the Kentucky Derby winner Riva Ridge.

The direct impact of Irish breeding on the English Classic races was constantly in evidence. During the thirty-four years from 1955 to 1988 Irish-bred horses won forty-two, or 24.7 per cent, of the 170 British Classic races run. This is a record which speaks eloquently for the high quality of Irish bloodstock because the English Classic races during this period were the target not only for the best of the home produced three-year-olds but for many choicely bred horses from North America and Continental Europe as well. The Irish-bred Classic winners included the Derby winners Hard Ridden, Psidium, Larkspur, Troy, Shergar and Kahyasi.

Troy's Derby victory was the climax for a triumphant season for Irish-bred horses on the British Turf in 1979; for horses bred in Ireland then won ten of the nineteen British Group 1 Pattern Races while home-bred horses won only three. If this was a success rate in the most competitive British races which even the most sanguine Irish breeder would scarcely have expected to see repeated consistently, it did provide telling evidence of the progress that Ireland had made as a source of Classic racehorses since Galtee More became the first Irish-bred Derby winner.

6

The Thoroughbred in
North America

There were no horses on the American continent in January 1519. The prehistoric ancestors of the horse had lived there for sixty million years, but had all died out. The later evolution of the horse and his domestication had been confined to Europe, Asia and Africa.

In February 1519 Cortes landed in Mexico with sixteen horses, the first representatives of the species to set foot on the continent for tens of thousands of years. The reason for the previous extermination has never been discovered. Whatever scourge of disease or predatory foes may have been responsible, there is nothing in the climate, soil and vegetation in large areas of the North and South Americas that is inimical to horses. The animals – eleven stallions and five mares – brought by Cortes, with many others afterwards imported by the Spanish conquerors, flourished and bred successfully. Some were purchased or stolen from the ranches and mission stations by Indians; and some again escaped from the Indian tribes to breed and multiply in the wild state and form the mustang herds of the prairies. Many different breeds were introduced or developed, and the thoroughbred has penetrated every corner of North America. In the 1980s every state of the Union and seven provinces of Canada produced some thoroughbred foals, even though production was averaging only about two per year in Alaska; and North America had the largest thoroughbred population in the world.

Nearly a century and a half after the Mexican landing of Cortes, Richard Nicolls captured New Amsterdam from the Dutch and became the first English governor of the colony under its changed name of New York. In the following year Nicolls laid out what is generally accepted as America's first regular racecourse at a place then called Salisbury Plain, but later known as Hempstead Plain, on

103

Long Island. Nicolls presented a silver cup to be run for each spring and autumn, explaining that he did so 'not so much for the divertisement of youth as for encouraging the bettering of the breed of horses, which through great neglect has been impaired'.

The kind of horses used for racing on Hempstead Plain is unknown. Governor Nicolls laid out his racecourse before the specialized breeding of racehorses had proceeded far in England itself, but there is no doubt that from the outset the colonists drew their ideas of the form that racing should take and the type of horse that was required from the English model. The colonists were importing horses of the evolving breed of the thoroughbred, mostly through Virginia, in the eighteenth century. In 1730, a twelve-year-old stallion called Bulle Rock, alleged to be by the Darley Arabian out of a mare by the Byerley Turk, was advertized by Messrs Samuel Patton and Samuel Gist, and Virginia breeders were urged to take advantage of his services in order to improve their bloodstock. Bulle Rock was followed by other stallions like Dabster, Jolly Roger, Janus and Fearnought, together with numbers of mares of similar quality. Janus, or Little Janus as he was sometimes called on account of his small stature – he stood only 14.0¾ h.h. (1.44 metres) – was by Lord Godolphin's Janus, a son of the Godolphin Arabian. His dam was an unnamed mare by Fox. Little Janus won races at Winchester and Salisbury, running in 4-mile (6400-metre) heats, as a five-year-old in 1751. He was sent to Virginia after a few seasons at stud near Oxford, and became a famous sire of fast horses. He lived to the great age of thirty-four, and inbreeding to him was practised intensively to produce speedy quarter horses for 2-furlong (400-metre) racing.

Little Janus was really outside the mainstream of progress towards a breed of thoroughbred horses in America. American racing in the middle of the eighteenth century, and for another 100 years, was based on races decided by 4-mile (6400-metre) heats as the supreme test. The importation of Selima, a daughter of the Godolphin Arabian, and the Cub mare at the same period as Little Janus had a more profound influence, since they were among the most productive of tap-roots. However, the War of Independence was long past before the breed of racehorses in America received a decisive impetus from the importation of Medley and Diomed.

Medley, an extremely handsome grey horse by Gimcrack foaled in 1776, won twelve races including a walk-over, and was imported

into Virginia as a nine-year-old. Later advertisements claimed that
'his stock are known to be the most elegant in the state', but it was
as a sire of broodmares that he had a lasting effect on the evolution
of the racehorse in the United States, for his daughters proved
eminently satisfactory mates for the amazing Diomed.

The story of Diomed is one of the most extraordinary in the
development of the breed of racehorses anywhere in the world. He
owed his unique place in the annals of the Turf to two separate
aspects of his career: he was the first winner of the most famous of
all races, the Derby, and much later had an epoch-making influence
on breeding in the United States.

Diomed was bred by Mr Richard Vernon, of Newmarket, and
was by Florizel, a son of Herod. He was sold to Sir Charles Bunbury, the first dictator of the Turf, before he went into training.
Although the future greatness of the Derby was then only dimly
perceived and his victory at Epsom caused little stir, Diomed was
undoubtedly a very good horse and went through his three-year-
old season without defeat. He won his first three races, including
the Fortescue Stakes and the Claret Stakes at Newmarket, the next
year, but met his first defeat in August when Lord Grosvenor's
Fortitude beat him in the Nottingham Stakes. From then on little
went right for him. He was beaten again by Boudrow in a match
at the Newmarket First October Meeting, paid forfeit in the only
race in which he was entered as a five-year-old and won only one
of his seven races, the King's Plate at Guildford, as a six-year-old.
His racing career came to an end when he went lame in the second
heat of a similar race at Lewes in July of that year.

Diomed began his stud career at a fee of 5 guineas. This was later
raised to 10 guineas, but his popularity diminished when his progeny
failed to come up to expectations, and many proved temperamental.
By 1798, when he was twenty-one years old, his fee had dropped
to 2 guineas and his usefulness as a stallion was apparently at an
end. Bunbury sold him for 50 guineas to John Hoomes, of Bowling
Green, Virginia, who was speculating on the rising bloodstock
market in the United States. Hoomes promptly passed him on to
Colonel Miles Selden, of Tree Hill in the same state, for £1000, but
this spectacular profit was reduced by the considerable cost of shipping him across the Atlantic. Weatherby's secretary wrote to a
correspondent in America: 'Mr Weatherby recommends you
strongly to avoid putting any mares to him; for he has had fine

mares to him here, and never produced anything good. A horse of his character on the turf must, at his age, have acquired some character as a stallion, and had that been a good one he would not have gone to America.' Other detractors added that he was none too virile.

Diomed, superannuated in England and dismissed as worse than ineffectual, could hardly have entered the Virginian stud in less auspicious circumstances. He quickly gave the lie to his critics. Far from lacking in virility, he began to cover mares with all the fire and impetuosity of a young horse; and he not only got his mares regularly in foal but enabled them to produce one high-class race-course performer after another. At the age of twenty-nine he was still perfectly fertile, and for the next season, his last, he was advertized to cover at 'fifty dollars the season, the money to be sent with the mare, or 100 dollars the insurance to be paid in October'. He died in 1808 at the age of thirty-one.

The best of all Diomed's progeny was Sir Archie. A rich bay, standing 16 h.h. (1.62 metres), a hand taller than his sire, Sir Archie was a horse of great power and substance and striking individuality. Sir Archie, foaled in 1805, was beaten in three of his seven races, but would have had a more impressive record if he had been allowed time to make a full recovery from a serious illness before running in his first two races. He ended triumphantly by distancing Wrangler, another very good son of Diomed, in the Jockey Club Purse at Fairfield, distancing his field again in the Jockey Club Purse at Petersburg, and beating one of the crack horses of the day, Blank, at Halifax, North Carolina. He was then retired to stud because there was no horse left who could give him a race over 4 miles (6400 metres), or in 4-mile heats.

Sir Archie was bought for $5000 after his last race by General William R. Davie, one of North Carolina's distinguished Revolutionary soldiers, the founder of the University of North Carolina, member of Congress and special envoy to France. His former owner and trainer, the 'Napoleon of the Turf' William Ransom Johnson, wrote to Davie: 'I have only to say that in my opinion Sir Archie is the best horse I ever saw, and I well know that I never had any thing to do with one that was at all his equal.'

Sir Archie was nearly as long-lived as his sire, and had cleared more than $70,000 in stud fees by the time he died at the age of twenty-eight. His success was phenomenal. He was so prepotent that he was able to sire useful progeny from mares of widely differing talents. One of the most distinguished of his sons was Henry, also known as Sir Henry, who was closely inbred to Diomed since his dam was by the first Derby winner. He took part in one of the most celebrated matches of all time when he met American Eclipse on the Union course at New York in May 1823. American Eclipse was by Duroc who, like Henry, was inbred to Diomed, as he was a son of Diomed and was out of a mare by Gray Diomed, the best horse sired by Diomed before he left England. American Eclipse was so called because he gave his breeder General Nathanial Coles such an impression of strength and speed when he was only five months old that he was considered worthy to bear the name of the greatest horse that had raced in England up to that time. Like his namesake, American Eclipse was a chesnut, standing 15.3 h.h. (1.6 metres) with a good deal of white on his face. He had reached the age of nine and gained the reputation of being practically invincible when he met Henry, five years his junior, in a $20,000 challenge. The race, with American Eclipse representing the North and Henry the South, had aroused so much interest that a crowd estimated at 60,000 turned out to watch. Henry won the first of the three 4-mile (6400-metre) heats by about a length; American Eclipse had appeared very distressed and was swishing his tail violently in the final stages of the heat; the reason was plain when he pulled up as his rider Crafts, in plying his whip wildly, had cut him deeply on the sheath and testicles. Odds were laid on Henry for the second heat, and there could be no more eloquent testimony to the toughness and courage of American Eclipse than that, with a change of jockey, he came back to win by two lengths. The match had developed into a battle of attrition. Both horses were exhausted when they came out for the final heat and the exceptional strength, stamina and determination of American Eclipse prevailed. The fact that American Eclipse took nearly a minute longer to cover the 4 miles (6400 metres) in the last than Henry had done in the first heat indicated the toll that his efforts had taken.

A male line descendant of Diomed and Sir Archie who was to have an even more profound influence on the evolution of the racehorse in America was Boston, by Sir Archie's son Timoleon. Boston was so called because he was won, as an unbroken two-year-old, in a card game of that name. The loser was the distinguished Virginia attorney John Wickham, and the winner

Nathanial Rives. Before long Rives was wondering whether the colt represented a fair settlement of the debt, because Boston was so bad-tempered and intractable in his early training that it was recommended that he be 'either castrated or shot – preferably the latter'. Fortunately Rives was determined to persevere and Boston, though never the most sweet-natured of creatures, became a racehorse of exceptional toughness and courage and a great sire. He won forty of the forty-five races in which he took part, and gained thirty of his victories in 4-mile (6400-metre) heats. One of his few defeats was by the mare Fashion in a match at the Union course in May 1842 which, in its North-versus-South implications, aroused as much public enthusiasm as the American Eclipse and Henry match nineteen years earlier. This time the result was a triumph for the South because Boston, having collided with the rail and sustained a long jagged cut on his hip in the first heat, was clearly below his best in the second heat and was beaten by 60 yards (55 metres).

Boston had covered forty-two mares in the spring of 1841, and the following year, after taking part in the Fashion match and two other races in May, did a further spell of stud service before returning to the track in the autumn. He used to make a habit of trying to bite any opponents who came near him in a race, and was a ferocious horse at stud. He was completely blind and terribly emaciated when he died in January 1850 but retained his fiery spirit to the end.

Boston was leading sire in 1851, 1852 and 1853. His greatest sons, Lexington and Lecomte, were products of his last stud season, and these two horses added piquancy to the fact by engaging in a series of close-fought duels on the racecourse. Lexington, a bay standing 15.3 h.h. (1.6 metres) with a lot of white on his legs, began his racing career under the name of Darley and carried the colours of his breeder Dr Warfield, but was really a partnership horse, the other partner being his trainer, a former negro slave. After winning his first two races the colt was bought by Richard Ten Broeck for $2500, and his name was changed to Lexington after the Kentucky town which became the centre of the breeding industry.

The black sheep of a distinguished family from Albany, New York, Ten Broeck was a gambler and a truculent fellow who made himself unpopular in respectable American Turf circles. Later he spent some years in England where he was more generally liked as a fine judge of racing. He raced some American-bred horses of his own and later acted as manager for James R. Keene, but finally returned to die in poverty and obscurity in the United States. He gained his principal successes with Lexington.

The first meeting of Lexington and Lecomte was in the Great State Post Stakes run on 1 April 1854 at Metairie racecourse, New Orleans, when they were four-year-olds. The race was promoted with the object of stimulating regional rivalry. In the field of four Lexington represented Kentucky and Lecomte Mississippi, and Lexington, revelling in the heavy going, won in straight heats to bring about Lecomte's first defeat. A week later Lecomte got his revenge in the Jockey Club Purse, also run in 4-mile (6400-metre) heats but on much faster ground. Lecomte won the first heat by six lengths and the second by four lengths, but Lexington was not beaten again.

Lexington and Lecomte met once more, but in the meantime Lexington took part in a match against time which was run in response to a challenge issued by Ten Broeck in a spirit of bravado. The match against time was run on the Metairie track and Lexington, permitted not only a flying start but pacemakers as well, stormed round to finish the 4 miles (6400 metres) in 7 minutes 19.75 seconds, beating the previous best time by 6.25 seconds and setting a record which stood for twenty years.

Lexington met Lecomte for the last time in the Jockey Club Purse at Metairie on Saturday, 14 April 1855. The race had been eagerly awaited, but proved an anti-climax. Lecomte had had an attack of colic a few days earlier and was probably not at his best. He certainly was no match for his old rival. Lexington won the first heat easily, and Lecomte was so distressed that his owner General Wells withdrew him from the second heat, leaving Lexington the victor.

Lexington was making his farewell appearance. He was having trouble with his eyes, and eventually became stone blind, like his sire. In 1856 Ten Broeck departed to England and sold Lexington for $15,000, then the highest price ever paid for an American horse. He stood at the Woodburn Farm, near Midway, Kentucky, where he lived to the age of twenty-five and became one of the greatest sires in American history. He was champion sire no fewer than sixteen times, fourteen times in succession. He got about six hundred foals, of whom 40 per cent were winners, with earnings of $1,159,321 on the American Turf. His very first crop included the best colts in the country, Norfolk, Asteroid and Kentucky. The first two were never beaten, while Kentucky's solitary defeat was at the hands of Norfolk.

Yet the stud career of Lexington, in spite of, or perhaps more properly because of, its resounding success, was to have serious repercussions in international racing affairs. The influence of Lexington saturated the pedigrees of good American horses by the end of the century. He appeared in the first three removes of the pedigrees of fourteen of the first twenty winners of the Kentucky Derby and his descendants were in the forefront of the waves of American horses that threatened to submerge European bloodstock markets at the beginning of the twentieth century. But Lexington was guilty of the original sin, in the eyes of the stud book purists, of having dubious elements in his pedigree, and his ascendancy was the pretext for the protectionist measures which culminated in the 'Jersey Act' of the English authorities in 1913.

Alice Carneal, the dam of Lexington, was a fine racemare herself. She was by the imported stallion Sarpedon, but her pedigree was not considered to be satisfactorily authenticated. Nor was the breeding of Lexington's grandsire Timoleon free from blemish, as he stood under several contradictory pedigrees in Virginia. That indefatigable researcher in American pedigrees Fairfax Harrison remarked somewhat sternly in his book *The St John's Island Stud*: 'Many of the traditional horse pedigrees deriving from the Roanoke Valley before the days of Stud Books are undoubtedly in confusion, but only a rash and superficial student of the available evidence for them dare adjudge generally that they are without foundation. When one of them is cited by a respectable horseman like Mr Jones [the breeder of Timoleon] for such a sterling individual as Timoleon it is the student's task rather to attempt to find an explanation.' Harrison seemed to be leaping to the defence of Timoleon's legitimacy, but his nerve failed him and he concluded lamely: 'In this case the explanation is, it must be confessed, difficult'.

If American pedigrees were saturated with the influence of Lexington by the end of the century, then it is also true that American pedigrees were saturated with the influence of his great great grandsire Diomed by the time Lexington himself was foaled in the middle of the nineteenth century. Inbreeding to Diomed had produced something like a fixed type of American racehorse, and breeders became convinced that more importations were necessary if further progress was to be made. As a result stallions like Leamington, Glencoe, Australian and Eclipse (by Orlando and not to be confused with either American Eclipse or the original English Eclipse foaled

110

in 1764) were imported from England, and each of these four horses made a vital contribution to the development of the racehorse in America.

Glencoe, imported in time for the stud season 1837, was the first of these to arrive by some twenty years. A beautiful golden chesnut horse bred by Lord Jersey, Glencoe had been third to Plenipotentiary in the Derby and had won the Ascot Gold Cup. Before leaving for America he had a season at stud in England and sired Pocahontas, who became one of the most successful broodmares in the history of the thoroughbred and produced the 'Emperor of Stallions' Stockwell, King Tom, and Rataplan. Before he died at Georgetown, Kentucky, at the age of twenty-seven, Glencoe had founded a male line that led, at an interval of four generations, to Hanover, the maternal grandsire of the 1907 Derby winner Orby and the maternal great grandsire of Durbar II, the winner of the Derby seven years later. But it was as an outcross for Lexington that Glencoe achieved his most striking success, and Lexington's three brilliant sons Asteroid, Kentucky and Norfolk were all out of Glencoe mares. The same cross was potent in the case of Hanover's sire Hindoo, winner of the Kentucky Derby, who was by Glencoe's grandson Virgil out of a Lexington mare.

Lexington also played a part in perpetuating the male line of Australian, a son of the 1853 Triple Crown winner West Australian. Australian sired Spendthrift as a result of a mating with a Lexington mare, and Spendthrift became the great grandsire of Man o'War, the greatest racehorse ever bred in America, whose deeds are still recalled with something like awe.

Eclipse founded one of the most enduring of the male lines established in the United States. His son Alarm had scorching speed, set up a record for the mile (1600 metres) and was hailed as America's first sprinter for his superb performances over 6 furlongs (1200 metres). This line has produced, in its various branches, such excellent horses as Domino, Commando, Peter Pan, Equipoise, Bimelech, Stymie and, in the second half of the twentieth century, the million-dollar-earner Dr Fager, the 1971 'Horse of the Year' Ack Ack, the 1976 French Derby winner Youth and the 1983 Derby winner Teenoso.

Alarm was a symbol of a new era in American racing. The stud career of Lexington, which straddled the Civil War, was a watershed marking a fundamental change in the character of American racing.

111

This change was from races in long-distance heats which were, above all, tests of endurance, to short races over distances from 5 furlongs (1000 metres) to 1½ miles (2400 metres) which were above all tests of speed. The change had begun to manifest itself before the war. The first set of racing statistics published by *The Spirit of the Times* to cover the season of 1836 showed sixty-two races in 4-mile (6400-metre) heats and 247 races at 1 mile (1600 metres). By 1860, the last full season before the outbreak of war, there were twenty-four races in 4-mile heats, while the number of 1-mile (1600-metre) races had increased to 313. Nevertheless, the 4-milers were still the kings of the Turf in 1860, whereas the speedy horses had succeeded them by the time peace was restored and racing was resumed on an orderly basis. The 4-milers had been mature horses. The speedy horses that came into their own in the last third of the nineteenth century were expected to shine at two and three years of age; and so the Civil War was accompanied by a peaceful revolution on the Turf that put a premium not only on speed but on precocity besides.

Another aspect of the post-Civil War Turf was that racing was no longer primarily a private affair with the object of finding the best horse. It had become a public entertainment with betting and bookmakers as essential ingredients. Large fields and keen competition were required, and these could not be ensured by restricting programmes to the old type of race in which good horses met at level weights. Handicaps, in which the runners were allotted various weights by an official for the purpose of equalizing their chances, and selling and claiming races were introduced to meet public demand and to provide opportunities for the bad and mediocre products of the swiftly growing breeding industry.

This was racing of the type that had long been established in England, yet the swing to speed and precocity went even further in the United States than in the country that had fathered those concepts. It is significant that the Kentucky Derby, which was founded at Churchill Downs, Louisville, in 1875 and became the greatest American Classic race, was run over 1½ miles (2400 metres), the same distance as the Derby at Epsom, for the first twenty years, but was then reduced to 1¼ miles (2000 metres), and has been run at the shorter distance ever since. The 1–1¼ mile horse, able to start quickly and maintain a fast pace for a limited distance and at an early age, became the ideal. The tobacco millionaire Pierre Lorillard, who was one of the leading owners and breeders of the period, gave expression to the new ideas animating the American Turf in some remarks quoted by William H. P. Robertson in his *History of Thoroughbred Racing in America*: 'I don't want to race anything but two and three-year-olds. After a colt has passed three years old I don't want him and shall sell mine as fast as they reach that age . . . I had rather race two-year-olds than any other class.'

Richard Ten Broeck had made the first American invasion of English racing in the 1850s. His filly Prioress deadheated with Queen Bess and El Hakim in the race for the 1857 Cesarewitch which represented Admiral Rous's greatest handicapping triumph, and showed indomitable courage to beat El Hakim by half a length in the run-off. He won the 1859 Goodwood Stakes with Starke and the Goodwood Cup with the same horse two years later. However, the status of American horses of that time was more accurately reflected by the performance of Ten Broeck's Umpire in the 1860 Derby, as this American-bred colt finished unplaced behind Thormanby after being in the lead soon after Tattenham Corner.

Appropriately Pierre Lorillard, as the representative American owner of the post-Civil War period, was the man to demonstrate the improvement of the racehorses being produced in the United States in the new era. Lorillard reconnoitred in 1879 with the six-year-old gelding Parole, who caused a sensation by winning the City and Suburban and Great Metropolitan on successive days at the Epsom Spring meeting. Satisfied with the results of the reconnaissance, he sent some yearlings to be trained at Newmarket the same autumn; among them was Iroquois, who was by Leamington out of Maggie B. B. by Australian, out of Madeline by Boston, and so blended the influence of two of the best horses imported from England in the mid-nineteenth century with the strain that had been most powerful in the previous age. Iroquois had the strenuous kind of introduction to racing prescribed by Lorillard, as he had twelve races at two years old and won four of them, and then heralded the arrival of the American horse as a leading player on the international racing stage by winning the Derby the next year. He had been second to Peregrine in the 2000 Guineas, and in September won the St Leger. If he was not invincible like Gladiateur, the horse who had signified the arrival of France as a first-class racing power by winning the Triple Crown sixteen years earlier,

Iroquois proved conclusively that American horses were as capable of excellence as any in the world.

While Iroquois proved the merit of American horses in England, Foxhall, owned by the Wall Street tycoon James R. Keene, carried out a similar mission in France. A son of Lexington, Foxhall began by finishing second to the previous year's Derby winner Bend Or in the City and Suburban and then went to France two months later to beat Fred Archer's mount Tristan in a magnificent race for the Grand Prix de Paris. In the autumn Foxhall won the two great handicaps of the Autumn Double, the Cesarewitch and the Cambridgeshire, and carried off the Ascot Gold Cup the next year. It was widely believed that Foxhall was an even better horse than Iroquois, but unfortunately he had been omitted from the entries for the English Classic races.

No other American-bred horse won the Derby until Never Say Die in 1954. The interval of seventy-three years between the first and second victories of American-bred horses in the Derby did not mean that there was a lengthy retrogression of American breeding standards. On the contrary, American-bred horses, and horses with strong American pedigree connections, made notable inroads in the English Classic races round about the turn of the century. In 1899 the American-bred filly Sibola won the 1000 Guineas and was second, beaten by a head by Musa, in the Oaks. Two years later the American-bred filly Cap and Bells II, owned by James R. Keene's all-round sportsman son Foxhall, gained a six lengths victory in the Oaks. In the intervening year the American-bred colt Disguise II had been third to the Prince of Wales's Triple Crown winner Diamond Jubilee in the Derby. The American-bred colts Norman III and Sweeper II won the 2000 Guineas in 1908 and 1912 respectively, and in the latter year another American-bred colt, Tracery, won the St Leger after being third in the Derby. Orby, winner of the Derby in 1907, and Rhodora, winner of the 1000 Guineas the next year, were out of the American mare Rhoda B. Moreover Durbar II, the controversial Derby winner of 1914, had the American mare Armenia as his dam although he was foaled in France.

These successes of American-bred horses in English Classic races took place against a background of recession, panic and disruption in the American racing industry. New racecourses had been mushrooming, meetings had been extended to absurd lengths, intertrack rivalries had multiplied, malpractices among bookmakers were prevalent, and in many states owners and racing promoters were at odds with the politicians. Disgust with the racing fraternity and all their works was widespread among decent citizens, and there was a great deal of public support for the anti-betting legislation that was passed in the majority of states. The amount of racing suddenly dropped catastrophically. In 1897 no fewer than 314 tracks in the United States and forty-three in Canada were operating, but by 1908 these numbers had fallen to twenty-five and six respectively. The most serious blow of all fell in 1910, when a new law, prohibiting all betting and making the race tracks responsible for its enforcement, was passed in New York. The result was a two-year suspension of racing in the state which was the home of the Jockey Club, the owner of the American Stud Book and the supreme legislative, judicial and administrative body for racing at that time. (In later times the powers of the New York Jockey Club were transferred to state racing commissions, but the Jockey Club continued to keep the Stud Book and retained great prestige and an advisory function of inestimable value.)

In the circumstances the bottom fell out of the bloodstock market. In 1909 J. B. Haggin sold 119 horses for $85,000 in Argentina and thirty-four horses for $17,747 in Germany. Two years later the average price for yearlings at auction had fallen as low as $230. With the imposition of the 'Jersey Act' in England and a similar protective measure in France in 1913, most foreign outlets for American horses were cut off and the fortunes of the American breeding industry were at their nadir.

Belmont Park, the New York track named after August Belmont, who had been a leading banker and racing man in the second half of the nineteenth century, opened its gates again on 30 May 1913. Racing began gradually to get back on its feet, and as it did so signs emerged that American breeding had suffered a severe temporary setback but had not been permanently crippled. Indeed it is arguable that the traumatic experience of the first two decades of the twentieth century, when the effects of anti-betting legislation were followed by the First World War, enabled the foundations of the future prosperity of American racing and breeding to be firmly laid. For one state after another outlawed bookmakers and permitted the tracks to install totalisators, or pari-mutuels, instead. A percentage deduction from the totalisator pools enabled the state treasuries to benefit by levying a proportion in taxes, and enabled the tracks

115

to make healthy profits and increase prize money. Thus the state governments acquired a vested interest in the prosperity of racing, while high prize money encouraged owners and breeders to invest larger sums in bloodstock.

Even now it is impossible to assess accurately the extent of the damage done to the breed of the racehorse in the United States by the anti-betting legislation of the early years of the twentieth century. Certainly, when others were unloading their bloodstock at almost any price in the dark days, some breeders had faith in the future of racing. Not everyone was trying to sell, for in 1906 Rock Sand, who had won the English Triple Crown three years earlier, was imported. Rock Sand became the sire of Tracery and, even more important, the sire of Mahubah, whose son Man o'War is still generally regarded as the greatest racehorse ever bred in the United States.

Man o'War was bred in 1917 by August Belmont II, who was chairman of the New York Jockey Club and had won the 2000 Guineas with Norman III and the St Leger with Tracery. Belmont sold Man o'War to Samuel D. Riddle, a Pennsylvania textile manufacturer, as a yearling because he had joined up in the American army despite his sixty-five years and was determined to devote all his energy to winning the war. Man o'War was a horse of tremendous power and fiery chestnut colour. He was nicknamed 'Big Red' by the stable lads as soon as he went into training, and the name stuck to him all through his life. His strength was matched by his vitality. He never had a day's sickness in his life, and it was unknown for him to leave an oat at feed times.

Man o'War was beaten in only one of his twenty-one races, and his defeat in the Sanford Memorial Stakes over 6 furlongs (1200 metres) at Saratoga as a two-year-old was due purely to the incompetence of his jockey Loftus, who managed to get hopelessly shut in in a small field. Inexplicably he was omitted from the entries for the Kentucky Derby, but won the other two races of the American Triple Crown, the Preakness and the Belmont Stakes, and other races now designated Grade 1 Stakes races like the Hopeful Stakes and the Futurity Stakes as a two-year-old and the Travers Stakes as a three-year-old. Although few owners were prepared to run their horses against him in his three-year-old days and he was seldom at full stretch, he broke seven track, American or world records during the season.

Riddle idolized Man o'War and conserved his strength so jealously when he was at stud that he restricted him to twenty-five mares a season, retaining most of the nominations for his own mares and selling the remainder to favoured friends at a fee of $5000. This policy was not calculated to give the horse the best opportunities, but Man o'War exerted a powerful influence on the evolution of the breed of the racehorse in spite of all disadvantages. He has an honourable place in the pedigrees of many top-class horses, including the Derby winners Never Say Die, Relko and Sir Ivor, besides numerous American-based champions like Buckpasser and Arts and Letters.

The career of Man o'War indicated the speed with which the American breeding industry was recovering from its setback. In the period between the two World Wars the recovery was accelerated by the importation from France of the brothers Sir Gallahad III and Bull Dog, and their sire Teddy. Sir Gallahad III not only got the Triple Crown winner Gallant Fox, but was leading sire of winners four times and leading broodmare sire twelve times. Bull Dog was the sire of Bull Lea, who was leading sire of winners once more than Sir Gallahad III and also got a Triple Crown winner, namely Citation. Other influential imported stallions of the same period were Hyperion's half brothers Sickle and Pharamond.

The next leap forward in racing standards in the United States was largely the result of what may be called the 'Aga Khan' series of stallion importations. These stallions, bred by the spiritual head of the Imami Ismailis who based his breeding operations in Ireland, included the Derby winners Blenheim, Mahmoud and Bahram (winner of the English Triple Crown), Hyperion's sons Alibhai and Khaled, and the brilliant and temperamental Nasrullah. Another imported notable son of Hyperion was Heliopolis, a product of the world famous stud of Lord Derby. Each of these importations, which spanned the Second World War and the years that immediately followed it, represented a powerful reinforcement of the breeding resources of the United States – except in the case of the hapless Bahram, whose sale in the darkest days of the war had been bitterly criticized as deeply prejudicial to the future prosperity of the breeding industry in England and Ireland. In addition Princequillo, imported as a yearling in 1941, became a top-class racehorse and stallion, heading the winning sires list twice and excelling as a sire of broodmares.

The impact of Nasrullah on the American breeding scene was positively epoch-making, and piquancy was added to his success story by the fact that the brilliant speed which he possessed, and transmitted to his offspring, could be traced back, generation by generation in his pedigree, to a filly Sibola and a colt Americus who had been exported from the United States to England in the 1890s. In a sense Nasrullah was repaying Europe's debt to America. Nasrullah had been leading sire once in England, and proceeded to head the list of winning sires in the United States five times. When mated with Miss Disco, whose sire Discovery traced back in direct male line to Australian and represented one of the oldest surviving American dynasties, Nasrullah got Bold Ruler, who won the Preakness Stakes and became the most consistently brilliant sire of fast, early maturing horses in the world. Although Bold Ruler died of nasal cancer at the age of seventeen, he surpassed the achievements of his own sire by heading the American list of sires of winners eight times. He was equally successful as a sire of sires, and seven of the ten winners of the Kentucky Derby during the 1970s (Dust Commander, Secretariat, Cannonade, Foolish Pleasure, Bold Forbes, Seattle Slew and Spectacular Bid) sprang from his male line.

Another feature of American breeding during this period was the way strains derived from Nasrullah and Princequillo seemed to complement each other, combining to form what in thoroughbred terminology is called a potent 'nick'. Both these great stallions stood at Claiborne Farm, one of the most famous of the Kentucky stud farms. The stamina and docility of Princequillo, who had been imported from Ireland as a yearling in 1941, was a perfect foil for the fire and brilliance of Nasrullah. The champions resulting from the nick included the American Triple Crown winner Secretariat (by Bold Ruler out of Princequillo's daughter Somethingroyal) and Mill Reef (by Nasrullah's son Never Bend out of Princequillo's daughter Milan Mill) who won the Derby, the King George VI and Queen Elizabeth Stakes and the Prix de l'Arc de Triomphe in 1971.

The Second World War left the United States dollar as the strongest currency in the world; and the well-developed gambling instincts of the American public, cultivated by the astute promotional activities of race-track managers, resulted in a rapid growth in revenue from betting which in turn brought unprecedented benefits to owners and breeders in the form of steadily rising levels of prize money. These two advantages, in conjunction with a tax system which offered incentives to invest in bloodstock, induced breeders to go out and buy the best horses of either sex wherever they were available. In this way the American breeding industry was able to expand without the loss of quality, at least in the top echelon of bloodstock, that would have been inevitable if the expansion had been achieved purely by the more intensive use of its own resources.

The unbeaten Italian champion and dual 'Arc' winner Ribot and Sea Bird II, winner of the Derby and the brilliant leader of the vintage 1965 French crop of three-year-olds, were probably the two greatest racehorses bred in Europe during the 1950s and 1960s, and both were acquired by Kentucky breeders on five-year leases. The volatile temperament of Ribot made the return journey to Europe an unacceptable insurance risk, and he remained at Darby Dan Farm until his death at the age of twenty in 1972. He was a potent Classic stallion who had a profound influence on both sides of the Atlantic. His great grandson Alleged won the 'Arc' in 1977 and 1978 and then returned to his native country to reinforce the stallion resources of Kentucky. Sea Bird II returned to France at the end of his lease but died of an intestinal blockage a year later, when he was only eleven years old. He had shown few signs of becoming as eminent a stallion as Ribot.

The outright purchase of foreign-bred stallions by American breeders was a much more common practice than leasing. The 'Aga Khan series' of importations was followed by an unending stream of stallion importations – a stream that was fed by fresh tributaries as American breeders looked to more and more thoroughbred producing countries for successful strains. The American net reached out to every part of the world where top-class horses were available, and the achievements of horses like Noholme II from Australia, Forli from Argentina and Hawaii from South Africa matched those of the best European horses in American studs.

The importations also included many choice fillies and mares like Gloria Nicky, La Mirambule, Masaka, Greengage, Aunt Edith and Reveille II who had been top-class performers in their native countries. There were also cheaper but judiciously selected mares, like Rough Shod II and Knight's Daughter who were bought by A. B. (Bull) Hancock of Claiborne Farm at the 1951 Newmarket December Sales. They were infinitely more successful at stud than they had been on the racecourse, and had a profoundly beneficial effect on the evolution of the American thoroughbred.

While the high rate of imports was a decisive factor in raising the standard of American breeding, other strains that had been in North America for many generations still contributed horses capable of gaining the greatest honours on the track and at stud. If attention is confined to the male lines, then it is notable that the Orlando-Eclipse line was responsible for Ack Ack, whose son Youth won the French Derby in 1976 and grandson Teenoso won the Derby in 1983; and the Australian-Man o'War line was responsible for In Reality, one of the leading stallions of the period and sire of the 1980 2000 Guineas winner Known Fact.

A male line of more recent importation but firmly enough rooted to be regarded as distinctively American came to the fore in the late 1970s as a strong challenger to the supremacy of the Nasrullah-Bold Ruler line. This was the line of Sickle (by Phalaris), a half brother of Hyperion imported from England in 1929. Sickle's great grandson Native Dancer, foaled in 1950, was a brilliant horse whose racing record of twenty-one victories from twenty-two starts was almost identical with that of Man o'War. He was desperately unlucky on the occasion of his solitary defeat by Dark Star in the Kentucky Derby. Native Dancer's daughter Hula Dancer and grandson Sea Bird II did particularly well in Europe. But it was Native Dancer's son Raise A Native, the breaker of track records at 5 (1000 metres) and 5½ furlongs (1100 metres) at Aqueduct, New York, in two of his four races as a two-year-old, who ensured the continuity of the line. Although a bowed tendon prevented Raise A Native from racing after he was two, he transmitted not only his blazing speed but also an unexpected measure of stamina to many of his progeny.

Raise A Native's sons Exclusive Native and Mr Prospector also were speed specialists who became leading sires and were capable of transmitting more stamina than they showed themselves. Exclusive Native did not win over a longer distance than a mile, but sired the 1978 American Triple Crown winner Affirmed and Genuine Risk – the first filly to win the premier American Classic race since Regret in 1915 – who won the Kentucky Derby two years later. Mr Prospector was a sprinter who broke the 6 furlongs track records at Gulfstream Park and Aqueduct, but sired the Belmont Stakes winner Conquistador Cielo besides a host of very fast horses including the 1000 Guineas winner Ravinella and the Breeders Cup Sprint winners Eillo and Gulch. Exclusive Native was leading American sire of winners in 1978 and 1979, and Mr Prospector followed suit in 1987 and 1988. Raise A Native's son Alydar was second to Affirmed in all the three Triple Crown races and also became a top class stallion, siring Alysheba, who won the Kentucky Derby and the Preakness Stakes in 1987 and the Breeders Cup Classic the following year.

The Canadian industry, which is included with the United States in North American breeding statistics, was also on the move in the second half of the twentieth century. Although Canada, with its long cold winters, has a less favourable climate for racehorse production than much of the territory of its southern neighbour, it found in the brewing and industrial tycoon Eddie P. Taylor the man to take it into the world racing league. Taylor's fortunes as an international breeder were founded on the importation of the mare Lady Angela from England in 1953. Lady Angela was by Hyperion and was in foal to Nearco so the resulting foal, named Nearctic, combined the influence of the two most eminent Classic stallions standing in England in the middle years of the twentieth century. Nearctic was voted Canadian 'Horse of the Year' as a four-year-old and was good enough to win important races like the Saratoga Special and the Michigan Mile in the United States at different stages of his career. But it is not as a racehorse, but as the sire of Northern Dancer that Nearctic will chiefly be remembered. Northern Dancer won the Kentucky Derby and the Preakness Stakes, the first two races of the American Triple Crown and, standing first in Canada and later in Maryland, became the world's leading Classic stallion.

He was a sire of exceptional prepotency, whose progeny included the British Triple Crown winner Nijinsky and further Derby winners in The Minstrel and Secreto. His greatness was demonstrated by a pre-eminence as a sire of sires reminiscent of St Simon's. Nijinsky sired the Derby winners Golden Fleece and Shahrastani, and his son Ile de Bourbon sired Kahyasi, winner of the Derby in 1988.

Other sons of Northern Dancer to attain the top rank as sires were Lyphard, Danzig and Nureyev, and a measure of Northern Dancer's dominance is that Lyphard, Nijinsky and Danzig were first, second and fourth in the American list of sires of winners in 1986. Lyphard's first place was due mainly to the exploits of his son Manila, winner of the Turf Classic and the Breeders Cup Turf, and Dancing Brave, who was trained in England to win the 2000 Guineas, the Eclipse Stakes, the King George VI and Queen Elizabeth Diamond Stakes and the Prix de l'Arc de Triomphe. Nureyev came into his own in the late 1980s primarily as the sire of the dual Breeders Cup Mile winner Miesque, though his son Theatrical was a top-class middle distance horse who won the Breeders Cup Turf.

Although Northern Dancer and Nijinsky spent the whole, and Lyphard and Nureyev most, of their stud careers in North America, many of the best of their progeny were trained in Europe where their prowess testified persuasively to the excellence of American bloodstock.

Canada has its own Classic programme based on the Triple Crown of the Queen's Plate and the Breeders Stakes at Woodbine, and the Prince of Wales Stakes at Fort Erie, but as these races are restricted to three-year-olds foaled in Canada they have no international standing. The principal Canadian races with more than domestic significance are the Rothmans International over 1½ miles (2400 metres) and the E. P. Taylor Stakes for three years old and upwards fillies and mares over 1¼ miles (2000 metres), both run on turf at Woodbine.

The diligent and, indeed, aggressive policy of acquiring the best genetic material wherever it is to be found has been one arm of the drive to improve the American thoroughbred in the second half of the twentieth century. The other arm has been selection on the domestic front based on the rigorous application of the racecourse test and the cultivation of top-class speed. A horse like Raise A Native, whose racing was confined to short distances as a two-year-old, is not typical. There were three winners of the American Triple Crown during the 1970s, and of those three brilliant Classic performers Seattle Slew and Affirmed both ran extensively as four-year-olds. The other Triple Crown winner, Secretariat, did not run as a four-year-old, but had twenty-one races in his two seasons and his reputation as a horse of superlative class and speed was not lightly gained.

Although Spectacular Bid did not win the Triple Crown in 1979, he was successful in the first two legs and was third to Coastal in the Belmont Stakes after treading on a pin before the race and injuring a hoof. He was a horse of the same standard as Seattle Slew and Affirmed. Like them, he raced as a four-year-old, and was not beaten in any of his nine races. Alysheba, who surpassed the achievements of the gelding John Henry to become the world's leading money earner with a total of $6,679,242, won eleven of his twenty-six races in three seasons.

Twenty years earlier Round Table, whose parents were the imported Princequillo and Knight's Daughter, had an even more strenuous programme. He ran no fewer than sixty-six times between two and five years of age, won forty-three races and was voted 'Champion Grass Horse' in each of his last three seasons. He became a top-class stallion and was leading sire of winners in 1972. Few American owners are affected by the almost pathological fear of defeat shown by many of their counterparts in Europe, and the odd defeat or two is not allowed to detract from the reputation or value of a good horse.

Credit for the searching campaigns to which the best American horses are generally subjected must be shared between the widespread conviction that no horse can be accepted as a true champion unless he has demonstrated his toughness and consistency over a lengthy series of races, and the existence of many tempting prizes for which four-year-olds and older horses are eligible to run. No fewer than six Grade 1 races for four-year-olds and upwards, plus four Grade 1 races for four years old and upwards fillies and mares, were programmed on the Californian tracks Santa Anita and Hollywood Park between January and April in 1988, and an equally attractive programme of Grade 1 races for which four-year-olds and upwards are eligible exists in the autumn, mainly in New York.

Although a number of the principal American courses have installed turf tracks for some big races — thirty-five of the one hundred and twenty-two Grade I Stakes races were scheduled to be run on the grass in 1980 — the intensive use of American tracks, with nine or ten races a day and meetings of several months duration, calls inevitably for dirt as the standard surface. The New York track Belmont is unique in having an outer dirt circuit of 1½ miles (2400 metres) and an inner turf circuit of 1¼ miles (2000 metres); but the large majority of American tracks are perfect and dead flat ovals of about 1 mile (1600 metres) in circumference, with chutes for some of the starts. The uniform fast surfaces, the need to sprint from the start to obtain a satisfactory position on the first bend, the sustained pressure to hold that position, all tend to make the American races of all distances true tests of speed and reliable criteria for selection.

The median distance of all American races is 6 furlongs (1200 metres), but the most important races for three-year-olds and older horses are run over middle distances from 9 furlongs (1800 metres) to 1½ miles (2400 metres). The Triple Crown Classic races for three-year-old colts and fillies are the Kentucky Derby over 1¼ miles (2000 metres) at Churchill Downs, the Preakness Stakes over 9½ furlongs (1900 metres) at Pimlico and the Belmont Stakes over 1½ miles (2400 metres) at Belmont. Belmont also stages a Triple Crown series for three-year-old fillies comprising the Acorn Stakes over 1 mile (1600 metres), the Mother Goose Stakes over 9 furlongs (1800 metres) and the Coaching Club American Oaks over 1½ miles (2400 metres).

In 1988 there were only four Grade 1 races for three-year-olds and upwards over distances less than a mile – the Breeders Cup Sprint, and the Carter and Vosburgh Handicaps and the Ballerina Stakes for fillies and mares. But if the American programme for top-class horses gives little encouragement to pure sprinters, it gives even less to specialist stayers. The San Juan Capistrano Handicap over 1¾ miles (2800 metres) at Santa Anita is the longest Grade 1 race since the reduction of the distance of the Jockey Club Gold Cup from 2 miles (3200 metres) to 1½ miles (2400 metres) in 1977.

While the American programme gives little encouragement to top-class specialist performers at either extreme of distance, it is equally unaccommodating to extreme precocity. The fifty-one Graded Stakes for two-year-olds in 1988 accounted for only 12.1 per cent of the 420 races which constituted the whole Graded Stakes programme, and of those two-year-old Graded Stakes thirty-one, or 60.8 per cent, were run over distances ranging from 7 to 9 furlongs between September and December.

The climactic period in the life of the male American Classic racehorse is from mid-September of its two-year-old to mid-June of its three-year-old season. Those nine months include the definitive tests of two-year-old excellence like the 7-furlong (1400 metre) Futurity Stakes, and the 1-mile (1600-metre) Champagne Stakes and Breeders Cup Juvenile: the preparatory races in the Classic canon, which include races of the first importance in their own right like the Florida Derby, the Santa Anita Derby, the Wood Memorial Stakes and the Blue Grass Stakes, and the Triple Crown races themselves, which are concentrated in a six-week period between early May and the middle of June. The time scale for Classic fillies is slightly longer because the Coaching Club American Oaks is not run until early July. The purpose of further racing after the climactic period is to confirm reputations, provide evidence of durability and to mop up prize money, and the introduction of numerous new and extremely valuable races for three-year-olds in the 1980s left the pre-eminence of the Triple Crown races unshaken.

This identification of a climactic period points to a definition of the American Classic racehorse. In American terms the model of excellence at which the breeder aims is neither excessively pre-cocious, nor pure sprinter, nor genuine stayer, but is capable of sustained first-rate performance in a limited period overlapping the two-year-old and three-year-old seasons. This masterpiece of the breeder involves the highest development of equine speed compat-ible with the proper balance of aptitude required for the varied tests in the programme.

Striking evidence of the progress of the American Classic race-horse can be drawn from the ascending scale of their achievements in Europe. The first dozen years after the Second World War brought only three successes in British Classic races for horses bred in North America: the St Leger victory of Black Tarquin and the Derby and St Leger victories of Never Say Die. Then the tempo of American success in the most important European races began to quicken as the prowess of American-bred horses became apparent, as higher levels of prize money first in France and later in Britain began to beckon irresistibly to American owners with a predilection for the European style of racing, and as stables based on American horse power, like that of Vincent O'Brien in Ireland, were assembled. Between 1960 and 1980 North American-bred horses gained twenty-seven successes in the British Classic races plus the King George VI and Queen Elizabeth Diamond Stakes and twenty successes in the French Classic races plus the Prix de l'Arc de Triom-phe. Those successes included the victories of Sir Ivor, Nijinsky, Mill Reef, Roberto, Empery, The Minstrel and Henbit in the most famous of all Classic races, the Derby. In 1970 Nijinsky became the first horse for thirty-five years to capture the British Triple Crown of the 2000 Guineas, the Derby and the St Leger; for good measure this bright star of the Vincent O'Brien stable also won the King George VI and Queen Elizabeth Stakes, though an attack of ring-worm during August took a toll of his health and, after winning the St Leger with less than his usual panache, he ended his racing career with surprising defeats in the Prix de l'Arc de Triomphe and the Champion Stakes. As Arab purchasing power made its deepest impact on the principal American yearling sales in the 1980s the success ratio for American-bred horses increased still further; the years 1981 to 1988 saw eighteen victories for American-bred horses in the same six British races.

The Classic racehorse accounts for a minute proportion of the North American thoroughbred population, indeed a much smaller proportion than in some other important racing and breeding countries. An unbridgeable gap separates this elite from the masses that run in 6-furlong (1200-metre) dashes week in and week out with deadening monotony and for meagre rewards to provide entertainment for the public, maintain betting turnover and generate revenue for the state governments through their percentage take-out. Of the 80,376 races run in North America in 1987 only 425 (0.5 per cent) were Graded Stakes. By comparison in Britain 99 (3.3 per cent) of the 3042 races run the same year were the equivalent of Graded Stakes, that is Pattern races. On the other hand it is relatively easy for the bad or moderate horse to gain some kind of reward for his efforts in North America, where there are more races than individual runners. In Britain the total number of individual runners in 1987 was 7411, and exceeded the number of races in the ratio of nearly 2.5 to 1.

The insistent demand for horses to fill an increasing number of revenue-generating races has caused many state governments to introduce breeding incentive programmes to boost local production. These programmes, financed by a percentage of betting take-out, include breeders prizes, stallion awards and races restricted to state-bred horses. The New York State fund was the richest of all and was responsible for a rapid expansion of the formerly insignificant local industry, raising its annual output of foals eight-fold to more than 2000 in the decade 1973–82.

The result of all these factors was a North American thoroughbred population explosion which raised annual foal production from 10,757 in 1957 to nearly 50,000 thirty years later. One effect of the state incentive programmes had been to cut the share of Kentucky, the traditional leader in thoroughbred breeding, from about 28 per cent to 16–17 per cent of North American production during the period. California and Florida, with more than 10 per cent each, were next in the production league.

The Kentucky state government shunned most of the measures designed to increase production in other states, though breeders' prizes for Kentucky-breds were added to the prize money for most races except those of the lowest class, that is claiming races. But if

Kentucky lost some of its lead in quantity production, it continued to demonstrate its primacy in quality by exceeding numerical expectations consistently in the races contested by horses of superior ability. With 16.1 per cent of total production, Kentucky provided 28.4 per cent of the winners of Stakes races (the stratum above claiming, maiden and allowance races) throughout the continent in the decade 1973–82 despite the fact that many Stakes outside Kentucky were restricted to the local state-bred horses.

Kentucky took over the leadership of thoroughbred breeding from Virginia in the middle of the nineteenth century, a transition symbolized by the fact that the mighty Lexington spent his whole stud career in Kentucky. After the Civil War wealthy industrialists from the north poured capital into the development of Kentucky breeding, and the foundation of the Kentucky Derby as the premier American Classic race in 1875 consolidated the state's leadership. The name of the race and the name of the track where it was run, Churchill 'Downs', were tributes to their British models. Nowhere is the ascendancy of Kentucky breeding more strikingly demonstrated than in the results of this greatest American race, as Kentucky-bred horses won eighty-four (73.7 per cent) of the 114 runnings of the Kentucky Derby from 1875 to 1988.

The primacy of Kentucky as a producer of quality thoroughbreds is an undisputed fact, but it is a more open question how the credit for this fact should be apportioned between favourable climate and environment, the heavy investment which was continuing as strongly as ever in the 1970s, the expertise of Kentucky breeders and other contributory factors. The heartland of the Kentucky breeding industry is the Bluegrass region of which the city of Lexington is the hub, 2500 square miles of rolling pastures and enclosed parkland in which stud farms adjoin each other in a density unknown elsewhere in the world. The road from Lexington to the small town of Paris runs straight for 17 miles (27.2 kilometres) without a break through immaculately fenced and tended stud paddocks.

Limestone lies close below the surface of those paddocks and, in association with calcium phosphate, various trace elements and a mineral-laden water supply from countless springs and streams, assists in the formation of hard but light bones and the strong tendons and elastic muscles necessary for racehorses. Although the mid-winters are often hard, the early springs and hot summers provide conditions in which the thoroughbred is able to thrive. As one French breeder who had transferred part of his operations to Kentucky remarked: 'It is the lack of humidity compared to Normandy which is so favourable, because humidity tends to debilitate thoroughbreds. When a mare has been in Kentucky for two or three months her whole skeleton seems to expand.'

Nevertheless it is possible to argue, in view of the degree of success already achieved by the relatively young Florida breeding industry, that investment has played at least as important a part as environment in securing the leadership of Kentucky. Most of the Florida stud farms are concentrated round the town of Ocala in the northern part of the state and were carved out of virgin woods and scrublands in the 1960s and 1970s. The mean annual rainfall in the district is 70 inches, but the soil is sandy and drains quickly, and Ocala enjoys many hours of hot summer sunshine. The patriarchal Florida stallion was Rough 'N' Tumble, who was not a top-class racehorse and was bought for $10,000, but who put the Florida breeding industry on the map by siring Dr Fager, the earner of more than $1 million and one of the best American racehorses of the 1960s. Up to 1988 Florida had produced four winners of the Kentucky Derby, including the Triple Crown winner Affirmed.

Such is the glamour of the Bluegrass; so choice is its broodmare population; so comprehensive are its back-up facilities of veterinary services and bloodstock sales staged by the Fasig-Tipton Company and the non-dividend-paying Keeneland Association; so inexhaustible are the funds that it is able to draw on for new investment, that the best potential stallions tend to be attracted inevitably to Kentucky irrespective of their state of origin and to stand at famous Kentucky studs like the long-established Claiborne Farm and the newer Gainesway Farm. Even Florida's Triple Crown winner Affirmed went to stud in Kentucky, and Mr Prospector was moved from Florida to Kentucky when his high quality as a stallion was realized. John Gaines was the most thrusting and ambitious of all the Bluegrass stallion promotors in the 1970s. His Gainesway Farm listed forty-one stallions for the 1981 season, more than either Spendthrift or Claiborne. It specialized in horses who had made their names in European racing like the 'Arc' winner Vaguely Noble and his Classic-winning sons Exceller and Empery, besides proven stallions like Sharpen Up plucked from an English stud and Riverman and Lyphard plucked from French studs by the magnetic power of dollars available for investment in the Bluegrass.

128

Anilin (1961).   The best horse ever bred in Russia, Anilin excelled in soundness and constitution. He proved himself on the fringe of world class by gaining places in the Washington DC International twice

Forli (1963).   One of the best horses ever bred in Argentina, Forli went to stud in Kentucky and became a potent influence in Classic breeding

Hawaii (1964).   Pictured winning the Man o'War Stakes at Belmont, New York, Hawaii was the first world-class racehorse bred in South Africa. He became a successful stallion in Kentucky and sired the 1980 Derby winner Henbit

Balmerino (1972).   Pictured winning the Valdoe Stakes at Goodwood in September 1977, Balmerino gave incontestable proof of the capacity of New Zealand to produce world-class horses when he was second to Alleged in the Prix de l'Arc de Triomphe a month later

Birkhahn (1945). Winner of the German Derby, Birkhahn became a champion sire in both East and West Germany. He had an influence extending far outside Germany, particularly as a sire of broodmares

Star Kingdom (1946). A horse of brilliant speed when racing in England, Star Kingdom helped to revolutionize Australian breeding as a stallion in New South Wales through his ability to transmit that brilliance to his progeny and through his excellence as a sire of sires

Ribot (1952). Unbeaten in sixteen races, the Italian-bred Ribot was one of the racehorses of the century. He spent most of his stud career in Kentucky, but his influence on Classic breeding was world-wide

Northern Dancer (1961). The winner of two of the three American Classic races, the Kentucky Derby and the Preakness Stakes, Northern Dancer became the foremost Classic sire of his day. His sons Nijinsky and The Minstrel won the Derby and he was a great sire of sires with world-wide influence

Pretty Polly (1901).   One of the greatest fillies ever to grace the Turf, Pretty Polly won twenty-two of her twenty-four races, including the 1000 Guineas, the Oaks and the St Leger. She was the ancestress of many Classic racehorses including Brigadier Gerard and the Derby winners St Paddy and Psidium

Tourbillon (1928).   Winner of the French Derby, Tourbillon was one of the cornerstones of the Marcel Boussac breeding empire which dominated the European Classic scene in the 1940s and 1950s

Hyperion (1930).   Winner of the Derby and the St Leger, Hyperion became the greatest British-bred Classic stallion of the twentieth century, headed the list of sires of winners six times, and had world-wide influence

Nearco (1935).   Unbeaten in fourteen races, Nearco won the Grand Prix de Paris on his only racing venture outside his native Italy. He spent his stud career in England and founded the world's most powerful Classic male line

Eclipse (1764).   Invincible on the racecourse, Eclipse became one of the great stallions that assisted in the transformation of the thoroughbred in the late eighteenth century. The large majority of modern thoroughbreds trace their descent from him in the male line

Diomed (1777).   The first Derby winner, Diomed went to North America late in life and became one of the strongest contributors to the evolution of the Classic American thoroughbred

St Simon (1881).   A horse of superb vitality, St Simon outclassed every horse he met on the racecourse and became leading sire of winners nine times. His influence on the Classic racehorse of the twentieth century was unsurpassed

Sceptre (1899).   Winner of the 1000 Guineas, the 2000 Guineas, the Oaks and the St Leger, Sceptre ranked as one of the greatest racemares. Her family has been prominent in Classic breeding, and her descendants include the Derby winner Relko and the French Derby winner Reliance II

A master showman, Gaines built for his illustrious stallion band new barns in which the most modern and practical design features contrasted with flights of ostentatious fancy like curved redwood beams, wrought iron box doors moving on solid copper wheels and, most flamboyant of all, circular red and green stained glass windows set high in the sharply pointed gables and reproducing the Gainesway symbol and racing colours. The Gainesway Farm complex received the American Institute of Architects 1984 Honor Award, the profession's highest form of recognition for excellence in design – a supreme accolade undreamed of in former days of purely utilitarian stud farm building and a sign of the heightened prestige of the thoroughbred industry.

As the Thoroughbred entered the final quarter of the twentieth century and the fourth century of evolution from the original stock, it was undeniable that the most productive sources of the Classic racehorse had shifted from the Old World to the North American continent, and predominantly to a tiny portion of that vast land mass called the Kentucky Bluegrass. The American breeding industry had an air of solid prosperity with the financial means to prolong that prosperity indefinitely into the future.

Yet the brightest picture usually has a darker side and even the booming American thoroughbred industry is no exception. It involves the fundamental anomaly arising from the fact that the bloodstock values of the late 1970s were sustained less by sound economics of racehorse ownership than by a tax system which offered powerful incentives to invest in thoroughbreds.

Louis E. Wolfson, whose Harbor View Farm bred and raced Affirmed, set out the difficulties of racehorse owners in a booklet entitled *The Problems Facing the Thoroughbred Racing and Breeding Industry* published in 1980. He quoted a report which stated that 90 per cent of racehorse owners lose money and that one-third of them drop out each year. He argued that the long-term financial stability of the industry depended on the introduction of a nation-wide off-course betting network providing for a fair distribution of revenue to state governments, racehorse owners and racecourse executives. Failing this, he warned, 'we will find that our best racing days are in the past'. Eight years later the impact of off-track betting and simulcasting of races at betting centres away from the track was still ambivalent and the finances of the New York Racing Association, whose tracks stage many of the most important races in the whole of the United States, were in some disarray. Moreover changes in the tax system had diminished the attractions of owning the breeding thoroughbreds for the newly rich and so tended to reduce the flow of fresh capital into the industry.

It was with the object of revitalizing the racing industry and raising public awareness of the charms of thoroughbred racing that John Gaines proposed, in a speech at the 1982 Kentucky Derby Festival luncheon, a series of multi-million dollar championship races. He envisaged a one-day programme of seven races for virtually every sex and distance division, 'giving a world-wide viewing audience the opportunity to witness all the pageantry and excitement of a true Thoroughbred Olympics'.

This brainchild of John Gaines developed into the Breeders Cup Day, which was held for the first time at Hollywood Park, California on 10 November 1984 and staged the Breeders Cup Classic (1¼ miles – 2000 metres) of $3 million, the Breeders Cup Turf (1½ miles – 2400 metres) of $2 million, the Breeders Cup Sprint (6 furlongs – 1200 metres), the Breeders Cup Distaff (1¼ miles – 2000 metres), the Breeders Cup Mile (1 mile – 1600 metres), the Breeders Cup Juvenile and the Breeders Cup Juvenile Fillies (both 1 mile – 1600 metres) of $1 million each. All the races, except the two Juvenile races for two-year-olds only, were for three-year-olds and upwards; and all the races were run on dirt except the Breeders Cup Turf and Mile.

Funding for these huge prizes was provided by the nomination of stallions paying an annual contribution equal to the advertized stud fee or 'farm gate' fee, together with a foal fee of $500 each for the progeny of nominated stallions to make them eligible for the benefits of the Breeders Cup, which included premiums in a series of races at tracks all over the country in addition to the Breeders Cup Day prizes. In 1984 1287 stallions representing thirty different States and five Canadian provinces contributed $12.9 million to the stallion fund alone.

Since the inaugural meeting at Hollywood Park annual Breeders Cup days have been held at the same time of year at Aqueduct in New York, Santa Anita in California, Hollywood Park again, and Churchill Downs in Kentucky. Horses trained, or previously trained, in Europe have had their share of success in the two Turf races, Lashkari, Pebbles and Theatrical (who beat the Prix de l'Arc de Triomphe winner Trempolino) winning the Turf and Royal

Heroine and Miesque, the latter brilliant filly in both 1987 and 1988, the Mile. However, the dirt races remained firmly the prerogative of American-trained horses. The Breeders Cup days brought extensive TV coverage and publicity to racing in the United States, but it would be an exaggeration to claim that Gaines's ideal of a 'true Thoroughbred Olympics' had been realized.

The original hope of the Breeders Cup founders was that the scheme would transcend national frontiers and embrace the principal European racing countries, but the differences between the racing systems and the requirements of the racing industries in the two continents constituted obstacles too great to be surmounted. Instead the principal European countries – initially Great Britain, Ireland and France, joined later by Italy and Germany – devised a parallel scheme based on stallion payments only and tailored to their own needs. This scheme, entitled the European Breeders Fund (EBF), involved the distribution of prize money on a broad basis which contrasted with the concept of a 'Thoroughbred Olympics' day. However, the two schemes were linked in a cross-registration agreement which made horses qualified by the due payments to one scheme eligible for many of the benefits of the other scheme.

There is no doubt that the magnitude of the American achievement in improving thoroughbred performance, demonstrated with so much panache on the Breeders Cup days, is remarkable and unique in the twentieth century.

The French veterinary surgeon Robert Lesaffre described this achievement succinctly in his book *Connaissance et Utilisation du Cheval de Course*: 'Les Americains ont croisé aptitude sur aptitude et modèle sur modèle pendant des générations et ont ainsi obtenu une race dont l'aptitude dominante est la vitesse pure. Il est remarquable que les temps moyens des épreuves moyennes aux U. S. A. sont nettement inferieurs aux temps correspondant chez nous.'* The brilliant American filly Hula Dancer, who won the greatest French two-year-old race, the Grand Criterium, in all-aged record time of 1 minute 37.6 seconds for the Longchamp mile (1600 metres) in 1962, was a portent. During the next quarter of a century hundreds of American-bred horses proved their marvellous speed and athleticism

---

* 'The Americans have been crossing aptitude with aptitude and type with type for generations and have thus obtained a breed whose dominant aptitude is pure speed. It is remarkable that the average speeds for ordinary American races are definitely faster than the average times for corresponding races in our country'.

by performances of a similar standard on all the principal racecourses of Europe.

7

The Thoroughbred in France

For a country that was to become one of the world's leading producers of high-quality thoroughbreds, France was surprisingly tardy, apathetic even, in organizing horse races and laying the foundations of a racehorse-breeding industry. There were scattered references to horse races from the fourteenth century onwards, but these were improvized affairs. Nor was the State Stud Administration Service founded by Louis XIV intended to promote a breed of racehorses; indeed the French in general and the kings in particular seemed to be ignorant of, or indifferent to, the value of oriental stallions for the purpose of improving equine breeds, and let a number of the horses that were to become potent formative influences in the English thoroughbred slip through their fingers. The Godolphin Arabian was the most important of these horses put to such successful use by the English, but the case of the Curwen Bay Barb and the Thoulouse Barb provided even more striking evidence of the casual French attitude in the matter. Volume 1 of the *General Stud Book* contained the following note:

Curwen's Bay Barb was a present to Lewis the Fourteenth from Muly Ishmael, King of Morocco, and was brought into England by Mr Curwen, who being in France when Count Byram and Count Thoulouse (two natural sons of Lewis the Fourteenth) were, the former, Master of the Horse, and the latter, an Admiral, he procured of them about the end of the seventeenth century, two Barb horses, both of which proved excellent stallions, and are well known by the names of the Curwen Bay Barb and the Thoulouse Barb.

Curwen's Bay Barb sired Mixbury, who was one of the best horses of his day despite being only 13.2 h.h. (1.33 metres), and other first-

133

class horses like Brocklesby, Brocklesby Betty and Creeping Molly; and Professors G. A. T. Mahon and E. P. Cunningham found in their report on 'Genetic Studies in Horses' published in 1978 that Curwen's Bay Barb was third only to the more famous Godolphin and Darley Arabians in the order of genetic contributors to the modern breed of the thoroughbred.

Charles X was the first French king to show any enthusiasm for racing. In 1776 the first regular course was laid out in the Plaine des Sablons under the supervision of the Duc de Chartres, the Comte d'Artois and the Marquis de Conflans. In November that year a 2-mile (3200-metre) race with a prize of 15,000 francs was run there and was won by the Prince de Guéménée's Abbé from Partner, owned by the Duc de Chartres. Any chance the sport may then have had of taking root vanished in the turmoil of the Revolution, and this upheaval, followed by the Napoleonic Wars, set horse racing in France back to zero at a time when the English Turf and its institutions were developing strongly through the initiative of the Jockey Club and the evolution of the English breed of racehorses was being regulated by the publication of the *General Stud Book*.

Although the thoroughbred stallions Truffle, Middlethorpe, Camerton, Coriolanus and Diamond were imported from England in 1817 and 1818, there was no immediate upsurge of horse racing in France after the restoration of the monarchy. In the end the drive and inspiration of an Englishman, Lord Henry Seymour, were required to put French racing on its feet. A son of the third Marquess of Hertford, Seymour was born in Paris and spent his whole life in France, but was imbued with the English passion for the Turf. It was mainly at his instigation and that of the heir to the throne, the Duc d'Orléans, that the Jockey Club was founded in November 1833, with Seymour as its first president. The intention was that the club should fulfil the joint functions of a race committee and a fashionable social club on the St James's model, but Seymour and Orléans soon discovered that most of their fellow members were more interested in playing cards than in racing and breeding. Accordingly, a few months later, they separated the racing aspect of the club from its social aspect by forming the 'Société d'Encouragement pour l'Amélioration des Races de Chevaux en France', leaving the Jockey Club as the smartest and most exclusive club in Paris, but with none of the administrative and legislative powers on the Turf that were wielded by its English namesake.

The Société d'Encouragement, as its name was generally abbreviated, was recognized by the government in March 1834 and granted the use of the Champ-de-Mars, on the left bank of the Seine where the Eiffel Tower now stands, for its race meetings, of which the first was held on Sunday 4 May, though the first racing had taken place on that course as early as 1806. The initial and vital decision of the Société d'Encouragement was that it was pointless to go back to the original stock and attempt to develop a French breed of racehorses, since they could not hope to improve on the achievements of the English in this respect. They declared that they must borrow the methods of the English and attempt to equal, and perhaps one day to surpass, their standards. For this purpose thoroughbred stallions and mares must be imported from England as foundation stock. These ideas were incorporated in the French Stud Book, founded at the same time by government decree, and the thoroughbred in France was designated the '*Pur-Sang Anglais*'.

These decisions of the Société d'Encouragement had been anticipated to a remarkable extent by the editors of the *General Stud Book* who stated in the Preface to Volume 2, published in 1821: 'If any proof were wanting of the superiority of the English breed of horses over that of every other country, it might be found in the avidity with which they are sought by foreigners. But this advantage some of our continental neighbours are of the opinion will not long remain with us: they are fully aware of the source from whence we derive this superiority, and are in consequence endeavouring to establish Races on the English plan, which, together with a more careful selection of stallions and mares that they observe, will very soon, they say, enable them to excel us, and they anticipate a day (not very distant) when the English must send to the Continent, if not for speedy, at least for sound horses.'

Seymour and Orléans dominated the development of French racing and breeding until 1842, when Orléans died as a result of a fall from his carriage and Seymour, somewhat disillusioned, decided to sell his stable. Seymour, who was born in 1805 and so was still a young man at the time of the foundation of the Jockey Club and the Société d'Encouragement, was an eccentric whose peculiar sense of humour finally lost him many friends. His addiction to practical jokes took two forms: the puerile form of distributing cigars fitted with explosive devices, and the blacker form of leaving nothing to his servants so that they would regret his death. Yet, for all his quirks of character, Seymour did a service of incalculable magnitude for French racing. During his presidency the dusty arena of the Champ-de-Mars and the avenues of the Bois de Boulogne, where impromptu races had been run in the 1820s, were supplemented by a magnificent new course in a lovely forest setting at Chantilly; and the Prix du Jockey Club, run over the Classic distance of 1½ miles (2400 metres), was founded in 1836 as the French equivalent of the Derby.

The races promoted by the Société d'Encouragement were confined to horses bred in France in order to give the necessary measure of protection to the infant French breeding industry. There was a marked increase in imports of top-class horses for stud. These included the Derby winners Cadland, Dangerous and Mameluke, and the St Leger winner Theodore, all brought from England in the 1830s. Seymour made his personal contribution to the growing store of Classic stock by importing the 2000 Guineas winner Ibrahim; but as happens not infrequently, his other stallion importation, the non-Classic Royal Oak, proved much the better stallion. Royal Oak was unplaced in the St Leger in 1826, but was a versatile horse who won eleven races, ranging from a 5½-furlong (1100-metre) handicap at Newmarket to a 2½-mile (4000-metre) weight-for-age race at Chesterfield, as a three-year-old and four-year-old. Royal Oak was one of the most important factors in the evolution of a successful breed of racehorses in France. Despite his own Classic failure, his influence was so beneficial that he richly deserved the honour of being commemorated in the name of the French race that corresponded to the St Leger until 1978.

Royal Oak was the sire of the last of Seymour's four winners of the French Derby, Poetess in 1841. Poetess became one of the greatest broodmares in the annals of the French Turf, as she was the dam of Hervine, winner of the French Oaks (the Prix de Diane founded in 1843 and run over 1 mile 2½ furlongs (2100 metres) at Chantilly) and of Monarque, who won the French 2000 Guineas and the French Derby. These two offspring of Poetess marked the arrival of French racehorses as a force to be reckoned with on the international stage. As a four-year-old in 1852 Hervine won the 2½-mile (4000-metre) Prix du Cadran, founded fifteen years earlier as the French equivalent of the Ascot Gold Cup, but was sent on an abortive expedition to Goodwood, where she was unplaced in the Goodwood Cup. However her owner Alexandre Aumont, the founder of the Haras de Victot in Normandy, was not dismayed and sent her back to Goodwood again the following year, when she was second to Jouvence in the Cup. Hervine may have been beaten, but the result was a triumph from the French point of view because Jouvence, successful in the French Derby and the French Oaks that season, was the first French-bred winner of an important race in England, although Juggler had won a ½-mile (800-metre) sprint at Newmarket in 1849 and the 1-mile (1600-metre) Great Yarmouth Handicap two years later. The French horses enjoyed big weight allowances – Jouvence carried 5 st 9 lb (35 kilos) and Hervine 7 st 11 lb (48½ kilos) in comparison to the 9 st 3 lb (57½ kilos) of the English horse Kingston who was third – but the one-two of the French mares in one of England's principal tests of stamina was a great tonic for French breeders.

Monarque, four years younger than Hervine, copied the disappointing example of his half-sister by failing in his first English campaign; after carrying all before him as a three-year-old in France, Monarque was unplaced in the Goodwood Cup and the Cesarewitch. On the other hand his connections were able to console themselves with the thought that his English form could not have been right because Baroncino, who had been second in the French Derby, had won the Goodwood Cup. He returned to Goodwood the next year to finish third in the Stewards Cup over 6 furlongs (1200 metres) and third again in the Goodwood Cup, a pair of performances which demonstrated his speed, stamina and versatility if nothing else. His perseverance was finally rewarded as a five-year-old in 1857 when, at the third attempt, he won the Goodwood Cup by a head from the three-year-old Riseber with Fisherman, the winner of twenty-six Queen's Plates and two Ascot Gold Cups, a bad third.

Monarque was certainly the best horse bred in France up to that time. He was tough, genuine and capable of winning an important long distance race in England. Nevertheless, French rejoicing over his victory at Goodwood had to be moderated two months later when the English horses Fisherman, Saunterer and Commotion went over to Chantilly to run in the Prix de l'Empereur, one of the few French races for which foreign horses were eligible, and occupied the first three places in that order, with Monarque unplaced. The following spring Monarque raided England once more and won the Newmarket Handicap, but ten days later, after his stable companion Mademoiselle de Chantilly had won the City and Sub-urban, his wonderful racing career came to and end when he broke down in the Great Metropolitan.

On balance the performances reflected immense credit on the French breeding industry, which had been in existence for little more than twenty years. Although the French had been saved a century and a half of experiment and evolution by the pioneering efforts of their English neighbours, they had raised their production to the fringe of international standard on relatively slender resources. In the early period there were only fourteen days racing per year at the principal meetings of Paris, Chantilly and Versailles; the number of horses running each year between 1834 and 1840 was only about sixty, and prizes of more than £100 were rare. At least the shortage of horses meant that those available were expected to race at frequent intervals and stay in training a long time, so that those that survived were guaranteed sound and of durable constitution.

The later stages of the racing career of Monarque coincided with two events which had the most profound significance for the progress of the thoroughbred in France: the first was the purchase by Comte Frédéric de Lagrange of all Alexandre Aumont's bloodstock, including Monarque, in 1856, and the second was the opening of the racecourse of Longchamp in the Bois de Boulogne on the last day of April the next year. Lagrange had the wealth, intelligence and ambition to give a powerful fresh impetus to the evolution of the racehorse, and Longchamp gave Parisians a splendid and picturesque racecourse on their doorsteps and brought a prosperity to the sport which helped to finance future progress.

A son of one of Napoleon I's generals, Frédéric de Lagrange was forty and had made a great fortune in mines, canals, railways and glass factories when he turned his attention to racing. He also had a leading position in Parisian society, and was a close friend of the Emperor Napoleon III, who was rumoured to have a financial interest in his stable. He was much more international in outlook than most of the French owners of his day, and for most of his career on the Turf maintained stables at both Chantilly and Newmarket, with the brothers Henry and Tom Jennings as the respective trainers. Both stables were supplied from his stud, the Haras de Dangu. In this way his breeding and racing ventures provided a continuous means of comparing thoroughbred progress on the two sides of the English Channel. For two periods, in 1861–62 when he collaborated with Baron Nivière in what was known as 'The Big Stable', and in 1874–78 when his partner was Joachim Lefèvre who had purchased his string at the outbreak of the Franco-Prussian War, he took part in tremendous joint ventures that were regarded with awe and dismay by owners operating on a more modest scale. 'The Big Stable' was fifth in the English list of winning owners in 1861 and seventh the following year, and, in 1876, the Lefèvre-Lagrange confederacy was leading owner in England with earnings of £17,650, though Lefèvre on his own had headed the list three years earlier with 105 victories, which stood as an English record until David Robinson won 109 races in 1970.

Nevertheless, Lagrange needed no partner to secure his greatest triumphs and demonstrate the attainment by the French breeding industry of equal status with the English. At the break-up of 'The Big Stable' he bought the filly Fille de l'Air for the equivalent of £340 and, trained in England, she proved a brilliant performer. As a two-year-old in 1863 she won those important races the Woodcote Stakes at Epsom, the Molecomb Stakes at Goodwood and the Criterion Stakes at Newmarket and the next year, after finishing unplaced in the 2000 Guineas, won the French Oaks and the Oaks at Epsom and then finished second to the colt Vermout in the Grand Prix de Paris. Her victory at Epsom, following her abject failure at Newmarket, provoked an ugly demonstration by a section of the crowd. Whatever the explanation of the discrepancy in her form, there was no doubt she was a very high-class filly on her day. At the Haras de Dangu she bred, to a mating with Monarque, Reine, the winner of the 1000 Guineas and the Oaks in 1872.

Fille de l'Air, though French-bred, was by the English sire Faugh-a-Ballagh. There was no such reservation about the 'Frenchness' of the most renowned of all Lagrange's horses, Gladiateur, who was foaled a year after Fille de l'Air. Gladiateur was by Monarque out of Miss Gladiator, whose sire Gladiator had been imported in 1846 by the State Stud Administration (Administration des Haras). In general the Administration des Haras was at loggerheads with the Société d'Encouragement, but in this instance they did bring a distinct benefit to the evolving French thoroughbred. Gladiator sired Fitzgladiator, an excellent racehorse and stallion who got the French Derby winner Gabrielle d'Estrées, the Prix du Cadran winner Compiègne, Palestro, who carried Lagrange's colours to victory over Gabrielle d'Estrées in the Cambridgeshire, and Dangu, who was

Lagrange's first runner in the Derby when he was fourth to Thormanby at Epsom in 1860. Miss Gladiator was not one of her sire's distinguished racecourse performers. She was a cripple who could not be trained, and her son Gladiateur was chronically unsound from navicular disease. But so unique was the combination of speed and stamina in the raw-boned Gladiateur, and such was his unquenchable fighting spirit, that he was one of the greatest racehorses ever bred. More than a century after his three-year-old season, 1865, his record of winning the English Triple Crown plus the Grand Prix de Paris remains unequalled. Although he was fairly hard-pressed to win the 2000 Guineas when only half fit, he outclassed his rivals to such an extent in his other Classic races that he was nicknamed 'The Avenger of Waterloo' by the exultant French.

Gladiateur was a freak and, like other freaks, he failed to transmit his great qualities to his progeny. His significance lay not in his influence on future generations, but in his power to symbolize the new status of the French thoroughbred. He shattered English complacency, which gave way to disquiet about the French challenge and later to resentment as the successes of French-bred horses in the Classic races continued. The victories of Fille de l'Air and Gladiateur were followed by the victories of Fille de l'Air's daughter Reine and Camelia in the 1000 Guineas, of Camelia and Enguerrande, who deadheated for the Oaks, of Chamant in the 2000 Guineas and of Rayon d'Or in the St Leger, all before 1880. These successes were built on the same virtues of toughness, courage and stamina that have already been noticed. The survival of the fittest principle was the basis of Lagrange's methods of selection. He made a practice of trying the produce of his Dangu Stud as yearlings in the rides cut through the forest of Compiègne. As the grassy rides could only take four or five horses abreast, these trials were arranged in the form of a knock-out competition with the survivors of the preliminary rounds meeting in the final. When Gladiateur was a yearling his rivals in the final were Gontran, Le Mandarin and Argences, who occupied the first three places in the French Derby two years later.

The introduction of the Grand Prix de Paris as the premier French Classic race, with a prestige even higher than that of the French Derby, was calculated to promote the same qualities. The Grand Prix, alleged to have been the brainchild of the Emperor for the purpose of enhancing the reputation of French racing and French horses, was inaugurated in 1863 with a prize equivalent to £4000, of which half was given by the City of Paris and the remainder by the five largest railway companies. The detailed planning was committed to the Duc de Morny, perhaps better known as the creator of Deauville, where his services are commemorated by the celebrated two-year-old race bearing his name. Two significant features of the Grand Prix, which was confined to three-year-old colts and fillies, were that it was decided over 1 mile 7 furlongs (3000 metres), an extremely severe test for animals of that age, at the end of June, and that it was open to horses bred outside France. French owners and breeders complained that the race would be a gift to the English, and indeed the first Grand Prix was won by the English colt The Ranger, who beat La Toucques, the winner of the French Oaks and the French Derby, by a length.

The score was levelled the next year when the Derby winner Blair Athol was beaten by Vermout and Fille de l'Air, but by 1886 the race had been won by further English horses in Ceylon, The Earl, Cremorne, Trent, Thurio, Robert the Devil, Bruce, Paradox and Minting, and the Hungarian-bred Kisber and the American-bred Foxhall had also been successful. It was clear that French-bred horses in general might have achieved parity of status with those bred in England, but had not achieved superiority. But in spite of the successes of English horses in the Grand Prix, or perhaps because these successes generated further ambitions, the fact that English horses were barred from the rest of the important French races while French horses were permitted to run freely in England rankled with English owners. In 1874 Admiral Rous wrote to Vicomte Daru, the president of the Société d'Encouragement, requesting that English horses should be given the same rights to run in France as French horses enjoyed in England, but received the evasive reply that French prizes were donated by municipalities, industrial companies and private individuals, so the racing authorities were powerless to act in the matter. Three years later Lord Falmouth, the leading owner-breeder, voiced the feelings of many of his compatriots when he pointed to the fact that French horses had won nearly £15,000 in England the previous year, and that a great deal of the money had come out of the pockets of English owners in the form of entry fees and forfeits. He demanded that either foreign races should be thrown open to English horses on equal terms or the most important English weight-for-age races should be closed to foreign horses. 'We are told that to pass such a rule as has been suggested would be tantamount to an admission of inferiority, or an act of submission. What we demand is to be placed in a position to attack,' he declaimed. However, fearing that his sportsmanship would be impugned, he dropped his agitation over what was known as the reciprocity issue after his Silvio had been third to the French-bred Chamant and the American-bred Brown Prince in the 2000 Guineas. His silence turned out to be golden when Silvio went on to win the Derby, with Chamant and Brown Prince unplaced.

The swing of the pendulum which enabled English horses to resist any continental challenge during the era of St Simon's greatness as a stallion, and declining Anglo-French competition on the racecourse, took the sting out of the reciprocity issue. In fact no French-bred horse won the Derby between Gladiateur in 1865 and Durbar II in 1914, and no English-bred horse won the Grand Prix between Minting in 1886 and Spearmint twenty years later. In the first decade of the twentieth century English breeders were too preoccupied with the American invasion, which was countered by the 'Jersey Act', to worry about the French.

The discontent of Falmouth and the majority of English breeders during the 1870s was understandable. The corollary of French delight in the triumphs of Fille de l'Air and Gladiateur should have been to open their important races to all-comers; the policy of protection which had been necessary to get the French breeding industry on its feet had outlived its utility, and it is possible that the thoroughbred would have made more rapid progress in France in the last quarter of the nineteenth century if the fresh wind of competition had been allowed to blow. At the same time it must be conceded that Falmouth's assessment of the cost to English owners of French victories would not bear examination. French-bred horses might have won £15,000, or more, or less, in prize money in any given season, but the figure, whatever it might be, did not represent the net cost to English owners because it did not take account of the substantial sums paid by French owners in entry fees and forfeits for horses that were unplaced or did not run. Moreover France had provided a valuable export market for English thoroughbreds for half a century, and it was the descendants of those exported thoroughbreds that were winning a share of English prize money in Falmouth's time.

Several of the stallions exported to France after 1850 played vital roles in the evolution of the thoroughbred in that country. Three of them – The Flying Dutchman, Flying Fox and Rabelais – founded powerful dynasties whose influence has persisted right down to the present day. The Flying Dutchman, winner of the Derby and St Leger in 1849 and conqueror of the next year's Derby and St Leger winner Voltigeur in the most famous match in racing history, was sold to France in 1858 for £4000 and there sired Dollar, who won the Goodwood Cup and ensured that the line put down firm roots in France. Five generations later the line produced Brûleur, foaled in 1910. Brûleur was no world-beater, as he was beaten into third place in the French Derby on his merits, but he was a very high-class stayer, as his victories in the Grand Prix, the Prix Royal Oak and the 2¾-mile (4400-metre) Prix la Rochette proved. If he had his limitations as a racehorse, he was undoubtedly a great sire, for his progeny included three winners of the Prix de l'Arc de Triomphe, four winners of the French Derby and one winner of the Grand Prix. If he had sired no other horse but Ksar he would have made a contribution of unsurpassed importance to the progress of the French thoroughbred in the twentieth century.

But for the death of his owner and breeder, the Duke of Westminster, after he had won the Triple Crown in 1899, Flying Fox would probably never have left the shores of England. He was put up for sale as a four-year-old at Kingsclere, where he was trained, and was purchased by Edmond Blanc for 37,500 guineas, a sum which remained the record for a horse in training at public auction until Vaguely Noble fetched 136,000 guineas at the Newmarket December Sales sixty-seven years later. Although Blanc was the most successful owner-breeder in France between 1880 and the outbreak of the First World War, he was never elected to the Committee of the Société d'Encouragement because the source of his fortune – his father was 'Fermier des Jeux' at Monte Carlo – was not considered quite respectable. As a measure of retaliation for this snub Blanc restricted Flying Fox to his own mares and to those of foreign breeders. Flying Fox sired a number of good horses, and his son Ajax, who was unbeaten as a three-year-old in 1907 and won the French Derby and the Grand Prix, was the link in the chain of heredity that led through his son Teddy to Tantième, one of the most potent Classic sires in France after the Second World War.

Rabelais, four years younger than Flying Fox, lacked the racing distinction of either The Flying Dutchman or Flying Fox, and was a long way from being the best of the sons of his sire, the mighty St Simon, on the racecourse. He was third to Rock Sand in the 2000 Guineas and fourth to the same horse, who won the Triple Crown, in the Derby, for which the field of seven was the smallest of this century. But though small and lacking the highest class, he possessed speed and stamina, winning the National Breeders Produce Stakes over 5 furlongs (1000 metres) as a two-year-old and the Goodwood Cup over 2 miles 5 furlongs (4200 metres) the next year. He was sold provisionally as a stallion to Russia, but the deal fell through on account of the outbreak of the Russo-Japanese War and he was sold to France instead for only £900. He proved a fantastic bargain, for his progeny included the 'half-bred' Derby winner Durbar II, the Grand Prix winner Verdun and the French Derby winner Ramus, while his male line continued strongly in France through Rialto to Worden II and Le Fabuleux and in Italy, through Havresac II, to the invincible Ribot.

The French breeding industry produced four real cracks in the last eight seasons before the First World War. They were Sans Souci II and his son La Farina, Alcantara II and Sardanapale. Sans Souci II, an elegant if rather delicate chesnut horse, won the Grand Prix in 1907, and the highly strung Alcantara II won the French Derby and the Prix Royal Oak four years later, but had a very rough passage and was beaten in the Grand Prix. The encounters of Sardan-apale and La Farina, belonging respectively to the cousins Edouard and Maurice de Rothschild, brought excitement and distinction to the French racing season until it was abruptly terminated by the outbreak of war. The leggy and light-framed La Farina came out the better in the Prix Lupin over 1 mile 2½ furlongs (2100 metres), but the massive Sardanapale, after winning the French Derby, got his revenge when he beat La Farina by a neck in the Grand Prix. All these great pre-war horses were links in male lines which con-tinued to exert their influence up to and beyond the Second World War, transmitting the stamina and tenacity that had become typical of the French thoroughbred. Sardanapale is worthy of special notice because he represented the oldest male line in France; he was a descendant of Monarque, not through Gladiateur but through another of Monarque's top-class sons, Consul, winner of the French Derby in 1869.

The First World War nearly killed the French breeding industry. The only races allowed were a few *épreuves de sélection*, without prize money or spectators, designed to discover the best animals for breeding. For profitable employment French horses had to go to Milan or to San Sebastian, just across the Spanish frontier. Ajax's son Teddy was one of the French horses sent to San Sebastian. Foaled in 1913, he was sold by his breeder Edmond Blanc for the equivalent of £200 in the depressed wartime market as a two-year-old. Teddy won the *épreuve de sélection* substituted for the French Derby and then carried off the San Sebastian Grand Prix and the San Sebastian St Leger. He made a great name for himself at stud. Two of his most famous sons, Sir Gallahad III and Bull Dog, followed by Teddy himself at the age of eighteen, went to the United States, but enough of his sons, notably Astérus and Aethelstan, remained in France to ensure that his influence would not be lost in his native country. Aethelstan was the great grandsire of Tantième, one of the most influential sires of the 1950s and 1960s, and Astérus was the grandsire or great grandsire of the Grand Prix winners Bagheera and Altipan and the French Derby winner Tamanar, besides being a notable sire of broodmares.

The depleted and weakened French breeding industry was vulnerable to raiders from England, where racing had been permitted on a severely reduced scale throughout the war, in the first few years after peace was restored. The English-bred and trained colts Galloper Light, Comrade and Lemonora won the first three races for the Grand Prix after the end of the war, and Comrade also won the first Prix de l'Arc de Triomphe, the new international race introduced at Longchamp in October 1920 to celebrate the return of peace. These early reverses were to be expected in the circumstances, and what was really more remarkable was the speed with which high-quality breeding was rehabilitated in France. Indeed Ksar, the first crack bred in France after the war, was probably the most brilliant three-year-old of either country in 1921, and the conspicuous lack of judgement with which he was ridden by George Stern was mainly responsible for his eclipse behind Lemonora in the Grand Prix. In the Prix Royal Oak he beat Fléchois and Harpocrate, who had been second and third in the Grand Prix, much more easily than Lemonora had done.

Ksar had a superb pedigree, as both his sire Brûleur, whose savage temper did not prejudice his success as a stallion, and his dam Kizil Kourgan were winners of the Grand Prix. Moreover he was inbred to Dollar's grandson Omnium II, the French Derby winner of 1895, who was the maternal grandsire of Brûleur and the sire of Kizil Kourgan. Bred by M. E. de St Alary at his Saint-Pair-du-Mont stud in the heart of the Normandy stock-raising region, he was sent to the Deauville Sales as a yearling and there bought by Edmond Blanc for the then record price of 151,000 francs. Asked why he had paid so much for a colt who, despite his pedigree, was awkwardly put together and had large plebeian feet and poor action, Blanc gave the shrewd answer: 'He is indeed ugly, but he is very like Omnium, and that is a kind of ugliness that I do not mind.'

The inbreeding that had reproduced Omnium's looks in Ksar had also reproduced his racing ability. Apart from his failure in the Grand Prix, he carried all before him as a three-year-old, winning such important races as the Prix Lupin and the Prix Hocquart besides the French Derby and the French St Leger, and confirming his superiority over Fléchois in the Prix de l'Arc de Triomphe. He turned back the English invasion decisively in the last named race, in which Square Measure, the best of the four raiders, was third three and a half lengths behind him. A year later Ksar again beat his old rival Fléchois in the Prix de l'Arc de Triomphe after winning three other important races, including the Prix du Cadran, earlier in the season.

Ksar was not merely providing the first dramatic sign of the post-war recovery of the French breeding industry; he was also, as a stallion, one of the chief architects of the excellence of the French middle distance Classic thoroughbred that was to be revealed in such sensational fashion after the Second World War. The second 'Arc' victory of Ksar had been preceded by another significant event the same year. This was the Classic success of Ramus, who gave Marcel Boussac the first of his twelve victories in the French Derby. Boussac had his second French Derby victory with Tourbillon, a son of Ksar, in 1931, and Tourbillon was to be one of the corner-stones of the Boussac racing empire that attained the height of its power in the dozen years that followed the end of the Second World War.

The 1920s and 1930s were the period of gestation of the greatness of the Boussac studs. During those years forays by Boussac-bred horses like Goyescas, Goya II and Abjer in England indicated the trend. On the other hand the main burden of demonstrating the continuing recovery of French thoroughbred standards was borne by the produce of other studs. Between the two world wars the victories of Rodosto and Le Ksar in the 2000 Guineas, of Kandy and Mesa in the 1000 Guineas, of Bois Roussel in the Derby, of Brûlette in the Oaks, of Massine in the Ascot Gold Cup, of Astérus in the Champion Stakes and of high-class horses like Sir Gallahad III and Epinard in big handicaps, had significance which the majority of English breeders chose to ignore.

In 1939 Boussac gained his fifth French Derby and his first Grand Prix victory with Pharis II, and the next year he gained his first Classic victory in England when Tourbillon's son Djebel won the 2000 Guineas shortly before the fall of France. An impenetrable curtain then fell between the English and French breeding industries. Both countries were able to keep racing going on a restricted scale during the Second World War, but the renewal of peace-time competition revealed that the French had outstripped the English in production of high-class horses capable of excelling over middle and long distances. From 1946 onwards the English breeding industry reeled under a French onslaught of unprecedented intensity, an onslaught which had the Boussac horses in the van. In the immediate post-war period Boussac won the Derby with Galcador, the Oaks with Asmena, the St Leger with Scratch II and Talma II, the Ascot Gold Cup with Caracalla II and Arbar, the Eclipse Stakes with Djeddah and Argur and the Champion Stakes with Djeddah and Dynamiter (twice), while he also won a corresponding share of other important middle and long distance races in England. The Boussac assault was the most concentrated, but certainly not the only assault launched by French owners and breeders on the prestige-bearing English races after the Second World War. Indeed so many other French stables joined in the cross-Channel raids that no fewer than twenty-four, or 20 per cent of the Classic races decided in England between 1946 and 1969, were won by French-bred horses.

Some special factors militated in favour of the Boussac empire in its challenge to the English. One was the application of a breeding formula which involved mingling the influence of three dominant sires – Tourbillon, Astérus, and Pharis II – in various combinations. A second was the ineligibility of one of those sires, Tourbillon, for the *General Stud Book* until the necessary changes in the conditions of entry were made in 1949. The reasons for Tourbillon's exclusion were twofold, as his dam Durban was by the 'half-bred' Derby winner Durbar II and Durban was out of the American-bred mare Frizette, whose sire Hamburg was 'half-bred' by English standards.

147

Frizette and Durbar II's dam Armenia were imported into France from the United States before the French version of the 'Jersey Act' was imposed in 1913, and for this reason the descendants of Armenia and Frizette were eligible for the French Stud Book but not for the English; and as Armenia and Frizette were mares of profound and widespread influence French breeders had unrestricted access to valuable strains which were denied to the English. Boussac, as the owner of Tourbillon, was the chief beneficiary of this anomaly.

The trouble with special factors is that they tend to wear thin in the course of time. The Boussac post-war successes were not, of course, confined to England. In 1956 he won the double of the French Derby and the French Oaks with Philius and Apollonia, and his empire seemed to be as secure as ever. No critic who had asserted in June 1956 that the might of the Boussac studs was on the wane would have been taken seriously, but this was the case. The magic of the Tourbillon-Astérus-Pharis formula had lost its potency, and efforts to introduce outcrosses in the shape of stallions from America were fruitless. While the volume of production from the Boussac studs was maintained, quality sagged alarmingly. After 1956 important successes for Boussac-bred horses were rare, and the only further Classic victories gained by them were those of Crepellana in the 1969 French Oaks and of Acamas in the French Derby nine years later. By the time of Acamas the Boussac textile and financial empire was disintegrating. When he died the following year his principal stud, the Haras de Fresnay-le-Buffard, was in the hands of the Greek shipping magnate Stavros Niarchos and his bloodstock had been sold by the liquidators to the Aga Khan, though part of the deal was contested in bitter and prolonged litigation.

Special factors also operated in favour of some of the other French breeders whose products scored heavily at the expense of the English in the post-war period – the international outcross practised with brilliant judgement by François Dupré and the introduction by Baron Guy de Rothschild of speedy elements into a stud previously dominated by staying strains. But special factors could hardly account for qualities that seemed to have become inherent in the French thoroughbred, qualities like toughness, courage, durability, middle distance ability and stamina reaching maturity at three and four years of age. In these respects the strains developed by the late Jean Stern at Saint-Pair-du-Mont, the former St Alary stud, may be

regarded as more typical of the French thoroughbred than the products of the breeding methods of Boussac, Dupré or Rothschild.
The Stern horses were submitted to the most stringent tests on and
off the racecourse in the true Lagrange tradition, and this system
resulted in such genuine and finely tempered horses as Sicambre,
Phaëton, Pasquin and Sigebert in the post-war years.

The French thoroughbred was essentially the product of adherence
to the guidelines laid down in the early days of the Société
d'Encouragement and confirmed by the introduction of the Grand
Prix as the premier Classic race. The ideal that the French breeder
aimed at from the 1860s to the 1950s was the horse capable of
excelling over 1 mile 7 furlongs (3000 metres) in June of his three-
year-old season. Not all the great French racehorses and sires of the
first half of the twentieth century won the Grand Prix, but they
were all – Ajax, Teddy, Brûleur, Alcantara II, La Farina, Sardanapale, Ksar, Brantome, Sicambre, Vieux Manoir, Djebel and Tantième – bred with that ideal in mind.

The type of racehorse produced in any particular country is the
creature of the pattern of racing established in that country, because
the selection processes of breeders are determined by the races which
bear most prize money and most prestige. If the horse capable of
winning the Grand Prix was the ideal towards which French breeders
directed their best endeavours for nearly a century, it is also true
that the French pattern of racing as a whole was loaded in favour
of horses able to shine over distances from 1 mile (1600 metres) to
1 mile 7 furlongs (3000 metres), with shorter shrift for precociously
speedy horses, sprinters and extreme stayers.

Tradition dies hard in racing, but can hardly survive radical
change. The French pattern of racing was subtly but decisively
modified in the last quarter of the twentieth century and by 1980
was recognizable as its traditional self only in its outward forms.
While the ancient race titles were retained, shifts in the distribution
of prize money had revolutionized the status of some races. The
most striking change of all concerned the relative importance of the
French Derby, run over 1½ miles (2400 metres) early in June, and
the Grand Prix, run over an additional 3 furlongs (600 metres) three
weeks later. In 1949 the Grand Prix was still indisputably the premier
French Classic race, with its first prize of 5 million old francs nearly
double the first prize of 3 million old francs for the French Derby.
The position had been reversed by 1980, when the French Derby

first prize of 900,000 francs was more than double the Grand Prix first prize of 400,000 francs, and the French Derby had just as surely taken over as the premier Classic race.

The shift of emphasis from stamina to speed was not confined to the most important Classic races. The prize money for the principal test of stamina, the 2½-mile (4000-metre) Prix du Cadran was pegged, while the prize money for the principal sprint, the Prix de l'Abbaye de Longchamp, was increased dramatically, as were the prizes for important mile races like the Prix du Moulin and the Prix Jacques le Marois. Moreover the Prix Royal Oak, losing its place as the final three-year-old Classic race corresponding to the St Leger, was debased to a nondescript race for three-year-olds and upwards though retaining, somewhat dubiously, its status of Group 1 Pattern race. The Prix de l'Arc de Triomphe was developed ambitiously as a great international middle distance race and the autumn counterpart of the King George VI and Queen Elizabeth Stakes run three months earlier.

In the 1980s this process was taken a stage further. The Grand Prix de Paris, deprived of its former preference in respect of prize money, sank lower and lower in the estimation of owners and breeders. Senior officials of the Société d'Encouragement spoke of it in disparaging terms, and the quality of its fields fell progressively. In 1987 the logic of the new priorities in French racing was applied and the distance of the Grand Prix was reduced from the traditional 1 mile 7 furlongs (3000 metres) to 1¼ miles (2000 metres). The first running of the Grand Prix in its new guise was won by Risk Me, by the sprinter Sharpo, who would not even have been considered a possible runner for the Grand Prix in its old form.

These changes appalled the traditionalists in the French racing establishment, but the fact was that they were sadly reduced in numbers and influence. Breeders like François Dupré, who had built a stud empire on the influence of the 1944 Grand Prix winner Deux Pour Cent, Elisabeth Couturié, who had bred and owned one of the greatest modern French racehorses Right Royal V, and Marcel Boussac, who reigned supreme as owner-breeder and President of the Société d'Encouragement for many years in the middle years of the century, were all dead. Not long before her death in June 1982 Elisabeth Couturié, owner of the famous Haras du Mesnil in the Sarthe, expressed her belief that while the French Thoroughbred might not be able to match the British for precocious speed or the

American for all-round brilliance, foreign breeders would always need to return to France at regular intervals to replenish their stocks of toughness and stamina. However, in the 1980s the validity of the tests for selection of those typically French traits was fatally undermined.

The chief agent in bringing about this change of attitude in the French racing establishment and the Société d'Encouragement, which had virtually absolute control over racing programmes and the distribution of prize money, had been the prowess of the American-bred horses which were appearing on French racecourses in increasing numbers in the late 1950s. One of the first of these was the brilliant filly Sly Pola, who won the Prix Robert Papin, the initial race in the French series of important two-year-old tests, in 1959. The same year an American-bred colt, Dan Cupid, was second in the French Derby; and three years later another American-bred filly, Hula Dancer, beat the best of the French-bred colts in the most important of all the French two-year-old races, the Grand Criterium, in the record time of 1 minute 36 seconds for the Longchamp mile (1600 metres). Hula Dancer was trained in France, but as a three-year-old made expeditions to England to win the 1000 Guineas and the Champion Stakes. In the next quarter of a century a stream of American-bred horses – Gazala, Yours, Sir Ivor, Lyphard, River-man, Pistol Packer, Dahlia, Mill Reef, San San, Allez France, Lianga, Nonoalco, Green Dancer, Caracolero, Youth, l'Emigrant, Alleged and Super Concorde among them – drove home the lesson that the North American thoroughbred was not only setting new and superior standards of precocious speed but was capable of sustaining speed over middle distances to a degree that few French thoroughbreds could match. The solid traditional virtues of the French thoroughbred were suddenly exposed as less than adequate to meet the ever more seaching demands of international competition. The changes in the French Pattern sprang from the acceptance of the implications of this unpalatable truth by the French racing authorities.

A law of 1891, which outlawed bookmakers and confined legal betting to pari-mutuels, or totalisators, operated by the racecourse companies, had brought great and steadily increasing benefits to the sport. The racecourse companies themselves were compelled by the same law to become non-profit-making bodies devoting the whole of their resources to the improvement of racing and racehorses. The introduction, after the Second World War, of the 'Tiercé', a special pool on selected important weekend races, multiplied betting turnover and thus the revenue available for distribution in prize money and breeders' premiums. The 'Tiercé' ushered in an era of unprecedented prosperity for French racing, and the promotion of the Prix de l'Arc de Triomphe, run over 1½ miles (2400 metres) at Longchamp on the first Sunday in October, as the European race with the greatest international prestige, symbolized the enormous accretion of wealth in the French prize money fund and the policy of distributing it in a manner calculated to give the highest rewards to quality. Control was in the hands of the closely knit bureaucracy of the omnipotent Société d'Encouragement, jealous of the reputation of French racing and determined to uphold its status by an apopropriate allocation of resources.

Disconcertingly, the wealth of French racing proved a two-edged weapon in the 1960s and 1970s. Huge prize money certainly had the effect of upholding the status of French racing, but it also attracted hordes of competitors bred in North America and other foreign countries. These incursions came at a time when not only the Boussac studs but also other once-powerful French studs were in decline, with the result that the French thoroughbred was ill-equipped to combat the challenge, and many valuable French races were at the mercy of the invaders. In the 1980s the levels of prize money in some of the great prestige races were raised even higher by the advent of commercial sponsorship; for example first Trusthouse Forte and then Ciga Hotels sponsored the Prix de l'Arc de Triomphe, Lancia the French Derby and Hermès the French Oaks.

The protectionist measures which had given so much offence to British owners and breeders in the last quarter of the nineteenth century had been lifted progressively over a long period, and the reciprocity issue had seemed to be finally buried on 25 October 1946, when the Société d'Encouragement decided to open all French races, with very few exceptions, to horses bred abroad. However, the growing number of successes by foreign-bred horses in the 1960s led to a revival of protectionist sentiment at the end of the decade, and only the introduction of the International Pattern Race system (see Chapter 13) averted an immediate crisis. Resentment smouldered during the 1970s as the proportion of French Pattern races won by French-bred horses fell below 40 per cent in some seasons. A series of measures designed to encourage French breeders and curb foreign competition was introduced. In the late 1970s breeders' premiums for French-bred horses were paid at the rate of 25 per cent in Pattern races and 15 per cent in other races, and further premiums of up to 50 per cent of the nominal value of races were paid to the owners of French-bred winners and placed horses. Restrictions on the running of foreign horses confined horses trained abroad, unless French-bred, to Pattern races, while 14.5 per cent of the races on the metropolitan courses (Longchamp, Saint Cloud, Maisons Laffitte, Evry, Deauville, Chantilly and Vichy) were reserved for French-bred horses. In the 1980s, however, the European Breeders Fund (EBF) made some inroads into French protectionist practices and opened up a number of races to foreign-bred and foreign-trained horses if they were EBF- or Breeders Cup-qualified.

The quality of French-bred horses revived strongly in the late 1970s. In 1979 the proportion of French Pattern races won by French-bred horses had risen to a healthy figure of nearly 60 per cent. A number of French breeders, like the trainer Alec Head and the breeder Comte Roland de Chambure, some of whose breeding interests were merged in the Société Aland, were operating on a scale which bridged the Atlantic and exploited American speed to the full. American-bred stallions like Lyphard and Riverman, though transferred to the United States when their stud success was assured, stood in France long enough to have a profoundly beneficial effect on the breed. Each sired a winner of the Prix de l'Arc de Triomphe. Lyphard sired the 1979 winner Three Troikas, bred by Head, and Riverman sired the 1980 winner Detroit, bred by the Société Aland.

This revival proved unsustainable. The truth was that changes in the fiscal system and the vastly increased social charges bore heavily on the racing and breeding industries, discouraging investment in racehorses and breeding stock by French nationals. Baron Guy de Rothschild, the owner of one of the last great private studs the Haras de Meautry and then President of the French Thoroughbred Breeders Association, painted a dark picture in his speech to the annual general meeting of the Association in 1980. The number of horses in training was declining because owners were liable to capital gains taxes for which neither capital losses nor expenses were deductable, and foal production was in a state of 'free fall' because breeders were suffering from the unfair burden of a new agricultural income system. He concluded: 'The current difficulties with reinvestment result from a taxation system which is poorly adapted to our very peculiar profession.'

Annual foal production actually fell from 4396 in 1975 to 3043 in 1980, a reduction of more than 30 per cent in a period of six years, and although it picked up steadily in the 1980s there was little sign of a corresponding improvement in the quality of production. For example, French-bred horses won only thirty, or 28 per cent, of the 107 Pattern races run in France in 1988. There were few proven high-class stallions in the country, and the death of Comte Roland de Chambure at the age of only fifty-four in 1988 led to the dissolution of the Société Aland and a serious depletion of the resources of quality bloodstock in France. Paul de Moussac, one of the small number of Frenchmen who invested heavily in bloodstock in the 1970s and 1980s, had founded a breeding operation in Kentucky to supplement his Haras de Mezeray in Normandy and give him access to better stallions than those available at home; significantly Trempolino, his winner of the 1987 Prix de l'Arc de Triomphe, bred in Kentucky, was by the Gainesway Farm-based stallion Sharpen Up and went to stud at Gainesway Farm.

Nevertheless, few outside observers were prepared to accept any suggestion that this decline might be permanent. French thoroughbred breeding has powerful and permanent natural allies. Climate, soil and environment generally in the principal breeding districts of Normany have proved, in the passing of a century and a half, extraordinarily kind to this specialized animal husbandry. Admiral Rous wrote to a prominent member of the Société d'Encouragement, Auguste Lupin, in the course of the controversy over 'reciprocity':

The question is what have you to fear – you Frenchmen who fear nothing? You have bought with great judgement our best stallions and mares; your paddocks are not tainted like ours by being overstocked with horses for many years; your climate is more favourable to their growth; consequently your two-year-olds are more precocious; you have had great success in your adolescence. Nothing can be more brilliant than your prospects.

The reference to precocity may seem odd. At that time two-year-old racing was prohibited in France until August, and there is still no two-year-old racing, except for a few selling races, on the main courses before May. On the other hand many French two-year-olds were winning in England during the agitation for reciprocity, and the Admiral was probably right in implying that early maturity was within the grasp of French breeders if they desired it.

The Admiral's attitude was far removed from that of the editors of the early volumes of the *General Stud Book*, who were convinced that British breeders had decisive but unspecified advantages over foreign competitors. The advantages of French breeders may be more specific. Most of the greatest thoroughbred studs are concentrated in the Orne and Calvados departments of Normandy, where the winters are mild, the paddocks are protected by dense hedgerows and the pastures continually refreshed by a natural compost of leaves and fallen apples, watered by gently flowing streams. These are the conditions that have nurtured the evolution of the French thoroughbred.

To the French breeders of 1980 the disadvantages described by Baron Guy de Rothschild probably seemed insuperable. But the lesson of racing history is that French breeders, granted a reasonably favourable taxation system, can tune their selection methods to the most exacting international standards, and there is no reason to doubt that at some future time they will again become fully competitive as producers of 'The Classic Racehorse'.

8

The Thoroughbred in Italy and Germany

The story of the thoroughbred in Italy has two unique features; the establishment of a successful breeding industry there depended on the efforts of a single man to an extent unparalleled elsewhere, and that industry has had an influence throughout the world greater than that of any other national breeding industry of comparable size. The man to whose genius the Italian thoroughbred owes so much was Federico Tesio, and, in 1966, his successors at the Dormello-Olgiata Stud, which it had been his life-work to create and develop, were able to make the following claims:

1. That 62.5 per cent of the pedigrees of prominent horses in England and Ireland that season contained Dormello blood.

2. That 36.99 per cent of the pedigrees of Stakes winners in the United States, Canada and Mexico that year contained Dormello blood.

These percentages in the home of the thoroughbred and in the country with the largest, richest thoroughbred industry in the world represent an almost incredible achievement by a single stud in a country with a thoroughbred population so small that annual foal production in the 1970s was little more than 1000. Tesio, a retired cavalry officer with limited capital, did not found his stud on the shores of Lake Maggiore until 1898, when the thoroughbred had been in the process of evolution for more than two centuries in England, and when breeders in France had a start of at least sixty years. Yes, Tesio, then twenty-nine years old, needed to be a genius

156

in his own line to force the Italian thoroughbred to the front of the world stage in such a short time.

Tesio won his first Italian Derby with Guido Reni in 1911, and had won the race twenty more times before he died in 1954. The Dormello-Olgiata Stud, carried on by his partners, the Incisa family, won it on five more occasions in the next fourteen years. He bred two world-beaters, Nearco and Ribot, and perhaps a dozen other horses of top international class. Nevertheless it would be an error, and would do less than justice to those of his companions who have played important roles, to suggest that all the credit for the progress and final excellence of the Italian thoroughbred belongs to Tesio. There had be·n racing in Italy long before his day. Regular race meetings began at Florence and Naples in 1837, and twenty years later the Lombard Society for Horse Racing was formed with a course at Segnano near Milan. Organized racing at Rome dates from 1868.

Importations of breeding stock were required to produce runners for these courses, which were supplemented by other meetings at Leghorn, Turin and Pisa in the second half of the nineteenth century. The English Derby winners Ellington and Melton, and other notable stallions in Hamlet, Andred and Melanion, were imported before the end of the century. Ellington was imported by King Vittorio Emmanuele II, whose influence and enthusiasm gave a powerful impetus to the development of the sport. The Italian Derby was inaugurated at Rome on 19 April 1884, and the first winner was Andreina, a daughter of Andred, owned and trained by an Englishman, Thomas Rook. Rook, a close friend of the leading English jockey Tom Cannon, went to Italy in 1854 to ride for the King. The royal stable became so powerful that there were few opportunities for anyone else to win a race, and in the end it was disbanded. Many of the King's horses were bought by Giovanni Ferrero, who appointed Rook as his trainer. Rook soon became the greatest name in Italian racing, and was the founder of the famous winter training grounds at Barbaricina, near Pisa, which were used intensively by the Dormello horses in later years.

Thus the foundations of a national racing system and breeding industry had been laid before Tesio embarked on his epoch-making venture. Nor did Tesio engineer single-handed the great leap forward that was to make the Italian thoroughbred a factor of international repute. The enterprise of two of his compatriots, Cavaliere

157

Odoardo Ginistrelli and Count Felice Scheibler, was of crucial importance in ensuring that Tesio had the right material to hand when it was needed. Ginistrelli, born at Naples in 1833, became a racing enthusiast at an early age. He was only twenty-six when he formed his own stable at Portici, and forty-two when, after a violent quarrel with a rival owner, he decided to transfer his stud and stable to Newmarket. One of the mares he took with him was Star of Portici, whom he had bred in Italy from the imported English mare Verbena. Star of Portici had been one of the best performers of her day in Italy, winning twelve races, and in due course Ginistrelli obtained a nomination to the mighty St Simon for her. The produce was Signorina, who showed brilliant speed as a two-year-old and won all her nine races including the Middle Park Stakes. She won only one of her five races as a three-year-old, though she was beaten by only three-quarters of a length by another exceptionally talented filly, Memoir, in the Oaks, and she came back the next year to win the £11,000 Lancashire Plate, then one of the most valuable races in the calendar, over 7 furlongs (1400 metres) at Manchester.

Signorina gained immortal fame as a result of her love-match with the otherwise undistinguished stallion Chaleureux which resulted in Signorinetta, the 100–1 winner of the 1908 Derby and subsequent winner of the Oaks. The romantic story is in perfect accord with the description of the Chevalier as 'fat, short-bearded, eccentric and entirely lovable', but Signorina's earlier and less glamorous mating with Best Man had far greater significance for the future of Italian racing. Signorina's colt foal by Best Man, the result of her first conception at the advanced age of fourteen, was somewhat confusingly named Signorino. He was a first-class but unlucky racehorse who won the Triennial Produce Stakes at Newmarket on his debut but never won another race, though he was third to the French horse Jardy in the Middle Park Stakes, second to Vedas in the 2000 Guineas and third to Cicero and Jardy in the Derby.

It is at this point that Count Scheibler comes into the story. Acting on behalf of the Italian National Stud, he bought Signorino for 3000 guineas as a stallion. Signorino proved a great sire, heading the sires list ten times. Equally important was Scheibler's purchase of the filly Madree, bred by the leading French breeder Edmond Blanc, as a yearling at Doncaster. Madree won the inaugural Italian 1000 Guineas, the Premio Regina Elena, and in 1911, to a mating with the Derby and Grand Prix de Paris winner Spearmint, produced the filly Fausta. Here Tesio re-enters the story of the Italian thoroughbred, for he bought Fausta as a yearling. Fausta won the Italian Derby, the only winner of the race that Tesio owned but did not breed himself, and then produced three winners of the Italian Derby, Meissonier (1919), Michelangelo (1921) and Melozzo da Forli (1922), all by Signorino. Michelangelo in his turn sired one of Tesio's best horses, Navarro, who got the outstanding 1946 three-year-old Gladiolo and was one of the greatest broodmare sires in Italian racing history. One of his best daughters was Tokamura, the dam of the Gran Premio d'Italia winner Toulouse-Lautrec and the Italian St Leger winner Tommaso Guidi. Although Navarro died in an air raid during the Second World War at the age of thirteen, he was a potent factor in Dormello pedigrees.

Ginistrelli and Scheibler, in their different ways, were responsible for strokes of genius which helped Tesio to launch his operations on a much more ambitious scale. However, Michelangelo, by a sire based in Italy out of a mare bred in Italy but not by Tesio, was not in his origins at all typical of the kind of horses with whom Tesio was to take his own country and later Europe by storm. The essence of Tesio's methods of improving the Italian thoroughbred was to purchase fillies and mares abroad, mostly in England, and mate them with the best sires wherever they were available in Europe, inside or outside Italy. These purchases continued throughout his career as a breeder of racehorses, though most were concentrated in the thirty years from about 1910 to the outbreak of the Second World War and included at least a dozen first-class producers – Spring Chicken, Catnip, Chuette, Vice-Versa, Duccia di Buonin-segna, Duet, Bunworry, Bella Minna, Angelina, Tofanella, Try Try Again and Barbara Burrini. As long as he was able to obtain the strains he wanted he was indifferent whether he acquired their female representatives as foals, yearlings, fillies out of training or mares who had already spent several seasons at stud.

In the early 1920s Tesio was ready to launch some of his horses at carefully selected targets outside Italy. Neither in the early days of his foreign ventures nor at any subsequent period was he prepared to send his horses to run abroad merely in a spirit of sporting challenge; he sent them with the well-defined purposes of testing the progress of his own bloodstock, winning more valuable prizes than were available in Italy and enhancing the reputation of his own produce. In due course of time he accumulated an impressive list of victories in France, Germany, Belgium and England and, as a result of his cautious judgement, had an extraordinarily low incidence of failures.

Scopas was the first of Tesio's produce to win abroad when he was successful in La Coupe at the Paris suburban course of Maisons-Laffitte in 1923, and proceeded to overwhelm his opponents in the Grosser Preis at Baden Baden in August the following year, when Tesio also won the Fürstenberg Rennen with Rosalba Carriera. In 1925 Apelle, by the pre-war French crack Sardanapale out of the English-bred mare Angelina, won the 6½-furlong (1300-metre) Critérium de Maisons-Laffitte and three years later, having been bought by the Englishman Mr Richard McCreery after winning the Italian Derby and failing in the Grand Prix de Paris in his second season, gained a thrilling victory over Silverdale and the St Leger winner Book Law in the Coronation Cup over the Derby course at Epsom.

Apelle was a milestone in the history of Italian breeding in general and of the Dormello Stud in particular, as he proved that horses of the top international class could be bred south of the Alps. He was soon followed by another top-class horse from Dormello, Cavaliere d'Arpino, who was unbeaten in the five races in which he took part in 1929–30. However, Cavaliere d'Arpino, though regarded by Tesio as the best horse he ever bred and superior even to Nearco, was an unsound horse and his racing career fell in an otherwise lean period for Dormello. Other powerful studs, like the Gornate Stud of Guiseppe de Montel and the Razza del Soldo, had gradually come into prominence since the First World War, and it was a horse of Montel's, Ortello, who confirmed the good impression of Italian bloodstock given by Apelle by winning the Prix de l'Arc de Triomphe at Longchamp the year after Apelle's Coronation Cup victory. Moreover Cavaliere d'Arpino was by Havresac II, a son of Rabelais imported by Montel and a great sire who headed the list of winning sires in Italy no fewer than eleven times. Four years later, in 1933, Crapom, owned by the Crespi brothers and bred by the Razza Bellotta, gave Italy her second victory in the Prix de l'Arc de Triomphe.

It was clear, in the 1929–33 period, that Dormello just was not producing enough good horses and was in danger of losing its pre-eminence. This was a time of crisis which was solved when Tesio went into partnership with Marchese Mario Incisa della Rochetta.

The new arrangements secured the injection of new capital which was necessary for expansion and to enable Tesio to take up the running again from his Italian competitors. The Dormello Stud became the Razza Dormello-Olgiata, with the Olgiata estate near Rome to supplement the older Tesio breeding grounds in the north.

The effects of the partnership were quickly felt. Although other Italian studs have produced international-class performers like the post-Second World War Prix de l'Arc de Triomphe winners Nuccio and Molvedo from time to time, there has been no sustained threat to the leadership of Dormello-Olgiata. In 1934 and 1935 Tesio bred two of his finest specimens of the thoroughbred, Donatello II and Nearco. Donatello II won eight of his nine races, including the Italian Derby and the Gran Premio di Milano, and suffered his only defeat when he succumbed unluckily by three-quarters of a length to Clairvoyant in the Grand Prix de Paris. Nearco avenged that defeat of his stable companion when he completed an unbroken sequence of fourteen victories by winning the Grand Prix the following year. Afterwards Donatello II and Nearco were both sold to England, where they became leading sires and principal agents for spreading the influence of Dormello to practically every part of the world where horse racing flourishes.

Nearco was one of the truly great horses of racing history in the tradition built up by horses like Flying Childers, Eclipse, Gladiateur, St Simon, Ormonde and Man o'War, and to be continued by Ribot and Sea Bird II – horses who outclassed the best of their contemporaries and for whom defeat was inconceivable except through sheer bad luck. His victory over the French Derby runner-up Canot and the English Derby winner Bois Roussel in the Grand Prix could be regarded as sufficient proof of his class, but even more striking evidence was provided by the trial which Tesio had previously staged to find out whether he stayed 1 mile 7 furlongs (3000 metres), the distance of the Gran Premio di Milano and the Grand Prix de Paris. Nearco's companions in the trial were Ursone, a proven older stayer, and the fast three-year-old Bistolfi, who jumped in for the last 7½ furlongs (1500 metres). Nearco won the gallop readily from Bistolfi, with Ursone a bad last. The magnitude of Nearco's achievement became evident when Bistolfi won the important Prix d'Ispahan comfortably earlier on the afternoon of the Grand Prix, and went on to win the City and Suburban at Epsom the following April under a big weight.

It would be fruitless to argue whether Nearco or Ribot, Tesio's second world-beater, was the greater racehorse. Neither was beaten, and Ribot, who raced until he was four in contrast to Nearco who retired after winning the Grand Prix, did his racing in a more internationally minded era so that his two victories in the Prix de l'Arc de Triomphe boosted his reputation sky-high. Unfortunately Tesio did not live to see Ribot run. The great breeder died on 1 May 1954, just two months before Ribot made his first public appearance on the San Siro track at Milan. Ribot was at the Dormello Stud for four seasons from 1957 to 1960, and then went to the United States on a five-year lease which was later extended up to the time of his death in 1972. He was a great Classic sire whose influence was seen to be spreading for many years after his death. His top-class progeny included the Prix de l'Arc de Triomphe winners Molvedo and Prince Royal II, the American Classic winners Tom Rolfe and Arts and Letters, the English and Irish Classic winners Ragusa, Ribocco, Ribero, Boucher, Long Look and Regal Exception, and the Italian Oaks winner Alice Frey. One of the most influential of Ribot's sons was Graustark, the most precociously fast of all his progeny. Graustark excelled as a sire of broodmares, his daughters producing performers of the shining quality of the triple British Classic winner Oh So Sharp.

Donatello II, Nearco and Ribot were Tesio's three horses who made the strongest impact on breeding in many countries, but they were not the only horses of the highest international class bred by Tesio during the last twenty years of his life. Others were Nearco's half brother Niccolo dell'Arca, who made a trip to Berlin during the war to win the Grosser Preis der Reichshauptstadt and was one of Nogara's five sons who were at stud in England at the same time; Ribot's sire Tenerani, who won the Queen Elizabeth Stakes and the Goodwood Cup in England; the Ascot Gold Cup winner Botticelli; and the Champion Stakes winner Marguerite Vernaut.

There has been abundant proof that Italy is capable of producing racehorses of top international standing. Inevitably, with limited investment and a declining thoroughbred population in the late 1970s, Italy has not been able to produce these top-class horses all the time or in large numbers, and a wide gap has existed between the performance standards of the occasional world-class celebrities and average standards. Italy has lacked the thoroughbred middle classes which give the breeding industries of France, England and Ireland, her chief European rivals, their consistent strength.

The Italian thoroughbred is essentially a middle distance horse. The only Italian Group I two–year–old race included in the European Pattern is the Gran Criterium over 1 mile (1600 metres), and the shortest of the other nine Group I races is the Premio Emilio Turati for three–year–olds and upwards over the same distance. The nucleus of the Italian Group I comprises the Italian Derby and the Gran Premio d'Italia for three–year–olds, and the Gran Pemio di Milano for three–year–olds and upwards, all over 1½ miles (2400 metres). The only sprint in the top two groups is the Group 2 Prix Melton for three–year–olds and upwards over 6 furlongs (1200 metres); and the longest race in the Italian Pattern is the Group 3 Coppa d'Oro over 1 mile 7 furlongs (3000 metres). The Italian programme makes very few concessions to precocity, pure speed or extreme stamina.

The Italian thoroughbred is inevitably the creature of the national pattern of racing, and the Italian Pattern was stamped with its indelible character when the Premio del Commercio was introduced as the key race, after the Italian Derby, in 1889. The Milan Racing Club (SIRE), by then firmly established at its present course San Siro, completed the mould in which the Italian thoroughbred was formed by founding in 1921 the Gran Premio d'Italia, regarded as a more genuine test than the Italian Derby on the easier Capannelle course at Rome, and by transforming the Premio del Commercio into the richly endowed Gran Premio di Milano three years later.

A little-known story concerning Neacro thows a revealing ray of light on the Italian racing set-up. In the early spring of 1938, when Nearco was officially just three years old, Tesio made a visit to England and tried hard to find a purchaser for the colt, in the belief that he was only a sprinter and much more suited to the English system of racing. Fortunately Nearco was not sold until after his glorious victory in the Grand Prix de Paris, and then came to England with the reputation of a brilliant middle distance horse; and as such gained his enormous success at stud. Yet Tesio never altered his opinion, and noted of Nearco in his private stud book: 'Not a true stayer though he won up to 1 mile 7 furlongs. He won these longer races by his superb class and brilliant speed.'

Nearco's dam Nogara also had her limitations of stamina, and of her Tesio noted: 'A first-class racer from six furlongs to a mile.' She won both the Italian 1000 Guineas and the Italian 2000 Guineas, and ran out of opportunities after that.

The triumph of Tesio was that he was able to cultivate and preserve the speed characteristics of his horses while operating within the somewhat rigid and limited Italian programme of racing. In his foreword to the illustrated Dormello-Olgiata private stud book published in 1962, John Hislop wrote: 'When those of my generation come to be asked by their grandchildren: "Who was the greatest breeder, the outstanding sire, the best racehorse of your time?" the answer will probably be: "Tesio, Nearco, Ribot." ' How did Tesio do it? What were the principles that guided him in making the breeding plans that raised the standard of the tiny Italian thoroughbred industry so sensationally and gave it world-wide influence? These questions cannot be evaded in any study of thoroughbred progress, but there can be no definitive answer to them.

During the train journey home from Baden Baden after the victory of Scopas in the Grosser Preis, Tesio gave a clue when he remarked of his sojourn among the wild herds of Patagonia before he founded Dormello: 'I studied the way to listen to the stars and to speak to the horse.' There was a visionary streak in his nature, and he had an almost mystical relationship with his horses. He trained them besides breeding them, and as a result of seeing them daily from the time they were foaled to the time they came out of training he had a deep understanding of the physical and temperamental traits of each individual. A less practical aspect of the mystical relationship was his tendency to conceive wildly fanciful ideas, some of which found their way into his book *Breeding the Racehorse*. Fortunately his wife, Donna Lydia, was an extremely practical woman with a flair for administration and a comprehensive knowledge of the stud book and breeding statistics, and her wise counsel acted as an invaluable counterweight to his flights of fancy. Uniting pragmatism with genius, they were perfect partners.

A corollary of Tesio's mysticism was a tantalizing reticence about his breeding policies. A few crumbs of information can be picked up in *Breeding the Racehorse*. He had a regard for the benefits of inbreeding and believed in the existence of 'nicks'. He wrote: 'Although we cannot reduce the number of a horse's ancestors, we can select his parents in such a way that one particular ancestor will occupy more than one place in his pedigree, thus ensuring a greater probability that certain desired characteristics will be inherited. Inbreeding is the surest way of obtaining this result, by reducing the number of different ancestors and thereby making it easier to fix or establish their characters.'

He defined a 'nick' as the phenomenon of two particular strains giving their best results when crossed with each other. One of his examples of successful 'nicks' was Isonomy with mares having the blood of Hermit. He wrote: 'It was with this last combination that I won my first Derby. We had in Italy a mediocre stallion Melanion by Hermit. In 1904 I went to England and bought a granddaughter of Isonomy with the intention of breeding her to Melanion and copying the successful Isonomy-Hermit cross. The outcome of this mating was a colt whom I named Guido Reni and who was to give me my first great satisfaction of winning my first Derby.'

Nearco and Ribot, his two greatest horses, could be chosen as examples of brilliantly successful applications of his belief in inbreeding. Pharos, the sire of Nearco, and Havresac II, his maternal grandsire, were both inbred to St Simon. The pedigree of Ribot contained an even heavier concentration of the influence of St Simon; four stallions occupying prominent positions in it – Havresac II, Apelle, Pharos and Papyrus – were inbred to St Simon. On the other hand Tesio is not known to have confirmed that the matings which resulted in Nearco and Ribot were planned with the intention of fixing and establishing the qualities of St Simon, one of the best racehorses and most prepotent stallions of all time.

In his memoir of Federico and Lydia Tesio *The Tesios as I Knew Them*, published in 1979, Mario Incisa dropped hints of his exasperation at Tesio's inability or reluctance to communicate his mating principles even to his own partner, let alone anybody else. Incisa related that Tesio said to him one day at Dormello: 'Come with me and I will show how to do the matings.' But when Tesio was seated in his study with his split-pedigree book open in front of him, no coherent advice or explanation was forthcoming.

Tesio sometimes declared that many of his matings were based on his 'impressions' of the stallion and mare. On the other hand his purchases of fillies and mares were strictly orthodox on the whole. Great play has been made of the fact that he bought many of his most successful mares for derisory prices. He bought Catnip, the granddam of Nearco, for 75 guineas as a five-year-old at the Newmarket December Sales in 1915, and Duccia di Buoninsegna, the granddam of Donatello II, for 210 guineas as a yearling at the Newmarket July Sales in 1921. Catnip, who was five years old when Tesio bought her, had moderate racing form, and had gained her only victory in a nursery handicap over 1 mile (1600 metres) at Newcastle. Duccia di Buoninsegna was a wretched-looking filly and a bad mover when she was put up for sale. Yet they were both superbly bred, as Catnip was by Spearmint out of the 1000 Guineas winner and Oaks second Sibola, and Duccia di Buoninsegna, who incidentally like many unprepossessing yearlings improved vastly in action and appearance and won the Italian 1000 Guineas and the Gran Premio d'Italia, was a granddaughter of the peerless Pretty Polly. Tesio adopted the only policy open to the ambitious breeder with limited means, which is to buy seemingly inferior members of illustrious families. Nevertheless, Tesio's eye often discerned virtues in fillies and mares which were hidden to other beholders. For instance Noble Johnson, the manager of the Eyrefield Lodge Stud where Catnip was bred, described her contemptuously as 'a light, narrow filly that carried little flesh'; but Tesio noted of her in his private stud book: 'Small, sound and well-made'.

Tesio never fell into the trap, which has caught many large-scale breeders, of retaining home-bred stallions and using them on many of his own mares. He patronized Derby winners assiduously, and paid little attention to the ups and downs of their stud reputations, believing that a top-class racehorse would sire some good progeny sooner or later. In this way he bred many excellent horses like Donatello II (by Blenheim), Niccolo dell'Arca (by Coronach), Botti-celli (by Blue Peter), Theodorica (by Owen Tudor) and Toulouse Lautrec (by Dante).

This faith in the breeding value of winners of the race which he described as 'the most important' was one of the most constant elements in his selection plans. His belief in the racecourse test as the basis of selection caused him to cull ruthlessly all fillies who proved unfit to run or failed the test. His training methods were so exceptionally severe that only the physically and mentally toughest horses could survive them. It was no coincidence that Tesio the successful breeder was also Tesio the hard trainer; for his training and breeding activities were the essential components of a single process aimed at producing the perfect racehorse.

Genius defies precise definition. When all attempts at logical analysis are exhausted the phenomenon that was Tesio of Dormello is still inadequately explained. It is undeniable that luck played its part in promoting some of his most spectacular breeding triumphs. For example, in the year that Nearco was conceived he had planned to send his dam Nogara to Fairway, but was refused a nomination; Nearco's sire Pharos was his second choice and, although Pharos and Fairway were brothers, their characteristics as stallions were very different. Nor did Tesio have any confidence in either of the parents of Ribot as potential producers of a great racehorse, and Tenerani and Romanella were both for sale at the time they were mated. 'Tesio disliked Romanella and despised Tenerani,' wrote Mario Incisa.

Nevertheless it would surely be wrong to ascribe a decisive role to chance in the Dormello story. Success was too frequent, too consistent, too overwhelming and too long-sustained to be explained in such terms. It is probable that an air of mystery will always cloak some aspects of the brilliant history of Tesio and his Dormello Stud, whose contribution must be regarded, in view of all the circumstances and the limited resources employed, as without parellel in the evolution of the Classic racehorse. The evidence of the enduring influence of his breeding was as strong as ever a quarter of a century after his death. In 1979, for example, twenty-two individual winners of Group 1 Pattern races in the British Isles had thirty-one crosses of Tesio-bred stallions in their pedigrees; and it is significant that the best of those horses, the Derby winner Troy, had the largest number of crosses of Tesio-bred stallions – three of Nearco and two of Donatello II.

Tesio put Italy on the map as a world power in the production of Classic racehorses, but one measure of his greatness is that it has failed to hold that position since his death. The whole Dormello-Olgiata stud enterprise, though continued by Mario Incisa, sank into a steep decline, and the dispersal of other once powerful studs like the Razza del Soldo weakened Italian breeding still further.

A determined effort to raise the standard of Italian racing and stimulate investment in the breeding industry was launched in 1966 when Dr Carlo Aloisi, the newly appointed president of the Government-controlled agency UNIRE, announced a 27 per cent increase in prize money. At the same time the majority of Italian races were opened to horses bred abroad, though the Italian Derby and the Italian Oaks did not become fully international races until 1981. However these measures, and the progressive increases of prize money that followed, did not have the desired effect. Instead Italian owners became persistent buyers at the yearling sales in Britain, France and Ireland, and foreign-bred and trained horses began to flock into Italy in search of the large sums of prize money that had become available to them. In the 1980s Italian owners were buying about 350 yearlings annually in other European countries and up to 100 annually in the United States. At the same time the quality of stallions standing in Italy was so poor that the Italian breeders were sending as many as 400–450 mares to be covered abroad, mostly in Ireland, Great Britain and France, each year.

These activities of Italian owners and breeders could not stem the decline of the standard of Italian racing or of Italy as a producer of Classic racehorses. A stringent appraisal of the Italian Pattern races undertaken in 1987 revealed that many of them had been attracting fields of a class far inferior to agreed international standards. With a sense of realism bordering on the heroic, the racing authorities reduced the number of Pattern races from forty-nine to thirty-eight the following year. Even so, only four of those remaining races were won by Italian-bred horses. The only consolation was that the Italian-bred Tisserand managed to beat a field which included nine foreign-bred horses in the Italian Derby. Tisserand was a scion of an old Tesio family which had been distinguished by top-class horses like Tissot and Torbido forty years earlier, and his fourth dam Tiberia was by Tesio's masterpiece Ribot. The fact that an Italian-bred horse good enough to win a Group 1 race had become a rarity only served to emphasize the ignominy of the collapse of Italian breeding since the death of the genius of Dormello.

Germany

The output of thoroughbreds in the Federal Republic of West Germany has generally been similar in numbers to that of Italy. However, not until the 1980s did clear signs emerge that qualitative improvement of the German Thoroughbred had wiped out the advantage that Italy had enjoyed in that respect in the days when Italian horses like Ortello, Apelle, Donatello II, Nearco and Ribot were making their mark in international racing and exerting a strong influence on the evolution of the breed.

This inferior status of the German Thoroughbred in comparatively recent times could not have been predicted by any student of the thoroughbred a century and a half ago, for several of the states and principalities that compose modern Germany were among the first foreign countries to endeavour to establish races on the English model. The *General Stud Book* records show that thirty-seven thoroughbred stallions, including the Derby winners Moses, Gustavus and Mundig, had been exported to Germany by 1845, whereas only fourteen stallions had been exported to France by that year. That gifted chronicler of various equine matters, 'Nimrod' (Charles Apperley), received the impression that German racing was thriving when he toured the continent in 1836. With singular lack of prophetic wisdom he expressed the opinion that racing had little future in France because it did not suit the taste of the people, and contrasted the stagnation of the sport there with the lively progress in Germany. There were regular race meetings at Gustrow and Dobboran and in New Brandenburg in Germany, and the Duke of Holstein Augustenburg had established a very promising meeting in his country. Racing had been founded at Berlin and Hamburg in the previous few years. 'Nimrod' added: 'His Serene Highness and his brother Prince Frederick have each a large stud of horses, from blood imported from England; and amongst the conspicuous German sportsmen who have regular racing establishments under the care of English training grooms are Counts Hahn, Plessen, Bassewitz, Moltke and Voss; Barons de Biel, Hertefeldt and Hamerstein.'

Baron de Biel was the principal importer of English bloodstock and the moving spirit in the spread of racing. He had five stallions and a large number of mares in his stud at Zieron, and held an annual sale of the produce. His ingenious method of distributing the potential racehorse fairly was to draw by lot the expected produce of six of the mares for himself about a month before foaling time, and sell the rest without reserve. 'Nimrod' commented that the Baron's efforts to introduce racing in that part of Germany had been crowned with complete success, a remark that was justified by the fact that by 1842 the German Stud Book listed 780 mares.

The German Derby, which had its centenary at Hamburg in 1969, preceded the corresponding race in Italy by some fifteen years, and Berlin's Hoppegarten course, opened on 17 May 1868, had such magnificent training facilities that it was called the Newmarket of Germany. The German horse Turnus, owned by Count Hahn, won the Stewards Cup and the Chesterfield Cup at Goodwood in 1850, three years before the first French horse won an important race in England. Thus German racing had an early start and every chance to become one of the pace-setters in Europe. Why, then, were these advantages lost, and why did the performance standards of German racehorses lag behind those of France and Italy?

One obvious reason was the Germany's 'men of rank and opulence', who, as the editors of the *General Stud Book* rightly pointed out must be the principal supporters of a successful breeding industry, did not follow up the promising start with sufficient skill and spirit; and as far as quality of production was concerned, Baron de Biel was no Tesio. But it seems certain that other factors helped to retard progress. One was the combination of cold winters and poor, sandy soil in large parts of Germany, notably Prussia, which created conditions unfavourable for thoroughbred breeding. Another was the prejudice of German breeders, who were apt to insist that their thoroughbred stallions should have the strength and substance of half-breds and the action of the Arab. Count George Lehndorff, the manager of the German Imperial Stud, criticized this attitude in his book *Horse Breeding Recollections*, published in 1883, in which he wrote: 'The good people forget that everything in the world has its limits, and that Nature herself is impotent when asked to produce an animal of the strength of the elephant with the agility of a gazelle.' Lehndorff himself may not have got his priorities entirely right, as he opened his book with the words: 'The principal requisite in a good racehorse is soundness, again soundness, and nothing but soundness.' No sensible person would dispute the importance of soundness, but Lehndorff seemed to lose sight of the fact that a racehorse without speed would be useless on the track.

Unfavourable environment and faulty methods of selection no doubt contributed to the failure of German thoroughbreds to compete with the standards of their chief foreign rivals. Nevertheless, Lehndorff did launch a determined attempt to improve the German thoroughbred by encouraging imports of high-class stallions. At the end of the nineteenth and early in the twentieth century these importations from England and France included the 2000 Guineas winner Chamant, the Triple Crown winner Galtee More, the Derby winner Ard Patrick, and other notable horses like Caius, Nuage and Dark Ronald. At the same time Lehndorff was responsible for importing mares of high quality like Orsova, Alveole and Festa. As a result there was a perceptible improvement in German-bred racehorses between the two world wars, and a few notable successes were gained in international competition. In 1935 German racegoers were able to cheer their Derby winner Sturmvogel to victory against the French horse Admiral Drake, the winner of the Grand Prix de Paris the previous year, in the Grosser Preis von Berlin; and a year later they had even greater cause for jubilation when the German Derby and German Oaks winner Nereide beat the brilliant French filly Corrida, who won the Prix de l'Arc de Triomphe later that season and again in 1937, in the Munich Brown Band.

Oleander, foaled in 1924, had probably been an even better horse than his daughter Nereide, though he did not gain such a sensational victory over foreign rivals. Oleander was bred at the Oppenheim family's Schlenderhan Stud, one of Germany's oldest and most famous breeding establishemnts near Cologne, which celebrated its own centenary in appropriate fashion by winning the centenary German Derby in 1969 with Don Giovanni, its fourteenth winner of the race. Oleander showed brilliant form as a two-year-old, but then broke his pelvis in an accident and was scratched from his Classic engagements. For a time his life was despaired of, but his trainer Arnull nursed him back to fitness and he carried all before him in his native country at three, four and five years of age, winning the Grosser Preis von Baden in each of those seasons. He ran in the Prix de l'Arc de Triomphe twice, finishing fifth to Kantar on the first occasion and third to the Italian horse Ortello and Kantar on the second, when his English jockey Joe Childs was alleged to have thrown the race away by coming too soon.

Oleander became the most successful stallion in German racing history, as he headed the list of sires of winners eight times, once more than Chamant in the 1880s and 1890s. In addition to Nereide he sired, among horses of international repute, Orsenigo, who was an extremely high-class horse in Italy during the Second World War and won the Italian Derby and the Gran Premio di Milano.

Oleander was by the Schlenderhan-based Prunus, who was a son of Dark Ronald, the founder of one of the two male lines that dominated German breeding for half a century – the other being the line springing from Louviers. Dark Ronald was a good two-year-old in England in 1907 but then broke down and did not reappear until he was four, when he won the Royal Hunt Cup and the Princess of Wales's Stakes. He had three stud seasons at home, siring the great stayer Son-in-Law amd the excellent racehorse and stallion

Dark Legend, before he was sold to Germany for £25,000. He was champion sire in his adopted country five times, and in Prunus and Herold got two sons who were able to carry on the line with marked success.

Louviers, who was second to Edward VII's horse Minoru in the 1909 Derby, never set foot in Germany. He retired to stud in England until 1913, and was then exported to Russia, where he disappeared during the Revolution. The German mare Ladora was sent to be covered by him in his last stud season in England, and the produce of this mating was Landgraf, the winner of the 1917 German Derby and the best German racehorse of the First World War period. Landgraf was the first in an unbroken father-to-son chain of German Derby winners that has continued through Ferro, Athanasius, Ticino and Orsini to Orsini's sons Ilix, Elviro, Don Giovanni and Marduk, of whom the last-named was successful in 1974. Another son of Ticino, Neckar, won the German Derby in 1951 and sired two more winners of the German Derby in Zank and Waidwerk.

The fortunes of the Dark Ronald line had sunk to an unusually low ebb at the end of the Second World War, but the line revived strongly in the 1960s and 1970s when it was responsible for the German Derby winners Alarich, Baalim, Stuyvesant and Surumu. Most of the credit for the revival belongs to the great stallion Birkhahn, the winner of the German Derby in 1948. Birkhahn began his stallion career at the Graditz National Stud in East Germany, where he was leading sire of winners five times. He was bought by Baroness Gabrielle von Oppenheim of the Schlenderhan Stud in 1960 and, although he died five years later, he was leading West German sire of winners three times posthumously. It was appropriate that Schlenderhan's sixteenth German Derby winner Stuyvesant – Alpenkönig in 1970 had been the fifteenth – should be a grandson of Birkhahn besides being a descendant in the female line of the brilliant Schlenderhan racemare Schwarzgold, who was supreme immediately before the Second World War and was commemorated in the title of the German 1000 Guineas.

Schwarzgold herself was a paradigm of the best German breeding; she united the two potent German male lines, for her sire Alchimist was by Herold and her dam Schwarzliesel was by Oleander. Between the two world wars German breeding was practically isolated from the mainstream of European breeding, with its crosscurrents of Phalaris, Gainsborough, Blandford and Tourbillon, and the lack of bloodstock imports involved concentration on the Dark Ronald and Louviers strains, which became characteristically German. This concentration was intensified by the fact that stallions like Ticino, Neckar and Birkhahn became as effective as sires of broodmares as they were as sires of winners. Consequently German pedigrees became saturated with the strains of Dark Ronald and Louviers in the same way that American pedigrees were saturated with the strains derived from Diomed in the middle of the nineteenth century; by the time peace returned after 1945 the German thoroughbred was crying out for suitable outcrosses.

The Schlenderhan Stud was one of the first to exploit the possibilities of outcrossing by sending Aralia (by Alchimist out of Aster by Oleander) to France to be covered by François Dupré's stallion Tantième in 1954. The produce of the mating was Agio, winner of the German St Leger. The same year Dupré sent his mare Rhea II, who though by the German sire Gundomar came from a French female line, to be covered by Ticino at another famous German stud, Erlenhof near Frankfurt-on-Main. The produce was Bella Paola, one of the most brilliant European racemares of the century who raided England to win the 1000 Guineas, the Oaks and the Champion Stakes.

Schlenderhan continued to pioneer the outcross by using the British stallion Tamerlane on German mares to breed the top-class miler Dschingis Khan and the German Derby winner Alpenkönig, and Birkhahn on the British-bred Dante mare Palazzo to breed Priamos, winner of the Group 1 Prix Jacques le Marois over 1 mile (1600 metres) at Deauville. Similar outcrossing procedures involving blends of typical German strains with strains drawn from the mainstream of European thoroughbred evolution have proved their worth as sources of Classic quality on numerous occasions. The produce of this kind of outcross include the 1967 Oaks winner Pia; the 1972 French 1000 Guineas winner Mata Hari, a sister of Marduk; the 1975 Eclipse Stakes and Prix de l'Arc de Triomphe winner Star Appeal; the 1974 2000 Guineas winner Nebbiolo and the 1980 Prix Jacques le Marois winner Nadjar. The most striking success achieved by this kind of outcross was represented by the 1985 Derby winner Slip Anchor. His owner and breeder Lord Howard de Walden had purchased his dam Sayonara from the Schlenderhan Stud, and she came from the finest of the Schlenderhan bloodlines, as she was by

Birkhahn out of Suleika, by Ticino out of Schwarzblaurot, a daughter of the great Schwarzgold. Lord Howard mated Sayonara with the Derby winner Shirley Heights, whose pedigree combined potent American and European strains, and bred Slip Anchor as a result.

The German thoroughbred industry had to recover from the devastation of the Second World War before the opportunities for outcrossing could be exploited. Much of the bloodstock had been dispersed or fallen into Russian hands, and the Hoppegarten and the National Stud at Graditz were lost behind the Iron Curtain. The recovery was very slow until 1956, when the Government began to take an interest in racing and allotted subsidies which permitted a 15 per cent increase in prize money. The benefits were felt instantly. Fields improved in numbers and quality, betting turnover increased, the yearling market was stimulated and there was a powerful incentive to invest in bloodstock. In the next thirty years total prize money multiplied five-fold and in 1986 amounted to more than DM26 million distributed among 228 race days on fourteen courses. German racing moved more firmly on to the international stage with the inauguration of the Preis von Europa, run over 1½ miles (2400 metres) at Cologne in 1963; before that the principal German international race had been the Grosser Preis von Baden run over the same distance at the big Baden Baden meeting in late August and early September.

Even in 1955 the number of thoroughbred mares in West Germany was as low as 520, only two-thirds of the number listed in the German Stud Book more than a century earlier, and only 331 foals were produced. In the next twenty years the breeding industry expanded rapidly, and by 1985 the number of mares had reached a peak of 2258, with foal production of 1143.

The Direktorium Für Vollblutzucht Und Rennen, with headquarters in Cologne, is the supreme authority for racing and stud book matters in West Germany. The rules protect young horses against exploitation , as no two-year-old is allowed to run before 1 June and two-year-olds are limited to eight races during the whole season. In 1988 the German Pattern of thirty-six races included only one race for two-year-olds, the Group 2 Moët and Chandon Rennen over 6 furlongs (1200 metres) at Baden-Baden. Older sprinters also got short shrift, as the only Pattern races for three-year-olds and upwards over distances less than a mile (1600 metres) were the

American-Express Sprinter Preis over 7 furlongs (1400 metres) at Hamburg and the Goldene Peitsche over 6 furlongs (1200 metres) at Baden-Baden.

Official concern for the performance and soundness standards of the German thoroughbred is expressed in a licensing system for stallions. Licences are issued only to stallions that attain a minimum performance rating, which in practice limits licences to about the top dozen three-year-olds in an average season, and to stallions certified free from hereditary diseases such as roaring.

The mainspring of quality in German breeding until the late 1970s was the Schlenderhan Stud, when it was confronted by a sustained challenge from the Fahrhof Stud located improbably on the cold north German plain near Bremen. Owned by Walther Jacobs, who also owned the largest coffee business in Germany, Fahrhof had its first German Derby victory with Surumu (by Birkhahn's son Literat) in 1977, and was a close second to Schlenderhan in the list of winning breeders of the same year. Six years later Fahrhof became Germany's leading breeder and held on to that position tenaciously, producing horses of the highest international class like Acatenango, winner of the Group 1 Grand Prix de Saint Cloud, and Lirung, winner of the Group 1 Prix Haras de Fresnay-Le-Buffard Jacques le Marois, in 1986. The Fahrhof policy was to use both the obvious methods of exploiting the international outcross; thus Acatenango was by Surumu out of the British-bred mare Aggravate, while Lirung was by the British stallion Connaught out of the German mare Liranga, who was by Literat.

This proof that German breeders, by enlightened investment and selection, could produce horses capable of holding their own in the international arena undermined the former protectionist stance that had excluded foreign-bred horses from a number of German Pattern races and other valuable weight-for-age races. In 1985, Germany, as well as Italy, applied and was accepted for membership of the European Breeders Fund. The terms of accession included a commitment to a progressive opening of those races so that all the Pattern races with the exception of the Classic races would be open to horses of all countries by 1989. A decision about the Classic races was to be made the following year.

In contrast to the Italian horses, German horses proved capable of putting up stout resistance to increased foreign competition in their own Pattern races. In 1988 they won fourteen, or 46.7 per

175

cent, of the thirty open Pattern races, and held on to two of the Group 1 international races for three-year-olds and upwards, the Preis von Europa with the four-year-old Kondor and the Grosser Preis der Berliner Bank with the five-year-old Helikon. By the late 1980s the German breeding industry could claim with justice to have made excellent progress as a producer of Classic racehorses.

9

The Thoroughbred in Australia

Kingston Town, who ruled the roost among the three-year-olds of the 1979–80 season, was a paradigm of the Australian Classic horse. He had enough precocious speed to win two of his three races as a two-year-old, and the next season revealed an exceptional and entirely admirable blend of brilliant middle distance ability, stamina, toughness and superiority to high-class older horses. In the first half of the season he began by winning a race over 6 furlongs and then enjoyed an easy win over his contemporaries in the Spring Champion Stakes over 1¼ miles (2000 metres) at Randwick, Sydney, and was unlucky when he failed by a short head to catch Big Print in the Victoria Derby over 1 mile 4½ furlongs (2500 metres) at Flemington, Melbourne. His true excellence was demonstrated in the second half of the season when, in the space of three weeks, he won four Grade I races on Sydney course – the Rosehill Guineas over 1¼ miles (2000 metres) and the H. E. Tancred Stakes over 1½ miles (2400 metres) at Rosehill, and the Australian Jockey Club Derby over 1½ miles (2400 metres) and the Sydney Cup over 2 miles (3200 metres) at Randwick. He was meeting older horses in the Tancred Stakes and the Sydney Cup, the Cup being one of the traditional long distance handicaps that have been regarded as supreme tests of the stamina and courage of the Australian thoroughbred. The Cup performance of Kingston Town was particularly meritorious because he dominated his sixteen opponents and won by three and a quarter lengths from the previous year's winner Double Century.

Kingston Town was less than the ideal Australian racehorse in only one respect: he is a gelding. He was gelded during the winter between his two-year-old and three-year-old seasons because he had

177

been difficult to train. Fortunately for this superbly talented black thoroughbred, geldings are eligible for the Australian Classic races, as they are for the Kentucky Derby, though they are excluded from the premier Classic races in all the principal European racing countries. The argument that the races which are crucial for the process of selection should be reserved for entire horses has failed to gain acceptance in Australia, so the case for Kingston Town as a splendid example of the Australian Classic horse cannot be gainsaid.

In respect of quality of performance, Kingston Town represented the apex of the pyramid of thoroughbred production in Australia – a pyramid with a very broad base. In 1979, when Kingston Town began to race, 14,900 foals were born, and eight years later the figure had reached 21,443, an increase of 43.9 per cent. Australia was then easily the second largest producer of thoroughbreds in the world after North America, which recorded 49,894 births in 1987. The land surface of Australia is roughly 85 per cent of that of the United States, but comparatively little of it is suitable for horse breeding owing to the aridity of much of the Australian continent. The size of the Australian thoroughbred population is even more remarkable in another respect, since the human population of Australia is barely 6 per cent of that of the United States.

The racehorse-breeding industry of Australia is even larger than the figures for thoroughbreds indicate. Non-thoroughbred horses have always been permitted to run in Australian races, and usually account for about one-third of all runners. It was estimated that about 55,000 mares were being employed for the production of racehorses by the end of the 1980s.

Although the prevalence of drought conditions and other quirks of climate restrict the areas of Australia that are suitable for horse breeding, the best pastoral regions are extremely favourable for the purpose. New South Wales, Victoria, Queensland, South Australia and Western Australia, in descending order of size, have flourishing breeding industries. Even the small island state of Tasmania has its breeding industry, though production there is relatively low, and has played its part in the evolution of the Australian Thoroughbred since the earliest days, when it was called Van Dieman's Land. Beer Street, winner of the Grade 1 Caulfield Cup in 1971, and Piping Lane, winner of the Grade 1 Melbourne Cup two years later, were Tasmanian-bred. One result of the escalation of yearling prices in the 1980s was renewed interest in the Tasmanian breeding industry, where thoroughbreds could be reared more cheaply than on the mainland and benefit from pastures considered equal to the best of New Zealand's.

There is no doubt, however, that the wide geographical spread of Australian breeding is accompanied by stark contrasts of quality between region and region and stud and stud. The best Australian horses are world class, but those forming the base of the population pyramid are dross by comparison. What applies to the breeding applies equally to the racing industry. So huge a country requires many race meetings to satisfy demand at local level, and in the 1978–79 season meetings were held on 532 courses throughout the country. No fewer than eighty-one courses, twenty-one more than in Great Britain, were in use in Victoria alone. The 28,000 individual equine competitors that took part in more than 22,000 races included thousands of minimal athletic ability bred on the cheapest and least ambitious lines.

High-quality racing is confined to a small number of horses and a small number of metropolitan racecourses. The 'Cataloguing Standards Book', sponsored by the Society of International Thoroughbred Auctioneers (SITA), showed that in 1986 the 225 Graded Stakes programmed in Australia were distributed among no more than twenty-four courses and accounted for only 1.02 per cent of all the races run. By comparison in Great Britain, where the quality of racing is more homogeneous, the Pattern races accounted for about 3.5 per cent of all races and were distributed among 38 per cent of all courses used for flat racing.

Nevertheless, when all necessary reservations have been made, there is no denying the success of Australian stud owners in exploiting the natural advantages of the best pastoral regions and taking high rank among the world's producers of racehorses. Those advantages include plentiful sunshine and ample space in addition to those qualities of soil and water required for building bone and sinew in healthy athletes. Although the horse was not among the original fauna of Australia, horses were introduced by the early English settlers and have been bred on the continent for two centuries. The first horses to set foot in Australia were landed from the First Fleet in January 1788, but the original elements concerned in the creation of the Australian bloodhorse did not arrive until some years later. In 1797 the four-year-old English thoroughbred stallion Young Rockingham, known more usually as Rockingham, was imported into New South Wales via the Cape of Good Hope, and was followed three years later by Washington, a stallion thought to be of the Spanish Eastern breed, imported from New England, also via the Cape. Washington on a Rockingham mare was a combination often found in the pedigrees of early Australian racehorses. Of even greater importance was the importation of Hector in 1807. A Persian Arabian formerly owned in India by Colonel Wellesley (afterwards the Duke of Wellington), Hector was presumed to be fourteen years old when he was landed, and by the time he died in December 1823 had left an indelible mark on the breed. According to the foreword to the bicentenary edition of the Australian Stud Book written by Brian Maguire, 'the vast majority of the colonial "cracks" of the period 1820 to 1840, and even beyond, carried his blood'. His daughter Betty was the tap-root of a family that was still represented in the latest volumes of the Stud Book.

The first official race meeting was held in Hyde Park, Sydney, in October 1810, and by the middle 1820s the sport was established on a regular basis. To supply the needs of the growing volume of racing more breeding stock had to be imported. Thoroughbred stallions like Peter Fin, Steeltrap, Camerton, Skeleton and Theorem were imported in the 1820s. The most influential of them all was Rous' Emigrant, imported by Captain Henry Rous (later Admiral and dictator of the British Turf) in 1828 when he was serving with a British naval squadron in Australian waters. Described as a black or brown horse of great quality standing sixteen hands, Rous' Emigrant became the property of a joint stock company after he was landed in Australia, with fifty gentlemen taking shares at £16 each and so making him the first syndicated stallion. The daughters of Rous' Emigrant were equally good on the racecourse and at stud, and several were found in the pedigrees of the colonial tap-root mares. One of his daughters, Flora McIvor, was the fourth dam of the great New Zealand-bred stallion Trenton (1881).

Thoroughbred mares as well as stallions were imported. The first mares of authenticated thoroughbred origin to reach Australia were Imogene (by Viscount) in October 1825 and Manto (by the St Leger winner Soothsayer) two months later. Imogene made little impact, but Manto was the most influential foundation mare in the history of the Australian Thoroughbred, not least because she was the granddam of Flora McIvor, and her name survived in high-class pedigrees in the later years of the twentieth century.

At a dinner given in Sydney by the Agricultural Society in the Captain's honour, Sir John Jamison predicted that 'in future years when our races will emulate those of the mother country the genealogies of our best horses will be interwoven with the names of those introduced by Captain Rous'. It is also clear that his counsel and example must have been at least partly responsible for the formation of the Australian Racing and Jockey Club which was set up by the Governor Sir Ralph Darling after a wrangle with the older Sydney Turf Club. However, it was not until 1840 that the decisive step was taken of forming the Australian Race Committee and issuing a manifesto which promulgated the aims of the Australian breeding industry. The manifesto stated:

The nature of this country is eminently adapted to meet the purposes of the horse breeder, and there can be little doubt in the minds of those who have considered the subject with attention that as soon as the number of horses bred here shall be sufficiently extensive to supply our colonial demand, we shall find in the neighbouring settlements and in India a sure and steady market for all our surplus; but to give our horses a reputation in foreign countries we must show to the world of what efforts they are capable, and prove that we devote both judgement and attention to the improvement of the breed.

The declared intention of the committee was to encourage a type of horse combining strength and endurance with as much speed as possible, so as to serve the dual purposes of sport and the daily needs of a mainly agricultural community with vast distances to cover. This encouragement took the practical form of a series of races to be run on the Sydney course of Home Bush the following year. These included the Metropolitan Plate to be run in 2-mile (3200-metre) heats, the Champion Stakes over 3 miles (4800 metres), and the St Leger, confined to three-year-old colts and fillies bred in the colony of New South Wales, over 1½ miles (2400 metres).

The St Leger was Australia's first Classic race. In 1842 the Australian Race Committee became the Australian Jockey Club, and the St Leger the Australian Jockey Club St Leger. Nineteen years later the race was transferred to Randwick, which had opened as Sydney's principal racecourse, and was supplemented by the Australian Jockey Club Derby in the New South Wales Classic programme. At first the Derby was run in September, but this date was considered too early in the spring and it was put back to the first week in October.

A more radical change was made in the 1978–79 season and the AJC Derby was transferred to the Sydney Easter Carnival.

Racing also thrived in other parts of Australia, and the various colonies founded their individual Classic programmes; it was not until 1901 that the Commonwealth of Australia came into existence, and those races were never merged in a single national Classic programme. Indeed Victoria had its own Derby at Flemington six years before the inauguration of the AJC Derby. The Classic programmes were supported by handicaps which carried equal or even greater prestige. Long distance handicaps like the Melbourne, Sydney and Brisbane Cups, all over 2 miles (3200 metres) and the Caulfield Cup over 1½ miles (2400 metres), became some of the most important races in Australia and were monuments to the original Australian Race Committee policy of encouraging horses of strength and endurance. This evolution of an Australian pattern of racing was accompanied by the crystallization of the Australian breed of racehorse. By the time Rous left Australia breeders were convinced the formula for success was to concentrate on imported English stock, and imports of Arabs and their use in breeding for the track declined. The middle of the nineteenth century saw the first great Australian-bred sire, Sir Hercules, make his mark. Sir Hercules, whose sire Cap-a-Pie and dam Paraguay were both imported from England, was sold as a yearling for £121 on the death of his breeder Mr Charles Smith. He never ran, but was an exceptionally successful stallion both in New Zealand, where he was sent for a spell of five years, and in New South Wales. The best of his sons, Cossack, won the St Leger at Home Bush and followed the example of his sire by doing well at stud, getting two St Leger winners. His top-class sons included the AJC Derby and St Leger winner Yattendon, the AJC St Leger winner Cossack and The Barb, who won the AJC Derby and the Melbourne Cup. Yattendon continued a native Australian dynasty with great success, and his grandson Merman developed into an excellent stayer when exported to England. Yattendon's daughter Yatterina was the tap-root of an enduring Colonial family.

The best imported horse of the same period was Fisherman, a horse of iron constitution and courage who won sixty-nine races in England including the Ascot Gold Cup twice. He was imported in November 1860 and, although he died less than five years later after standing in Victoria and South Australia, acted as a powerful reinforcement of the stamina of the Australian thoroughbred.

The compilation of breeding records had been initiated tentatively in the early days of Australian racing, though it was not until 1859 that Fowler Boyd Price's *Stud Book of New South Wales* was first published. By the 1870s New South Wales, Victoria and Tasmania had all published their own stud books. It was at that time that William Yuille, a Melbourne bloodstock agent and auctioneer, conceived the idea of compiling a stud book to cover the entire continent. It was a daunting task, because Australia was not then one nation but a collection of self-governing colonies linked by the most primitive communications, while many breeders were either dilatory in correspondence or reluctant to supply information. However, by 1878 Yuille, assisted by his son Archie, had overcome all the obstacles and published Volume 1 of the Australian Stud Book. The Yuilles continued to be responsible for compiling the book until Volume 9 in 1909, when the Australian Jockey Club and the Victoria Racing Club bought the copyright.

Eligibility for the General Stud Book was the main criterion for admission to the Australian Stud Book, but the Yuilles also admitted many families whose origins were unrecorded in the early colonial days. The new owners conducted a purge of mares whose pedigrees were poorly authenticated or whose influence had dwindled to vanishing point. Nevertheless, sixteen Australian tap-roots were retained, and this number of 'colonial families' was increased to nineteen by subsequent re-admissions. The Sappho family has been one of the most vigorous of the colonial families and has continued to flourish down to modern times. Royal Sovereign, foaled in 1961, was an illustrious scion of the family. He won the AJC, Victoria and Queensland Derbys, a treble achieved only twice before, by Florence in 1870 and by Tulloch in 1957. Another scion of the family, Powerscourt, sired Comic Court, the best horse of the 1950–51 season, and winner of the Melbourne Cup in record time.

By the end of the nineteenth century a distinct Australian type of racehorse had evolved from mingling the old colonial strains with the English thoroughbred stock that was being imported constantly. The most striking characteristic of this Australian type was toughness. Australian breeders, as much as any in the world, bred horses to race, and reputations were not to be cheaply earned. 'Race them hard and race them often' could be taken as the maxim of Australian owners and breeders. Some of the best horses to have raced in Australia, and some of the most successful home-bred Australian stallions, have run more than fifty times. Heroic, who set up a record by heading the winning sires list for seven consecutive seasons beginning in 1932–33, ran in fifty-two races and his victory in the AJC Derby as a three-year-old was followed the next season by a victory in the 6-furlong (1200-metre) Newmarket Handicap, one of the most important sprint races in Victoria. Spearfelt, who was leading sire of winners in 1942–43 after being second to Heroic twice, ran five times more than Heroic; he won only nine of his races, but had victories in the Victoria Derby and the Melbourne Cup to his credit.

One of the toughest of them all was David, foaled in New South Wales in 1917. He piled up a total of 124 racecourse appearances, mostly over long distances, and gained the most important of his twenty victories in the Sydney Cup. He became a successful sire, and most of his progeny were distinguished by their ability to carry big weights over long distances. David was by Maltster, who won the AJC and Victoria Derbys and was leading sire of winners five times between 1910 and 1915.

Home-bred stallions like Maltster, Heroic, Spearfelt and Carbine's son Wallace, who was leading sire in 1915–16, proved that Australia can produce high-class stallions. Nevertheless, for thirty years after Spearfelt's day the top place in the list of sires of winners was monopolized by imported stallions, and this state of affairs has given rise to a good deal of controversy. Some commentators expressed the opinion that for a long period Australian breeders harboured an irrational prejudice against home-bred stallions, preferring to send their best mares to imported stallions whose qualifications in terms of constitution and racing ability may have been inferior. They found it inexplicable that so many breeders recognized the value of the Australian climate and environment for raising sheep and cattle while denying their virtues for raising thoroughbreds.

Clearly many Australian breeders lost confidence in the merits of home-bred stallions for a lengthy period, but it is difficult to determine whether that loss of confidence was justified or not. The 1940s, 1950s, and 1960s may have been years of dearth of Australian-bred stallions of real worth, leaving the field wide-open to imported rivals. On the other hand if the superiority of imported stallions was a myth, general acceptance of the myth by breeders would have helped to make it come true. Breeders send their best mares to the stallions they believe to be the best, and the stallions that consistently get the best mares have an overwhelming advantage.

Once a prejudice of this kind has become fixed only the most powerful contrary evidence is capable of removing it. The chain of circumstances that was to lead finally to restoration of the faith of Australian breeders in their home-bred stallions originated, paradoxically enough, in the advent of the best of all the imported stallions, Star Kingdom, in 1950. Bred in Ireland in 1946, Star Kingdom raced as a two-year-old and three-year-old in England, where he was known as Star King. Although he was a small and light-framed chesnut, he was very athletic in build. He was by Stardust, one of the best of the early sons of Hyperion. Stardust was second in the war-time substitute races for the 2000 Guineas and the St Leger in 1940. However, his most notable asset was first-rate precocious speed, and he had been equal second best English two-year-old the previous year. This asset was augmented in Star Kingdom by the influence of his maternal grandsire Concerto, a pure sprinter. Consequently Star Kingdom was so brilliantly fast that he won five of his six races, including the important Richmond and Gimcrack Stakes, and suffered his only defeat as a two-year-old when he went under by a short head to Abernant, regarded as one of the best sprinters ever to race in England, in the 5-furlong (1000-metre) National Breeders Produce Stakes at Sandown. As a three-year-old Star Kingdom exploited his wonderful speed to win three races afterwards classified as Group 3 Pattern races – the Greenham Stakes and the Hungerford Stakes over 7 furlongs and 60 yards (1455 metres) at Newbury and the Jersey Stakes over 7 furlongs and 155 yards (1542 metres) at Ascot.

The concentration of speed in the parents of Star Kingdom and so signally expressed in his own performances and progeny had a revolutionary impact on the Australian thoroughbred. He was leading sire of winners five times (in 1958–59, 1959–60, 1960–61, 1961–62 and 1964–65) before he died at the Baramul Stud near Sydney at the age of twenty-one. He was second on the list twice and third three times, and was leading sire of the dams of winners three times. His success depended on his ability to sire horses with his own exceptional speed and precocity; he began his career by heading the list of first season sires, and was leading sire of two-year-olds seven times. Some of the best of his progeny, like Noholme and Sky High, stayed well enough to be top-class middle distance performers, but the 2 miles (3200 metres) of races like the Melbourne Cup were usually beyond them.

Star Kingdom not only injected a fresh element of brilliance into the Australian thoroughbred. He also wrought a subtle change of thinking in the Australian racing community. Breeders, owners, trainers and public alike were enraptured by the special quality of his progeny, for the excitement generated by their scorching speed was infectious. Responding to this new obsession with pure speed, the Sydney Turf Club in 1957 introduced the Golden Slipper Stakes, a valuable race for two-year-olds over 6 furlongs (1200 metres) at Rosehill. The first Golden Slipper winner was Star Kingdom's most gifted son Todman, and Skyline, Fine and Dandy, Sky High and Magic Night followed on to give the Star Kingdom progeny a monopoly of victory in the first five runnings of the race.

The influence of Star Kingdom on the Golden Slipper Stakes was not confined to his immediate progeny. Todman sired two winners of the race, Sweet Embrace and Eskimo Prince, and another son of Star Kingdom, Kaoru Star, sired Luskin Star, whose victory in the 1977 Golden Slipper Stakes was one of the most scintillating in the history of the race. Marscay, by Star Kingdom's son Biscay, won the Golden Slipper Stakes in 1982 and proved a typical member of the dynasty by becoming a prepotent sire of fast horses before the end of the decade.

The prize money and prestige of the Golden Slipper Stakes increased so rapidly that in the 1978–79 season its total endowment of $A250,000 made it the joint most valuable race in the continent with the Australian Derby run at Ascot in Western Australia. Ten years later the value of the Golden Slipper Stakes had risen to $A1.65 million, the same as Australia's greatest traditional race, the 2-mile (3200-metre) Melbourne Cup. Nor was the Golden Slipper Stakes alone in providing a rich reward for precocious excellence. Supporting races of the same kind include the Blue Diamond Stakes over the same distance at the Melbourne course Caulfield. The Star Kingdom influence has been apparent also in the results of the Blue Diamond Stakes, which was won in 1977 by Blazing Saddles (by Todman) and two years later by Star Shower (by Star Kingdom's son Star of Heaven).

Star Kingdom had a dual significance for Australian breeding. Firstly he transformed the Australian thoroughbred by injecting a pervasive dose of precocious speed; secondly, he sired progeny of such sublime excellence that breeders could not ignore them, and the prejudice against home-bred stallions was broken down in a manner that was timely and ineluctable in equal proportions. Todman was the supreme example of a Star Kingdom horse who captured the imagination of breeders. He and the New Zealand-bred Tulloch were the principals in 1956–57 which was one of the finest vintage seasons for two-year-olds in Australia. Although Tulloch outstayed Todman in the AJC Sires Produce Stakes over 7 furlongs (1400 metres), Todman got his revenge by outpacing Tulloch and beating him by six lengths in the Champagne Stakes over 6 furlongs (1200 metres) four days later. He outclassed his rivals in the Golden Slipper Stakes, when Tulloch was not in the field.

The burgeoning male stock of Star Kingdom has permeated high-class breeding to an extraordinary degree. It can produce performers of Classic middle distance standard with suitable help from the distaff side of matings, as the case of Kingston Town proved conclusively. Kingston Town sprang from a pure speed branch of the line, as neither his grandsire Biscay (by Star Kingdom) nor his sire, the pony-sized Bletchingly, revealed any ability to stay further than sprint distances. His dam Ada Hunter, who was imported unraced from Italy, had a pedigree packed with stamina. She was by Ribot's son Andrea Mantegna, and her dam Almah was a half sister by the great English stayer Alycidon to the French Oaks winner Tahiti.

The 1980s saw the consolidation of the dominant influence of Star Kingdom in Australian breeding. His grandson Bletchingly was leading sire of winners for the three seasons 1979–80, 1980–81 and 1981–82. He then gave way to the New Zealand-based Sir Tristram, but continued to be one of the most consistently successful stallions. As late as 1987–88 he was second to the New Zealand-based Zamazaan in the general list in which no fewer than thirteen of the top fifty sires belonged to the Star Kingdom male line, and was first in the list of the sires of two-year-olds with Marscay second and Biscay, the sire of both Bletchingly and Marscay, in third place.

Although the Star Kingdom line was the prime force in revolutionizing Australian breeding and the attitude of Australian breeders, it was not a Star Kingdom horse that made the first breakthrough to become the first home-bred leading sire of winners since Spearfelt. This honour fell to Matrice, who headed the list in the 1973–74 season thanks mainly to his three-year-old son Taj Rossi, winner of the Victoria Derby and three other Grade 1 Stakes races. Matrice, by the imported Blue Peter horse Masthead, was twenty-three years old when he finally reached the top.

Three seasons later home-bred Australian stallions triumphed on a much broader front when Century (by the once despised imported horse Better Boy) and Vain (by the imported horse Wilkes) occupied the first two places in both the general list of sires of winners and the list of sires of two-year-old winners. Century's double achievement was a record, because he was the first horse ever to head both lists with only two crops of runners to represent him. His progeny covered a wide range of successful performance, as one of his daughters, Century Miss, won the Golden Slipper Stakes, another daughter, Valley of Georgia, won the AJC Oaks, and his son Double Century won the Sydney Cup. Vain, who had been second to Century, had his hour of glory when he interrupted the reign of Sir Tristram and became the leading sire of winners in 1983–84.

Comparison of Australian horses with those of Europe and North Amercia has always been difficult on account of the difference in seasons in the two hemispheres. Horses in Europe and North America have their official birthdays on 1 January, those in Australia on 1 August. The covering seasons fall in the spring and summer in each hemisphere. Consequently horses bred to southern hemisphere time count as three-year-olds in the northern hemisphere when they would still be running as two-year-olds in Australia. In 1975 the Jockey Club introduced modifications to the official weight-for-age scale making allowances to horses foaled between 1 July and 31 December in the southern hemisphere so as to compensate for this disadvantage, but the problem has inhibited the testing of the best Australian horses against northern hemisphere opposition in the past, at least until they were fully mature. The Hon. James White, the leading New South Wales owner and Chairman of the Australian Jockey Club in the 1880s, was determined to overcome the difficulty by having three of his mares covered to northern hemisphere time. As a result Kirkham, named after his stud, carried his colours in the 1890 Derby, but finished unplaced behind Sainfoin after running prominently in the early stages of the race.

Kirkham failed to win in three races in England, but showed respectable ability by finishing third to Heaume, winner of the French 2000 Guineas and Derby, in the Hastings Plate over the Ditch Mile (1600 metres) at the Newmarket First Spring Meeting.

Later ventures were successful in attaining objectives less ambitious than the Derby. The Australian filly Mons Meg, also bred to English time, won the Ascot Gold Vase as a three-year-old the year after Kirkham's Derby failure. Paris, after winning the Caulfield Cup in 1892 and 1894, was sent to England where, as Paris III, he won small races at Northampton, Gatwick and Lewes. It was the other way about with Merman; he had comparatively modest form in Australia but, after reaching England as a five-year-old in 1897, became a high-class stayer and won the Cesarewich, the Jockey Club Cup, the Goodwood Cup and the Ascot Gold Cup, besides finishing second in the Grand Prix de Deauville, in the course of a campaign covering four seasons.

Merman, who stood as a stallion at studs in Wiltshire and Surrey, was a dark chesnut horse combining power and quality, standing on the best of limbs and blessed with an excellent temperament. He was a fine advertisement for the Australian thoroughbred, as were Newhaven II and The Grafter, who were sent to England after winning the Melbourne Cup, then the most glamorous and coveted prize on the Australian Turf, in 1896 and 1898 respectively. Newhaven II was third and last to Merman in the Goodwood Cup, but was beaten by only a little more than two lengths. He showed more speed than Merman, winning the Epsom Cup over 1½ miles (2400 metres), the City and Suburban over 1¼ miles (2000 metres) and the March Stakes over the Newmarket Rowley Mile (1600 metres) twice. The Grafter took some time to become acclimatized, but as a seven-year-old won two important handicaps over 1¼ miles (2000 metres), the City and Suburban and the Prince Edward Handicap.

These and other Australian-bred horses like Australian Star, winner of the City and Suburban, and Dalkeith, winner of the Newbury Spring Cup, proved conclusively that good Australian horses were capable of holding their own in high-class company in England. Nevertheless, many horses with first-rate form in Australia failed patently to do themselves justice when they were sent to Europe. The problems of acclimatization, on top of the costs of transportation and the long duration of the sea voyage, caused the flow of Australian horses to run in England to dry up. Yet Merman and company had made their point.

It was after the Second World War that Shannon led the way in demonstrating the prowess of Australian-bred horses in the United

States. Foaled at the Kai-Ora Stud in New South Wales in 1941, Shannon was one of the best horses in Australia during and just after the war. Having won fourteen of his twenty-five races in his native country, he was exported to the United States where he won six more races including the Golden Gate Handicap, the Forty Niners Handicap and, most important of all, the Hollywood Gold Cup. He was an excellent advertisement for the quality and durability of the Australian thoroughbred. He did well as a stallion at Spendthrift Farm in Kentucky until he died at the early age of fourteen. His son Clem was one of the best horses in the United States in 1957 and 1958.

The foundation of the Washington DC International at Laurel in 1952 provided a new yardstick for measuring the progress of thoroughbreds from different countries. Two Australian-bred horses, Sailor's Guide and Tobin Bronze, finished in the first three in the first seventeen runnings of the race. Sailor's Guide was awarded the race on the disqualification of the English-bred Tudor Era in 1958, and Tobin Bronze was third to the American horses Fort Marcy and Damascus in 1967. Sailor's Guide was conceived in England and imported into Australia *in utero*, but owed a lot to the Australian environment and training. He was a thoroughly tough and genuine performer, as his career record of nineteen successes from sixty-two races attested. His most important victories before the Washington DC International were gained in the Victoria Derby and the Sydney Cup.

If the problems of distance and season have restricted direct competition between racehorses bred in Australia and those bred in the northern hemisphere, more plentiful evidence about the relative quality of the Australian Thoroughbred can be obtained from the influence exerted by Australian bloodstock on breeding in other countries. Shannon is only one of many who have demonstrated the breeding value of Australian bloodstock abroad in the period 1945–80. Another was that superb galloping machine Bernborough, who graduated from the bush meetings of Queensland to become the idol of crowds on the metropolitan courses. He broke his near foreleg while running in the L.K.S. Mackinnon Stakes at Flemington as a seven-year-old. He was saved for stud, joined Shannon at Spendthrift Farm and sired many good horses including Berseem and Hook Money, who were leading sprinters in the United States and England respectively. His influence lives on, as one of the best of his daughters, the Grade 1 Acorn Stakes winner Parading Lady, became the granddam of Briartic, the sire of the 1979 champion Canadian three-year-old Steady Growth.

Royal Gem, the winner of the Caulfield Cup in 1946, also went to stud in Kentucky and left an indelible mark on the American Turf when his son Dark Star administered the only defeat ever suffered by the brilliant Native Dancer in the Kentucky Derby of 1953. The influence of Royal Gem and Dark Star persisted in the French 1000 Guineas and Oaks winner Gazala, the French Derby winner Youth and the leading international performer of the late 1970s Exceller.

Tobin Bronze became a successful stallion in California and Dhaulagiri, who won seventeen of his sixty-seven races in Australia, went to France and sired the Grand Prix and French St Leger winner Dhaudevi, but soon became infertile. Not surprisingly in view of the dominance of Star Kingdom at home, two sons of Star Kingdom, Noholme and Sky High, were among the most successful Australian-bred stallions abroad. Sky High, winner of the Golden Slipper Stakes and the Victoria Derby, had the advantage of being at one of Kentucky's most famous studs, Claiborne Farm, and sired many good horses including the Grade 1 Jockey Club Gold Cup winner Autobiography. The success of Noholme, a younger brother of Todman, was more remarkable because he began his stud life in Arkansas, remote from the main American thoroughbred-producing areas, where there were few quality mares. He forced himself on the attention of breeders far beyond the confines of Arkansas by the sheer excellence of some of his early progeny like Nodouble, nicknamed the 'Arkansas Traveller' as a result of his achievement in winning important races from the east to the west coast, from the extreme north to the extreme south of the United States. Nodouble and another of Noholme's high-class sons, Shecky Greene, have carried on the line with distinction, while Noholme's daughter Carnauba won the Italian Oaks. Nodouble was the leading North American sire of winners in 1981, and Shecky Greene sired Green Forest, who was the European champion two-year-old colt the same year when he won three French Group 1 races – the Prix Morny, the Prix de la Salamandre and the Grand Critérium.

The high standard of the Australian Thoroughbred in modern times has been founded on the enthusiasm of the people for racing and betting and the huge revenues flowing into racing from betting with bookmakers and from the Totalisator Agency Boards (TAB) which have a legal monopoly of off-course betting. In 1987 3.5 per cent of betting turnover was returned to the industry, producing income equivalent to £68 million for racing; in Great Britain the corresponding figures were 0.88 per cent and £27 million. Consequently racing flourished all over the country, and was able to make rapid strides in respect of prize money and amenities. In Western Australia, formerly the poor relation of the other mainland States as far as racing was concerned, the principal racecourse Ascot, controlled by the Western Australia Turf Club, was able to stage races like the $A931,300 The Australasian, the $A500,000 Australian Derby and the $A300,000 Perth Cup in the late 1980s. Australia moved into the international racing arena in 1987 when the H. E. Tancred Stakes, run since 1963 at the Sydney course Rosehill, became the Tancred International and high-class foreign horses were invited to compete with expenses paid. The result of the first running was a triumph for the Australian-trained but New Zealand-bred Beau Zam, who won decisively from the British-trained Highland Chieftain and the French-trained Very Pleasant. However the race shed little light on relative thoroughbred standards in Europe and the Antipodes because the foreign runners were a long way below the best in their own countries; Highland Chieftain had a rating of only 116 in the previous year's International Classifications, 18 lbs less than the top rated Mtoto.

The prosperity of Australian racing was reflected in steeply rising bloodstock values once the market had stabilised after the worldwide recession of 1974–75. The spending power of Australian breeders increased both absolutely and in relation to foreign competitors, and as a result there was an influx of high-class stallions. In the 1980s Australian stallion resources were enhanced by horses of the high quality of the Arlington Million winner Tolomeo, the Group 1 Sussex Stakes winner Noalcoholic and the French 2000 Guineas winner Melyno. Arrangements with the leading Irish stud Coolmore meant that top-class stallions like Godswalk, Salmon Leap and Bluebird spent covering seasons in Australia. The immensely talented trainer Colin Hayes, who founded the Lindsay Park Stud in the Barossa Valley of South Australia in 1965, played a leading part in securing these stallions. A great coup for Australian breeding was the importation in 1987 of Kenmare, who was the leading sire in

France the following year after being third once and second twice in the previous three seasons.

The other side of the coin of Australian racing prosperity was a thoroughbred population explosion possible only as a result of relaxation of normal criteria of selection. Inevitable loss of quality could be compensated only partially by imports. Nor could promotional gimmicks like the Magic Million Sale on the Gold Coast in Queensland fail to distort the time-honoured principle of the best horse earning most and the worst horse earning least, which gives breeders the strongest possible incentive to concentrate their efforts on improving the thoroughbred. The Magic Million Sale involved 200 colts and 200 fillies which were qualified exclusively to contest two $A1 million two-year-old races the following season and a single three-year-old race of the same value twelve months later. This baneful example had been followed by sales companies in Ireland and France by the end of the decade, and an extension of the original scheme was proposed for 1992 with the introduction of a so-called Magic Million Championship Classic for three-year-olds and upwards over a mile (1600 metres) worth $A4 million.

Besides combating the ever-present risk that over-rapid expansion would lower standards, Australian breeders striving to produce Classic racehorses had to face the powerful competition of breeders in New Zealand, which boasts an ideal environment for raising thoroughbreds. This New Zealand competition may not be significant in the category of precocious speed, and no New Zealand-bred horse had won the Golden Slipper Stakes up to 1988. It is a different story in the middle distance Classic and weight-for-age races, and most conspicuously in the well-endowed long distance races like the Melbourne Cup, in which New Zealand-bred horses regularly take a substantial share of the honours.

Some Australian commentators became so resentful of the persistent success of New Zealand horses that they advocated the abolition or conversion of the traditional Cup races. Why, they asked, should big prizes be provided for a type of horse that was virtually obsolete in Australia, with the result that most of the benefits accrued to New Zealand horses and the New Zealand breeding industry? The answer surely must be that a drastic break with tradition would be in conflict with the wishes of the betting public, and that the destruction of the character of the Cup races would detract from the variety and attractiveness of the overall Australian racing pro-

193

gramme. It seemed that Australian breeders needed either to find a more positive solution to this dilemma or to accept that the New Zealand breeding industry had a permanent and important ancillary role to play on the Australian racing scene.

10

The Thoroughbred in New Zealand

In respect of thoroughbred production New Zealand and the Irish Republic play corresponding roles in the southern and northern hemispheres. Both countries have exploited the assets of their mild climates and basically pastoral economies to develop thriving blood-stock industries and become important suppliers of thoroughbreds to richer and more populous neighbours – Australia in the case of New Zealand and England in the case of Ireland; and have been so successful in this specialized kind of livestock breeding that they have the highest ratios of thoroughbred to human population of any countries in the world.

In the 1980s New Zealand was slightly ahead of Ireland in this respect. They had similar human populations of about 3 million, but New Zealand produced 6982 thoroughbred foals in 1987 compared with 5280 in Ireland, having held the lead throughout the decade. Ireland last held a small numerical advantage in 1977. Nor do these figures convey a faithful picture of total production of racehorses in New Zealand, where non-thoroughbreds are eligible to race and account for about 7 per cent of all the horses in training.

Physical toughness and high-class middle distance ability and stamina are accepted as the hallmarks of the New Zealand horse, and are the reasons why New Zealand breeders have been able to secure a lucrative share of the Australian market. The description of New Zealand as a neighbour of Australia may be loose in terms of distance, because they are separated by 1200 miles of the Tasman Sea. But the two countries are, geographically speaking, components of Australasia and there is no country close to Australia with an environment as favourable for thoroughbred breeding as that of New Zealand. Although the two main islands of New Zealand cover a distance of about 1000 miles from south-west to north-east, they lie wholly within the temperate zone and no part of the country is more than eighty miles from the sea. The annual average rainfall is from 25 to 60 inches (600–1500 millimetres), a range regarded as ideal for plant growth in the temperate zone. Much of the country has at least 2000 hours of sunshine per year, with a high proportion during the winter months. Consequently New Zealand does not suffer extremes of temperature and, with soil of high mineral-bearing content, produces excellent pasture and conditions generally for producing thoroughbreds in regions like Auckland, the Waikato valley, Hawkes Bay, Wanganui and the Manawatu Plains in the North Island and the Canterbury Plains in the South Island.

The majority of New Zealand horses are reared under natural conditions. Most studs have shelter plantations and foals, having been born in the open, run with their dams in the paddocks day and night until weaning without risk from the elements. Mares are covered in the open on many studs, though this practice has been known to have baleful consequences. On one stud a rabbit, pursued by two dogs, darted between the legs of a mare while the stallion was in the act of covering, and in the resulting turmoil mare and stallion sustained injuries which persuaded the stud owner that it would be wise to build a covering barn before the next stud season. Such incidents are rare. Many young horses never see the inside of a box until a few weeks before the yearling sales, when they are brought in and prepared. The benefits are twofold. Firstly, horses reared under this system tend to be healthy and hardy; secondly, the open-air regime brings significant economies in manpower and installations, and in New Zealand it costs only half as much as in England to put a yearling in the sale-ring.

In the early days of colonization New Zealand had to rely on horses imported from Australia and Tasmania for racing and breeding. Although Captain Cook explored the islands in 1769, extensive British settlement did not begin until 1840, by which time racing and breeding were well established in Australia. The first stallion of mainly thoroughbred origin to be landed in New Zealand was Figaro, who was imported from New South Wales to Wellington the same year. Figaro's pedigree was recorded as by Operator (by the 1823 Derby winner Emilius) out of a mare by Theorem. Several localities have laid claim to have been the site of the first race meeting. Figaro took part in one of the early meetings when he won a 10-guinea sweepstakes on the beach at Petone, near Wellington, in 1842. Mr H. A. Thompson arrived in Wellington about the same time, bringing with him an unraced mare, also by Emilius. Mated with Figaro, this mare bred Il Barbiere, who sired Rosebud, Ladybird and Opera, who became influential tap-roots for New Zealand breeding.

Of great importance for the evolution of the New Zealand thoroughbred was the arrival of The Libel's son Traducer as a five-year-old in 1862. Traducer's only victory had been gained in the Wynnstay Handicap over 6 furlongs (1200 metres) at Chester as a three-year-old, but he was not devoid of class and had been third in the 2000 Guineas. Unfortunately he had inherited the uncertain temper of his sire, which may have helped to account for the fact that he changed hands at least seven times while he was in New Zealand. Despite the savagery which greatly restricted his use at stud, he sired nine New Zealand Derby winners, three winners of the Great Northern Derby and eight winners of the Canterbury Cup, a weight-for-age race over 2¼ miles (3600 metres). He was equally successful as a sire of broodmares, and his daughters were appearing in a high proportion of New Zealand thoroughbred pedigrees late in the twentieth century. The best of his daughters, Lurline, was out of Mermaid, who had accompanied him on the voyage from England and survived such appalling storms that both horses were nearly lost. Foaled in 1869, Lurline was far the best performer of her day in New Zealand at three and four years old, and at five raised the prestige of New Zealand in Australia by winning five races, including the VRC Australian Cup and the Adelaide Cup. She bred the Victoria Derby and St Leger winner Darebin.

The greatest of the early imported mares was Flora McIvor, by Rous' Emigrant out of Manto. Manto, the first mare of authenticated thoroughbred pedigree imported into Australia, produced Flora McIvor as an eleven-year-old in 1828, but Flora McIvor had reached the advanced age of twenty-six before Henry Redwood of Nelson took her to New Zealand. Nevertheless, she was so wonderfully vigorous and long-lived that she still had time to produce two fillies destined to have a profound influence on the breed of the racehorse in her adopted country. Sired by the great Australian stallion Sir Hercules, who had a spell of five years at stud in New Zealand, they were Io, the ancestress of Trenton, and Waimea, the ancestress of such top-class horses as the New Zealand Derby and Melbourne Cup winner Nightmarch and Scorn, one of the best fillies ever to race in New Zealand.

Men like Redwood and George Gatenby Stead were the pioneers of thoroughbred evolution in New Zealand, but their example was eagerly followed. The volume of racing, and the size of the breeding industry required to supply horses to it, increased rapidly in the 1860s.

In 1897 control of racing on a national basis was established by the formation of the New Zealand Racing Conference, to which all the metropolitan and provincial clubs were affiliated. Conference laid down the principle that race programmes should encourage the breeding of the middle distance and staying type of horse.

Musket, imported as an eleven-year-old in 1878, not only embodied this principle but played a vital part in putting New Zealand on the map as a racehorse-producing country. He did not run as a two-year-old, but was successful in nine of his twelve races during the next three seasons and won over distances ranging from the 1¼ miles (2000 metres) of The Flying Dutchman Handicap at York to the 2½ miles (4000 metres) of the Ascot Stakes and the 3 miles (4800 metres) of the Her Majesty's Plate at Shrewsbury and the Alexandra Plate at Ascot. He left his son Petronel to win the 2000 Guineas and the Doncaster Cup, and in the six years he was at stud in New Zealand sired two horses, Carbine and Trenton, who were to go to England and leave an indelible mark on the evolution of the thoroughbred, and another, Martini-Henry, who was destined through his daughter Achray to appear in the pedigree of the Derby winner Nimbus and the potent sire Grey Sovereign.

Foaled in 1885, Carbine was unbeaten as a two-year-old in his home territory, the South Island of New Zealand. He then moved to Australia, where he ran in all sorts of races over all sorts of distances, ending as a five-year-old with a career score of thirty-three wins, six seconds and three thirds from forty-three races. He reached his peak as a five-year-old when he won ten of his eleven races including the Melbourne Cup, the most coveted prize in Australia, which he won in the then record time of 3 minutes 28¼ seconds carrying the all-time record weight of 10 st 5 lb (65 kilos). He was a horse of tremendous character and consummate ability.

Having retired to stud in Victoria at the then record fee of 200 guineas, Carbine sired Wallace, named after his owner Mr D. S.

Wallace. Wallace won the AJC St Leger and the Sydney Cup and became one of the rare home-bred stallions to head the Australian list of winning sires. In 1895 the Duke of Portland, seeking an outcross for his mares by St Simon and Donovan, bought Carbine for £13,000, then a record price for an Australian horse, and installed him at his Welbeck Stud, where St Simon also held court. Understandably he was overshadowed by St Simon, but his contribution to the progress of the breed was still significant. He sired the Derby and Grand Prix de Paris winner Spearmint, and was the grandsire and great grandsire of two more Derby winners, Spion Kop and Felstead. In addition to Spion Kop Spearmint sired Plucky Liège, a truly great broodmare and dam of the Derby winner Bois Roussel, the Grand Prix de Paris winner Admiral Drake and the brothers Sir Gallahad III and Bull Dog who as sires had a profound influence on the modern thoroughbred in the United States. Carbine's daughter Queen Carbine is found prominently in the pedigree of Petition, the sire of Petite Etoile and the important stallion Petingo.

Martini-Henry won the Melbourne Cup with the light weight of 7 st 5 lb (46½ kilos). Trenton alone of Musket's three famous sons did not win the Melbourne Cup, but as a four-year-old was third, beaten by two heads, and as a five-year-old was second, beaten by a neck by Arsenal, to whom he was trying to concede 29 lb (13 kilos). Trenton won eight of his thirteen races. He excelled at stud. In Australia he sired the winners of 404 races worth £101,933 including the Melbourne Cup winners Auraria and Revenue, and was leading sire in 1901–02. He was fifteen by the time he arrived in England, and had been such a sick horse on the voyage that he was able to cover only four mares in his first season at the Cobham stud. He recovered to sire Rosaline, whose daughter Rosedrop won the Oaks and became the dam of the Triple Crown winner and great sire Gainsborough. Trenton's son Torpoint sired Hamoaze, the dam of the Eclipse Stakes winners Buchan and Saltash and the Derby runner-up St Germans.

Phar Lap was bred in 1926 at Timaru on the east coast of the South Island, and became one of the greatest racehorses ever bred in New Zealand. He was a son of Night Raid, a moderate racehorse in England and Australia but the sire of another high-class performer called Nightmarch. His racing career began unpretentiously, but his brilliance was undoubted once he had matured and struck form as a three-year-old. He had been so big and backward as a yearling that he was gelded. Fortunately geldings were eligible for the Australian Classic races and Phar Lap was able to win the AJC Derby and St Leger and the Victoria Derby and St Leger. His best performance was to win the Melbourne Cup as a four-year-old. Although he had 9 st 12 lb (62½ kilos) on his back, his reputation was such that he started at 11–8 on, the shortest price in the history of the race.

Phar Lap had the chance to show his superb racing merit outside the confines of Australasia when he was sent to the United States as a five-year-old. Anti-betting legislation had halted racing in California but at Tanforan, just across the Mexican border, he won the Agua Caliente Handicap in the course record time of 2 minutes 2.8 seconds for 1¼ miles (2000 metres). Shortly after that triumph Phar Lap died when turned out at Menlo Park in California. He was thought to have eaten grasses treated with a poisonous spray, but the cause of his death was never verified.

Phar Lap was known as the 'Red Terror' on account of his fiery chesnut colour, formidable stature and apparent invincibility when at his best. He was also described as 'a phenomenal racing machine'. In colour and size he resembled Man o'War in the United States and Hurry On in England. In these respects he could hardly have been less like another great New Zealand-bred horse, Tulloch, who was foaled twenty-eight years after Phar Lap. A giant in racing ability, Tulloch was physically a midget, and never stood more than 15.2 h.h. (1.57 metres) while he was in training. He was bred by Mr Seton Otway at the Trelawney Stud in the lush Waikato valley, where his sire Khorassan had succeeded the great Foxbridge. Though he was by the non-staying Big Game, Khorassan had the Oaks winner Udaipur as his granddam. Florida, the dam of Tulloch, was a tough little mare who stayed 1½ miles (2400 metres) and revelled in heavy going. Tulloch was an insignificant bay yearling, but the leading Sydney trainer Tommy Smith took a liking to him on account of his game head and beautiful swinging walk and bought him for 750 guineas. He proved an amazing bargain. He had the hallmark of the brilliant racehorse – the ability to hold his own against the fastest of his contemporaries over distances less than 1 mile (1600 metres) as a two-year-old combined with overwhelming superiority over longer distances at three years of age and upwards. The AJC handicapper rated him equal best two-year-old of 1956–57 with the outstandingly fast Australian-bred Todman, whom he beat in the AJC Sires Produce Stakes over 7 furlongs (1400 metres) but who beat him in the Champagne Stakes over 6 furlongs (1200 metres). As a three-year-old he won the AJC, Victoria and Queensland Derbys and the AJC and Victoria St Legers, and proved his excellence by beating good older horses in the Caulfield Cup.

His career reached its peak in the first half of his three-year-old season. After that he was inhibited by a mysterious internal ailment, and the fact that he struggled to his target of £A100,000 in prize money, and reached it with a glorious victory under 9 st 12 lb (62½ kilos) in the 2-mile (3200-metre) Brisbane Cup, was eloquent testimony to class and courage.

Tulloch's illness thwarted plans to send him to run in England as a four-year-old. How good a horse was he by international standards? His trainer gave his own idea of the answer when he remarked: 'I saw Round Table, the United States champion, and Tulloch would have given him 7 lb and beaten him.' There is bound to be a subjective element in such judgements. Scraps of evidence, such as the fact that he ran the 1½ miles (2400 metres) of the Caulfield Cup in 2 minutes 26.9 seconds, lowering by nearly a second the record which had stood for twenty-two years, testify to his exceptional class. Veterinary surgeons unearthed the intriguing fact that his heart weighed 31½ lb (14 kilos), and that Phar Lap's heart weighed only ½ lb more although Phar Lap was 1.2 h.h. (15.3 centimetres) taller and a much bigger horse in every respect.

Although the evidence about the international standing of Tulloch was inconclusive, there was no doubt whatever of the world class of the New Zealand-bred Balmerino, who followed him two decades later. Several New Zealand horses, notably Daryl's Joy, who won the Grade I Oak Tree Stakes and the Grade 2 Del Mar and San Luis Obispo Handicaps in California, advertised the merits of New Zealand breeding in the meantime. Like so many horses destined for glory on the racecourse, Balmerino began life inauspiciously. His breeder Ralph Stuart, a farmer at Cambridge in the Waikato valley, usually sold his colts as yearlings, but abandoned this practice in the case of Balmerino because he was such a miserable specimen at that age and had a lump on his thigh which required surgical removal. But he quickly grew out of his early troubles, and foreign observers who became familiar with his appearance in maturity found it hard to believe that he had ever been anything but a handsome thoroughbred.

He had a quiet season as a two-year-old in 1974–75, when he won one of his four races. He blossomed into an outstanding three-year-old, and became the first horse ever to be placed top of the three-year-old Free Handicaps of both New Zealand and Australia. His fourteen victories from eighteen races that season included the New Zealand Two Thousand Guineas, the New Zealand Derby and the Wellington Derby in his native country and the Grade I Rawson Stakes over 8¾ furlongs (1750 metres) and Brisbane Cup over 2 miles (3200 metres) in Australia.

Balmerino was given time as a four-year-old to show that he had made the right progress, which he did by winning the Group I Air New Zealand Stakes over 1¼ miles (2000 metres) at the Auckland course Ellerslie, and was then launched on a campaign abroad with the aid of sponsorship by the principal New Zealand thoroughbred sales company Wrightson Bloodstock. The object was promotion of the New Zealand thoroughbred, and Balmerino did not let his country down. He did not appreciate the hustle and bustle involved in being stabled at an American racecourse at his first stop, California, though he did win one of his four races there. A decision was made to move him on to England. He was in poor and nervous condition when he reached John Dunlop's stable at Arundel in Sussex in August 1977. Dunlop's training grounds in lovely Arundel Park, on the southern slopes of the South Downs, are among the most peaceful in the world, and in these surroundings Balmerino's restoration to mental and physical health was astonishingly rapid. Within two months of his arrival he had won the Valdoe Stakes over 1¼ miles (2000 metres) at nearby Goodwood and proved himself to be in the top flight of world-class middle distance performers by finishing second to Alleged in the Prix de l'Arc de Triomphe. His 'Arc' performance was all the more creditable because he had far from the best of luck in running and came late on the scene.

The 'Arc' second was the peak of Balmerino's achievement. Although he continued to run well in international company and won the Clive Graham Stakes at Goodwood the next May, there were signs that much travelling and strenuous racing had taken their toll. By the time his European campaign terminated in the late summer of 1978 he had been second in three more Group I races, namely the Gran Premio del Jockey Club in Milan (in which he finished first but was relegated to second place by the Stewards in favour of Stateff), the Coronation Cup and the Joe Coral Eclipse

Stakes. He had also been third in the Hardwicke Stakes, fourth in the Washington DC International, fifth in the King George VI and Queen Elizabeth Diamond Stakes and sixth in the Benson and Hedges Gold Cup. He had done more than enough to establish himself as one of the leading international performers of his time and fulfil his mission to promote the virtues of New Zealand blood-stock. He made a favourable impression in all the European countries in which he raced, and his wonderfully fluent action was particularly noted.

Balmerino returned to New Zealand to stand at the Middlepark Stud in the Waikato valley where his sire Trictrac also had stood. Trictrac was not otherwise a successful stallion, but had been a good-class racehorse in his native France, where he won the Group 2 Prix Eugene Adam over 1¼ miles (2000 metres) at Saint Cloud as a three-year-old. New Zealand breeding has always been heavily dependent on imported stallions, and no wholly New Zealand-bred stallion has headed the list of winning sires since Stepniak in 1908, though Martian, who was leading sire seven times beginning in 1941, was foaled in New Zealand after being imported *in utero*. Several of the most renowned staying male lines have had notable success in New Zealand. For example, the Son-in-Law line has been represented by the two potent stallions Beau-Père and Foxbridge. Beau-Père, sold for the derisory sum of £100 when he was exported from England, also was a successful stallion in Australia and the United States, where he was the maternal grandsire of Swaps. Fox-bridge, by Son-in-Law's Gold Cup winning son Foxlaw, was the most influential of all the Trelawney Stud stallions. Beginning in 1941, he was leading sire of winners for eleven consecutive seasons, and was equally influential as a sire of broodmares.

Le Filou, the first French-bred horse to head the list of winning sires in New Zealand, was by Vatellor, the sire of the Derby winners Pearl Diver and My Love and a source of abundant stamina. Bought in England for 500 guineas on behalf of Mr Jack Macky, owner of the Pirongia Stud in the Waikato valley, he had sired the winners of more than $NZ1½ million by the time he was withdrawn from service at the age of twenty-two in 1968, and was leading sire four times.

Alycidon, the greatest stayer to grace the English Turf after the Second World War, had a strong impact on New Zealand breeding through his son Alcimedes and his grandson Oncidium, who was by the St Leger and King George VI and Queen Elizabeth Stakes winner Alcide. Alcimedes, another high-class stallion to stand at the Trelawney Stud, sired the Melbourne Cup winners Galilee and Silver Knight and the AJC Derby winners Prince Grant and Divide and Rule. Oncidium, who stood at another famous stud, Te Parae in the Wairarapa valley, was even more successful. He was the leading sire on New Zealand and Australian combined earnings three times, and his death from cancer at the age of fourteen in 1975 was a grave loss for New Zealand breeding.

Most striking of all in the context of stamina was the consistent success of stallions from the male line of the 1916 substitute St Leger winner Hurry On. Hurry On, a horse of commanding size and power, founded one of the most persistent staying strains in England and his sons and descendants, particularly those derived from his Ascot Gold Cup winning son Precipitation, have thrived in New Zealand as surely as rhododendrons in the Bagshot sands of England. The first member of the line to make his mark was Hunting Song, by Hurry On out of a daughter of the romantic Derby winner Signorinetta. He was champion sire six times in succession, beginning in 1933. The Derby winner Coronach, by Hurry On, ended his days in New Zealand, having been transported there after the outbreak of the Second World War, and sired a winner of the Auckland Cup, though he scarcely achieved the eminence expected of an Epsom Classic winner.

The sons of Precipitation began to play a dominant role in the 1950s. The most influential of them were Admiral's Luck, Count Rendered, Summertime and Agricola. Admiral's Luck died after only four seasons at stud, but still managed to sire a champion in Mainbrace, who won twenty-three of his twenty-five races and slammed all the best horses of his time. Count Rendered, who was champion sire twice, Summertime, who was champion sire three times, and Agricola were all of material assistance in the onslaught by New Zealand-bred horses on the big Australian races. A half-brother of Alycidon, Agricola was the sire of the spectacularly successful filly Lowland, who won the South Australian St Leger and the AJC Oaks and beat the dual Melbourne Cup winner Rain Lover in the Sydney Cup.

Summertime was the sire of Sobig, the most successful native-bred stallion of modern times in New Zealand. Foaled in 1961 and the winner of twelve races including the Great Northern Derby,

Sobig began his stud career with two important advantages. One advantage was that his dam Passive had been a top-class performer, heading the 1956–57 Free Handicap and including the New Zealand Derby, Oaks, St Leger and the Great Northern Derby among her thirteen victories. The other advantage was that he was owned by Gordon Mitchell, who had good mares and the determination to give him every possible chance to distinguish himself at his Santa Rosa Stud in the Manawatu Plains near Palmerston North. Sobig never headed the New Zealand list of winning sires, though he made a habit of heading the New Zealand-bred sire list. His principal impact was in the wider field of Australasian earnings, and he was second twice and third three times in the combined New Zealand and Australian rankings. The most notable of his progeny in Australia included the dual Melbourne Cup winner Think Big, the Caulfield Cup winner Sobar and the Grade 1 W. S. Cox Plate winner So Called; and his top-class progeny in New Zealand included Kirrama and Corroboree, who were the top-rated colts in the three-year-old Free Handicaps of their years, the New Zealand Oaks winner Devante and the Wellington Cup winner Big Gamble. Kirrama, a scion of the Australian 'colonial' Yatterina family, became a fairly successful stallion in New Zealand. In the 1980s Balmerino and Vice Regal were New Zealand-bred horses who made their names as high-class sires, and towards the end of that decade McGinty was raising hopes that he was another home-bred stallion of the superior class of Sobig. A winner of six Grade 1 races in New Zealand and Australia, McGinty was the sire of the 1988 New Zealand Derby winner The Gentry.

Without doubt the same prejudice against native-bred stallions which prevailed for so long in Australia, and its converse, preference for imported stallions, have affected the attitudes of New Zealand breeders. Nor has the frequent practice of gelding colts early in life, more for the convenience of trainers than for sound physical or temperamental reasons, helped to preserve a wide choice of native-bred stallions for breeders. However these are not the only, or perhaps the most cogent, factors which tend to restrict the general use of native-bred stallions. The very success of New Zealand breeders as exporters has been a prime cause, since foreign buyers cream off a high proportion of the best-bred yearling colts, and therefore the most attractive stallion prospects, at the yearling sales.

The National Yearling Sales were founded at Trentham racecourse, near Wellington, in 1927, as a cooperative venture by the two main sales companies. At the first National Sales the two companies obtained averages of 315 and 275 guineas for their offerings. The top price of 1500 guineas, significantly enough, was paid by an Australian, and Australian buyers continued to provide the backbone of the market as the importance of the National Sales in the context of the entire Australasian racing scene increased during the next sixty years. Turnover and average prices at the National Sales were rising rapidly in the 1980s, partly in line with world trends in bloodstock values and partly as a result of the prosperity of Australian racing and the soaring reputation of the New Zealand Thoroughbred. Turnover rose from $NZ6,484,750 to $NZ32,987,000 (408 per cent) and the average price from $NZ18,013 to $NZ78,332 (335 per cent) between 1980 and 1986. In 1986 56 per cent of the turnover was accounted for by Australian buyers and a further 13.4 per cent by other overseas buyers, while 54 per cent of the turnover at the second most important yearling sales, Waikato, was attributed to overseas buyers. In 1988 the National Sales moved from Trentham to a brand new complex of the most up-to-date design near Auckland, the largest city in New Zealand, with superior air communications calculated to enhance the appeal of New Zealand thoroughbreds in the international market.

Although New Zealand breeders are forced to recruit stallions abroad to ensure the future of their success as exporters, exports in the past did not provide sufficient funds to buy those stallions at top world prices. Forced to choose between pedigree and performance, New Zealand breeders have usually opted for pedigree in the horses they have bought abroad. The guiding principle has been the maxim enunciated by Seton Otway, that potential stallions must have a good dam and come from a strong female line.

Battle-Waggon and Mellay, two of the most prolific sires of winners in the 1970s, illustrated the working of this principle. Battle-Waggon won only one unimportant race in England, and Mellay never ran. They were both by the Derby and St Leger winner Never Say Die. Battle-Waggon was out of the Oaks winner Carrozza and came from the same family as the Triple Classic winner Sun Chariot, and Mellay was out of the Triple Classic winner Meld and came from the same family as Precipitation.

New Zealand breeders tend to be fiercely independent in outlook, and many of them prefer to own stallions and try to make their reputations by letting them serve most of their own mares, rather than endure the loss of personal control involved in syndication. This system of individual stallion ownership may bring resounding success when the stallion proves prepotent and nicks with the mares on the stud; it may even be necessary to give a stallion a fair chance, as in the case of a native-bred stallion like Sobig. But the system does entail at least partial suspension of proper criteria of selection based on pedigree and conformation, and must mean that the potential genetic excellence of the thoroughbred population is not completely realized over the national breeding industry as a whole.

Nevertheless, heavy investment by foreign breeders like the American Bunker Hunt, the Irishman Tim Rogers and the Australian Arrowfield Group in the 1970s and 1980s heralded a revolution in the outlook and the prospects of the New Zealand breeding industry. Patrick Hogan personified a new spirit of enterprise, recruiting stallions of the highest class and applying the most modern ideas of marketing and promotion to his operations at the Cambridge Stud in the Waikato valley. He achieved spectacular success with Sir Tristram, a tall and powerful son of the Derby winner Sir Ivor, who had achieved only moderate success on the racecourse in France. The progeny of Sir Tristram took Australian racing, and consequently the yearling market, by storm, heading the list of sires of winners in Australia four times between 1982–83 and 1986–87. One of Sir Tristram's best sons, the VRC Derby winner Grosvenor, proved such an instant success when he retired to stud at Matamata that hopes of the foundation of a potent New Zealand male line were kindled. Sir Tristram sired performers of note from two-year-olds to Classic winners, to the gigantic mare Empire Rose, the winner of the Melbourne Cup in 1987. In 1984 Sir Tristram was joined at the Cambridge Stud by the superbly bred Danzatore, by the world's foremost Classic stallion Northern Dancer and himself the best Irish two-year-old of 1982 when he was the unbeaten winner of three races including the Group 2 Panasonic Beresford Stakes. Danzatore lost no time in establishing himself as a Classic Sire when his son Wonder Dancer won the 1988 Australian Derby. In 1987 John Messara, chairman of the Arrowfield Group, announced the purchase of the top-class proven stallion Ahonoora from the Irish National Stud by a syndicate headed by the Irish Coolmore Stud and the Australian Segenhoe Stud. Ahonoora was to serve dual stud seasons annually at Coolmore and the Ra Ora Stud near Auckland.

The essence of New Zealand racehorse breeding lies in the wonderfully sound and hardy female strains which have been developed in the country for many equine generations. The large majority of mares in the *New Zealand Stud Book* trace without flaw to *General Stud Book* sources, but some have one or more sires not warranted pure-bred in their pedigrees, others spring from imported Arab taproots, and others again belong to prominent so-called 'Colonial' families not traced to *General Stud Book* sources. The Cutty Sark, Gipsy, Sappho, Yatterina, Moth, Princess, Rosebud, Sharkie, Slander, Vesta and Woodstock Colonial families were represented in Volume 22 of the *New Zealand Stud Book* published in 1975, and of these the first four are also accepted in the *Australian Stud Book*. Several of these families are still active in the production of high-class performers. For example Sobig's son Kirrama and Battle-Waggon's daughter Battle Eve, a leading stakes winning mare with twenty-five victories to her credit, sprang from the Yatterina family; and Disraeli, the winner of the New Zealand St Leger in 1977–78, was a member of the Woodstock family.

Many of the top-class horses who have traced their descent from original *General Stud Book* mares belong to strains that have been extant in New Zealand for numerous generations. Tulloch was a seventh generation and Balmerino was a sixth generation native-bred New Zealand horse. The family from which Balmerino sprang came to be known by the name of his dam Dulcie and also produced the brilliant filly Surround and Beau Zam, the easy winner of the first running of the Tancred International at the Sydney course, Rosehill, in March 1988. Beau Zam was rated with 63 kilos in the 2000 metres plus section of the official Australia-New Zealand Classifications for the 1987–88 season, the highest rating awarded to a three-year-old since Kingston Town's 64 in the 1979–80 season. Another great New Zealand family was that of Eulogy, imported from England in 1915. Athenaia, the winner of the New Zealand Oaks in 1978, was a sixth generation descendant of Eulogy, and Bonecrusher, an outstanding performer of the 1984–85 season when he beat another New Zealand-bred horse Waverley Star in a titanic struggle for the Grade 1 W. S. Cox Plate at the Melbourne course Moonee Valley, was an eighth generation descendant of Eulogy. On the male side of his pedigree Bonecrusher was a third generation descendant of Star Kingdom through Kaoru Star and Pag-Asa.

The typical New Zealand female strains are not only sound and hardy; they are also imbued with such a potent degree of stamina that it is transmitted to their offspring no matter how they are mated. Essentially speedy imported stallions like Pakistan II, Copenhagen and Sovereign Edition have proved capable of siring top-class middle distance performers when mated with New Zealand mares. Surround herself was a striking example of this process. Though New Zealand-bred, she was elected Australian 'Horse of the Year' in 1977 on the strength of her marvellous feat of winning the AJC, the Victoria and the Queensland Oaks. She was by Sovereign Edition out of Micheline, a half sister by Le Filou to Balmerino. On the other hand Beau Zam, who won the record sum of $A2,111,175 in the 1987–88 season, had a more orthodox middle distance pedigree as his French-bred sire Zamazaan (by the Prix de l'Arc de Triomphe winner Exbury) won three Pattern races over distances up to 1 mile 7½ furlongs (3100 metres) in his native country.

New Zealand breeders are deeply conscious of the fact that Australia is capable of producing all the horses it needs, and that Australian owners and trainers go to New Zealand only in search of horses of superior quality. In practice New Zealand breeders have been consistently successful in supplying that quality. New Zealand-bred horses have a long record of victory in the Australian Cup and middle distance Classic races, and the flow of New Zealand winners of those important races showed no sign of abating in the 1980s. In the 1984–85 season, for example, New Zealand-bred horses won all the six Australian Grade 1 Derbys – the AJC, the Victoria, the Queensland, the Australian, the West Australian and the South Australian.

Nevertheless the huge increases in prize money for two-year-old races and the proliferation of speed tests in Australia were of concern to New Zealand breeders. Determined efforts were made to increase the elements of speed and precocity in the New Zealand Thoroughbred by importing horses like Sovereign Edition, Star Kingdom's speed record-breaking grandson Zephyr Bay and the English sprinter Three Legs, of whom the last-named was the leading New Zealand sire of winners in the 1984–85 season. Nor has this kind of investment been confined to stallions. Encouraged by tax concessions which enabled them to invest profits in high-priced mares and write them off over a short period, New Zealand breeders upgraded their operations by extensive buying in Australia. The leading Australian trainer and breeder Colin Hayes was quoted as saying:

'New Zealand breeders will continue to drain our best blood because New Zealand is a tax haven for the breeder.' The influence of Star Kingdom, so prevalent in the male line, was also harnessed to the distaff side of New Zealand pedigrees. For example Dulcify (by Decies), who won the AJC Derby, and Good Lord, who won the Wellington Cup in his own country twice and proved himself a genuine international performer by winning the Sydney Cup in Australia and the Eddie Read Handicap in California, were both out of mares by Star Kingdom's brilliant son Todman.

The Golden Slipper Stakes, the supreme test of precocious speed in Australia, continued to elude the grasp of New Zealand breeders up to the late 1980s. McGinty was probably unlucky not to break the ice in 1983, as he beat the subsequent Golden Slipper Stakes winner Marscay in the Todman Slipper Trial two weeks beforehand but split a cannon-bone in doing so. Evidence of success in the drive to enhance the speed of the New Zealand Thoroughbred was found in the Australian 1984–85 season when New Zealand horses won eight of the ten Grade 1 sprints at 7½ furlongs (1500 metres) or less.

The growing importance of the thoroughbred industry in the New Zealand economy convinced breeders and the racing authorities that it was necessary to promote the New Zealand Thoroughbred more actively and make their Pattern of Racing more intelligible to foreign observers. One promotional exercise was Balmerino's world tour. The most important step in respect of the Pattern of Racing was the rationalization of the Classic races which came into effect in the 1973–74 season. The individualism of New Zealand breeders has always been matched by the independent spirit of the regional racing clubs, with the result that races with Classic labels had proliferated in different parts of the country. It had become impossible to identify a horse's true status from the names of the races he had won. The agreement on rationalization involved the creation of a national Classic series on the English model with each race identified by a prefix 'New Zealand'. The series comprised:

The New Zealand 1000 Guineas for three-year-old fillies and the New Zealand 2000 Guineas for three-year-olds of both sexes, both run over 1 mile (1600 metres) at Riccarton (Christchurch) in November.

The New Zealand Derby for three-year-olds of both sexes, run over 1½ miles (2400 metres) at Ellerslie (Auckland) in January.

The New Zealand Oaks for three-year-old fillies, run over 1½ miles (2400 metres) at Trentham (Wellington) in January.

The New Zealand St Leger for three-year-olds of both sexes run over 1¾ miles (2800 metres) at Trentham in March.

The special importance conferred on these races by their titles was enhanced by stakes subsidies granted by the Racing Authority, the body set up by law and charged with the duty of channelling funds drawn from the off-course Totalisator Agency Board into the racing industry. The New Zealand Classic races thus became a reliable guide to the best horses of each generation.

The rationalization of the Classic races was followed by the designation as Graded Stakes of a programme of important and well-endowed races providing opportunities for the best horses of differing ages, sex and aptitudes, which corresponded to the British Pattern races. The Graded Stakes, divided into three groups in order of their importance, were kept under continuous review and by the 1987–88 season comprised a total of eighty races. The seventeen races in Group 1 included the Classic races and the two great traditional 2-mile (3200-metre) handicaps, the Auckland Cup and the Wellington Cup. Only two of the Group 1 races were confined to two-year-olds; indeed no more than nine (11.25 per cent) of all the Graded Stakes were confined to two-year-olds, a small proportion compared to Great Britain where 25 per cent of the 1988 Pattern races were for two-year-olds only. In March 1989 New Zealand racing moved decisively into the big international league with the first running of the country's first $NZ1 million race, the DB Draught Classic over 10½ furlongs (2100 metres) at Ellerslie.

Rising investment, enlightened breeding policies embracing a wide range of thoroughbred aptitudes, greater awareness of the enormous advantages of the New Zealand climate and environment and a firmer will to exploit them, and aggressive marketing were transforming the New Zealand Thoroughbred in the 1970s and 1980s. The capacity of the New Zealand breeding industry for producing Classic racehorses and shaping the evolution of the Thoroughbred was being enhanced systematically and gaining ever increasing international recognition as the end of the twentieth century approached.

211

11

The Thoroughbred in Eastern Europe and Japan

Nowhere is the ideal of the Classic racehorse upheld in purer form than in the countries of Eastern Europe. Opportunities for two-year-olds to run over short distances are restricted, good class sprint races for older horses are almost non-existent, and concentration on middle distance tests for the best horses almost complete. Staying power is valued more highly than in most other regions, notably North America. The Soviet Union even stages a searching test of high-class stamina in the Douga Narodov Priz over 2½ miles (4000 metres), the same distance as the Group 1 Ascot Gold Cup in Britain and the Group 1 Prix du Cadran in France, the two greatest races of their kind in the world.

Although each Eastern European country has its own programme of Classic and other important races, the climax of the season is the International Meeting held in late summer and rotating between the main participating countries of the Soviet Union, East Germany, Poland, Hungary and Czechoslovakia. Victory in the principal race of the meeting, the Grand Prix of the Socialist Countries, or Nations Cup, brings enormous prestige. Significantly the Cup is run over 1¾ miles (2800 metres) rather than the 1½ miles (2400 metres) of the principal international races in Western Europe, the King George VI and Queen Elizabeth Diamond Stakes in Britain and the Prix de l'Arc de Triomphe in France.

The International Meetings, inaugurated in 1950, have been dominated almost invariably by the Russian representatives. The Soviet Union has far the largest thoroughbred population in Eastern Europe, with about 800 mares compared with between 400 and 500 each in Hungary, Poland and Czechoslovakia in the late 1970s. Moreover the Soviet Union has invested in good-class stallions from the West and made the most persistent efforts to improve its bloodstock during the last thirty years.

The involvement of Russia in thoroughbred breeding has a very long history. That Russian breeding has never been prominent in the production of quality racehorses on a world scale is due to a combination of many different causes. The climate of vast areas of the country is unfavourable to the thoroughbred, and revolution and world wars have ravaged the racehorse population repeatedly. Nevertheless, there is no doubt that the failure to found a strong thoroughbred industry in pre-revolutionary days was to a large extent the result of ill-conceived policy, or perhaps the lack of any coherent policy at all.

Few countries were as quick to begin importing thoroughbreds in considerable numbers as Czarist Russia. By 1826 the Russians had imported eleven thoroughbred stallions including the St Leger winner Soothsayer, but these horses were used more for the purpose of improving existing Russian breeds than to found a breed of racehorses on the English plan. When the imported horses were used for racing they were often subjected to wanton cruelty. Perhaps the most outrageous abuse of these horses occurred near St Petersburg in 1825, when the victims were the thoroughbreds Sharper and Mina. The seven-year-old Sharper had arrived from England only that year. According to a note in the *General Stud Book*, Sharper and Mina 'were matched to run 75 versts (49¾ miles) on the public road against two Cossack horses; Mina falling lame was pulled up early in the race, which Sharper won with ease, notwithstanding the loss of a stirrup, and the consequent inability of his rider to restrain him for several miles. The Cossack horses had nearly 3 st advantage in weight, and one of them fell at the end of 25 miles and died.' If the result was a tribute to Sharper's powers of endurance and to the superiority of the thoroughbred over the best of the native breeds, the staging of the race was a grim exposure of the flagrant inhumanity and folly of the Russian horse owners of the time. By comparison Gimcrack's ordeal of running 22½ miles (36,000 metres) within the hour seems innocuous.

It is pleasant to be able to record that the excesses of the Sharper episode soon gave way to a more rational concept of horse racing. The authorities acknowledged the need for properly organized races to test their stock, and in the same year the first racecourse was opened at Lebedjan. Within the next sixteen years other courses were opened at Moscow and Tsarkoie Selo, and the first Russian Stud Book was published. However, it was not until the second half of the nineteenth century, when Count Woronzoff-Dashkoff was Director of the Russian Imperial Horse Breeding Board, that any real incentives to improve racing standards were given. Woronzoff-Dashkoff was responsible for installing pari-mutuels under State control on racecourses and for making deductions from the pools for the benefit of breeding and for increasing prize money. At the same time active encouragement was given to the importation of high-class stallions, and between 1856 and 1874 the Derby winners Andover and Caractacus, the St Leger winner Van Tromp and the Dee Stakes winner Ithuriel were imported from England.

The good work of Woronzoff-Dashkoff was continued by his successor the Grand Duke Dmitri Konstantinovich, an uncle of Tsar Nicholas III. The Grand Duke authorized the purchase of the Triple Crown winner Galtee More, the best horse ever imported into Russia, for 20,000 guineas in 1898. The French Derby winners Boiard and Clover were secured from France. By the end of the nineteenth century more than 1500 mares were registered in the Russian Stud Book and more than 1200 races were run annually on thirty-two courses.

The thirty years before the 1917 revolution saw a high rate of importation. During that period eighty-seven colts and stallions and 265 fillies and mares were imported from England. They included, in addition to Galtee More, the Derby winners Minoru and Aboyeur, and Louviers, who was second to Minoru in the 1909 Derby. During this period Russian studs were turning out horses good enough to compete successfully abroad, and the Russian horses Ksiaze Pan and Mosci Ksiaze gained easy victories in the Grosser Preis von Baden at the Baden-Baden international meeting in 1910 and 1913 respectively.

Galtee More sired Irish Lad, a record stakes winner and by reputation the best racehorse bred in Russia up to the revolution. Nevertheless, attempts to improve the Russian thoroughbred were less effective than they might have been, partly as a result of the twin catastrophes of the First World War and the Russian revolution, and partly because they seemed to be strangely half-hearted. Inexplicably, since he was a first-class stallion, Galtee More was sold to go to Germany after he had been in Russia only six years, and Galtee More emphasized the gravity of this mistake by siring the winners of

214

309 races in Germany before his death in 1917. Louviers disappeared without trace during the revolution, and the fact that his son Landgraf, sired in England immediately before he was sent to Russia, founded the most successful of German male lines suggests that his influence would have been highly beneficial in Russia.

The fate of Minoru and Aboyeur has never been verified. There is strong evidence that they were taken on foot from Moscow to the Black Sea, a journey of 1000 miles, in 1919 and shipped to Constantinople with the help of British troops and the Royal Navy. However, the trail petered out after their arrival in Turkey.

Little could be done to rehabilitate the Russian thoroughbred until 1925, when purchases were made in Hungary with the intention of improving the surviving Russian strains. During the next ten years hundreds of thoroughbreds were purchased in France, Germany, Italy, England and Ireland; these imports included such first-class stallions as Diligence, Press Gang and Cyclonic. Diligence, a product of the British National Stud, has an honourable place in the breeding of his native country as maternal grandsire of the great filly Sun Chariot, winner of the 1000 Guineas, the Oaks and the St Leger in 1942. However Press Gang, by the wartime St Leger winner Hurry On out of the wartime Oaks and St Leger winner Fifinella, had a more profound influence on Russian breeding. Although he did not found an enduring male line, his name was still in the pedigrees of high-class Russian horses nearly half a century after his importation.

Unhappily the Russian breeding industry was hardly back on its feet before it was shattered again by the Second World War. Information about the fate of the industry in 1941 and after is scanty and to some extent contradictory. Michail Petrovich Noskov, writing in the 1956 edition of the *Bloodstock Breeders Review*, gave this account:

The second world war changed fundamentally the shape of Soviet breeding. The leading Soviet studs with their well established male and female lines were totally, or partly, destroyed and immediately after the armistice foreign stock was brought in from Eastern and Central Europe, mainly from Hungary and Germany. No wonder that in these circumstances the once leading Russian lines, such as those of Potysz, Princessa, St Macheza, Asia, Sornette, Zaza and Talija, have completely lost their importance. Similarly with the stallions. The once leading lines of Tagor, and especially that of Brimston, have been pushed into the background by stallions acquired after the war and their descendants.

215

On the other hand Evgeni Dolmatov, the director of Moscow racecourse, gave a more cheerful report on the survival of the old Russian strains when he was interviewed in 1961 during his visit to England to supervise the unsuccessful running of the Russian horses Grifel and Reljef in the Grand National:

There was inevitable dislocation because most of the studs in the south, in the areas of the Ukraine and the Don, were overrun by the German invasion. But much of the stock was recovered and sent to studs in safe areas east of the Volga, where the managers showed great skill in rehabilitating the various strains that were still available.

Subsequent events have indicated that there was some truth in both accounts. Although the male line of Brimston was not extinct in the late 1970s, it was hanging on by no more than a slender thread; but the influence of Tagor was as strong as ever, not only in the direct male line but as an ingredient of high-class pedigrees in many different ways.

Tagor owed his existence to A. M. Lazarev, a leading Russian breeder for twenty years before the First World War. Lazarev operated on an international scale, and in 1907 sent his Russian-bred mare Paraguay to be mated with Florizel II, a brother of the Triple Crown winner Diamond Jubilee and the dual Classic winner Persimmon, at Newmarket. The produce of this mating, Floreal, won the Russian and Polish Derbys and then went to stud in Russia, where his son Tagor, a chestnut with three white legs, was foaled in 1915. Tagor's racing opportunities were severely curtailed by the war and the revolution, but he survived unscathed to play a vital part in the resuscitation of the Russian thoroughbred in the 1920s.

The most important son of Tagor was Granit II, foaled in 1929. Granit II showed high-class form as a two-year-old, but afterwards developed a habit of breaking blood vessels. Despite this infirmity, Granit II became a successful stallion and the chief agent in prolonging the dynasty. He was the great grandsire of Aden, who joined the select few Russian-bred horses who have distinguished themselves in the West when he won the Group 1 Preis von Europa at Cologne in 1978. Incidentally Derzkiy, the sire of Aden, was out of a mare by Press Gang.

Tagor also appears prominently in the pedigrees of the other two horses who have done most to advertise the virtues of the Russian thoroughbred since the Second World War, by name Zabeg and

Anilin. Zabeg was third to Bald Eagle and Harmonizing in the Washington DC International as a three-year-old in 1960 and Anilin was third to Kelso and Gun Bow as a three-year-old in 1964 and second to Behistoun in the same race two years later. Zabeg's maternal grandsire Zagar was by Granit II, and Anilin's granddam Giurza was by Tagor's son Zator.

On the male side of their pedigrees Zabeg and Anilin both sprang from sources acquired when the Russian armies overran Central Europe at the end of the Second World War, and which constituted the first wave of recruits for the ravaged Russian breeding industry. Zabeg's sire Baltic Baron was brought from Hungary, as was Anilin's maternal grandsire Agregat; Anilin's paternal grandsire Etalon D'Or, bred in France, was taken from Austria.

Anilin was the nearest that Russia, under any regime, has come to producing a world-class performer. He was a horse of steel in limb, constitution and spirit. His racing career, which lasted from two to six years of age, brought him twenty-two victories from twenty-eight races. He was unbeatable in his native country, and also won races in East Germany, West Germany and Hungary, apart from acquitting himself with immense credit on his two appearances in the United States. His finest performances were given in West Germany, where he won in each of his last four seasons, and carried off the Group 1 Preis von Europa at Cologne three times with top-class West European horses like Salvo, Carvin, Luciano and Taneb behind him. The only country where he did not do himself full justice was France, and he could finish no nearer than fifth and eleventh on his two appearances in the Prix de l'Arc de Triomphe, though the winner on the former occasion was the mighty Sea Bird II and he was certainly not disgraced.

Anilin did not breed a horse as good as himself before he died of a twisted gut at the age of fourteen, but he did head the list of sires of winners in the Soviet Union in 1975, 1978 and 1979.

Russian breeding was reinforced by occasional importations from Western Europe during the thirty years after the Second World War. Some of the horses concerned, like Ivory Tower (by Luminary), Gay Warrior (by Fighting Don) and Kontakt (by Never Say Die), were imported as yearlings and raced with distinction in the Soviet Union before becoming successful stallions there. Others, like the Ascot Gold Cup winner Balto, the St Leger winner Athens Wood, the Group 2 Queen Elizabeth II Stakes winner Trusted and the

217

Group 2 Great Voltigeur Stakes winner Whitstead were imported after proving their ability on the racecourse.

There is no private ownership of racehorses or breeding stock in the Soviet Union. The breeding stock are divided among a dozen State Studs, which also maintain their own racing stables on the principal racecourses at Moscow, Pyatigorsk and Rostov-on-Don. The Voskhod Stud in the Kuban, where Anilin was bred and stood as a stallion, was consistently the most successful over a long period.

Selection in the Soviet Union has been based on rigorous application of the racecourse test to both sexes. Anilin showed that the Russian breeding industry has the capacity to produce a performer of world class, but Anilin was an isolated case whose achievements have not been equalled, even by the admirable Aden. The industry is too small, and has not drawn often enough on the resources of the principal racehorse-producing nations of the West, to have much hope of breeding a top-class international performer more than once in a decade. There is a danger that the Russian racing and breeding industry, with its strict adherence to the ideal of a Classic racehorse at the upper end of the middle distance range, will lose ground in an international racing system which tends to put growing emphasis on the lower end of the middle distance range.

On the other hand it must be said that there is little evidence that the Russian racing authorities have serious ambitions to compete regularly with the best horses in the West. It is possible that they are content to maintain their dominant position in Eastern Europe and make occasional excursions to Western Europe when a suitable opportunity presents itself. After the inauguration of the International Meeting of Eastern Europe Russian horses generally proved superior to those of Hungary, though Hungary had been the source of the influential stallions Baltic Baron and Agregat and had a tradition of producing high-class racehorses going back nearly a century.

Hungary

Hungary made its mark as a producer of the Classic racehorse when in the successive years 1873 and 1874 the Derby winners Kisber and Kincsem, one of the most remarkable thoroughbreds of all time, were foaled at the Imperial Stud at Kisber. They were both of predominantly English pedigree. Kisber was by Buccaneer, by the

Derby winner Wild Dayrell, out of Mineral by Stockwell's brother Rataplan; Kincsem was by Cambuscan, who had been third to Blair Athol in the 1864 St Leger, out of the Hungarian 1000 Guineas winner Water Nymph by the English horse Cotswold. Nevertheless, they were officially products of Hungarian breeding and proved that top-class thoroughbreds could be reared in that land-locked country.

Kisber was bought as a yearling for the equivalent of £500 by the Baltazzi brothers, who were anglicized members of a family of Levantine merchants and had been educated at Rugby. The Baltazzis sent him to be trained at Newmarket, and Kisber was regarded as a potential Derby winner from the moment he won the Dewhurst Plate over 7 furlongs (1400 metres) as a two-year-old. His victory at Epsom was gained by the convincing margin of five lengths, and shortly afterwards he emphasized his exceptional class by crossing to France and winning the Grand Prix de Paris. Unhappily he was the victim of foul play before the St Leger and was too sick a horse to do himself justice, finishing unplaced. He did not run again, and at stud failed to sire a son or daughter capable of passing on his admirable qualities.

Kisber was a top-class racehorse by international standards, but could not compare with the amazing constitution and consistency of Kincsem, who ran fifty-four times in four seasons and was never beaten. Although she was foaled at Kisber, Kincsem was bred by Mr Ernest de Blascovich, who normally sold all his produce as yearlings. However Kincsem was considered plain, presumably because she was a dull liver chestnut without a single white hair, and failed to find a buyer. Blascovich kept her, and she grew up into a grand filly with wonderful action and a habit of galloping with her head close to the ground which was expressive of her indomitable will to win.

Some thoroughbreds fret when they are away from home and lose stones in weight on a long journey. Not so Kincsem, who loved travelling and enjoyed every moment of the tedious railway journeys which were the inevitable concomitant of international racing at the time. It was this trait which made her fantastic career possible. As a two-year-old she won ten races on ten different courses in Germany, Austria and Hungary. Her victories the following year numbered seventeen and included the 1000 Guineas, the 2000 Guineas, the Oaks and the St Leger in Hungary, the Derby and the Emperor's Prize in Vienna, and the Grosser Preis at Baden

Baden and the Grosser Preis at Hanover in Germany. As a four-year-old she visited England to win the Goodwood Cup, beating Pageant who afterwards won the Doncaster Cup from the doughty Hampton; and she won the Grand Prix de Deauville and the Grosser Preis at Baden Baden on the way home. In her final season she won twelve more races, including the Grosser Preis at Baden Baden for the third, time.

Kincsem was a remarkably successful broodmare in spite of her arduous racing career and the fact that she died when she was only thirteen. One of her daughters, Budagyongye, won the German Derby, and her descendants won scores of races, mostly in Central Europe. The best of her descendants outside that region was Calandria, who won the French St Leger (Prix Royal Oak) and the Group 1 Prix Vermeille in 1929; and Calandria's great granddaughter Orberose followed her example by winning the Prix Vermeille twenty-two years later.

In general, however, Hungarian breeders failed to build on this early evidence of ability to produce horses of the top international class. Nevertheless, one more international performer did emerge from Hungary in the 1960s. This was Imperial who, like Kisber and Kincsem, was bred at Kisber, by then a State-owned stud. Imperial was unbeaten in Hungary, where his victories included the Derby and St Leger; and ran in five countries abroad to win nine races including the Austrian Derby, the Group 2 Grosser Hansa Preis in West Germany and the Skanska Fältrittklubbens Jubileumslöpning in Sweden. At the same time it is necessary to place Imperial's achievements in perspective by adding that he was beaten by the English horse Espresso in the Grosser Preis at Baden Baden as a three-year-old in 1963, but returned to Budapest five days later to outclass his opponents in the most important race of the Eastern European International Meeting, the Nations Cup, and win by nine lengths.

Imperial was by Imi, who was leading sire of winners in Hungary eight times and traced back in the male line, through Caissot, to the 1917 British Triple Crown winner Gay Crusader. Imperial also became a leading sire and his son Prince Ippi, bred and owned by the West German Gestüt Röttgen, showed international form superior even to his own by winning the Group 1 Preis von Europa at Cologne in 1972 and the Group 1 Gran Premio d'Italia at Milan the next year.

No national breeding industry suffered worse in the Second World War than that of Poland, whose broodmare band had been reduced to twenty-two at the time the war ended. The number was raised to more than 100 by the return of the mares that had been removed to Germany and Austria. By the late 1970s the thoroughbred population had crept up to more than 450 mares, with about twenty stallions in service and annual foal production of 250. More significant than the increase in quantity, however, was an improvement in quality which had resulted from a determined policy of importing good-class stallions from Western Europe during the previous ten years. In 1979 the Polish three-year-old Czubaryk won the coveted double of the Moscow Prize and the Nations Cup at the International Meeting held at the Hoppegarten in East Germany, and then travelled to Cologne to finish a close second to the West German horse Nebos in the Group 1 Preis von Europa; and a year later the then West German-trained, but Polish-bred, six-year-old Pawiment went one better by winning the Preis von Europa and the Gran Premio del Jockey Club at Milan. Czubaryk, too, was trained in Germany when he added to his laurels as an international performer in 1981. Although he was last when sent to England to run in the Eclipse Stakes, he gave performances which reflected well on the Polish standard of breeding when finishing second again, this time to the English horse Glint of Gold, in the Preis von Europa and third in the Group 1 Premio Roma. Czubaryk was a third generation Polish horse in the male line, his grandsire Turysta being by Ribot's grandsire Bellini, but his maternal grandsire was the imported English horse Deer Leap. Pawiment was by the imported Mehari, a top-class stayer who was beaten by a short head by Parbury in the Ascot Gold Cup in 1967 and won the Group 2 Prix Kergorlay over 1 mile 7 furlongs (3000 metres) at Deauville. Horses bred in the Eastern bloc countries made little impression in the West in the 1980s after the exploits of Pawiment and Czubaryk. However the Polish-bred Omen, trained by Germany's leading trainer Heinz Jentsch, won the Group 3 Preis der Spielbanken des Landes Nordrhein-Westfalen at Dusseldorf in 1988. He was by the imported English horse Dakota and his granddam was by Mehari. His success confirmed Poland's second place, behind the Soviet Union, as a producer of the Classic racehorse among the nations of Eastern Europe.

Japan

In respect of numbers Japan is one of the most important producers of thoroughbreds in the Northern Hemisphere. In the 1980s Japan was breeding more thoroughbreds than such eminent producers as Great Britain, Ireland and New Zealand, and, with annual production of more than 7600 foals, was fourth in the world league behind the USA, Australia and Argentina. But the situation was different in respect of quality, because by the late 1980s not a single Japanese-bred horse had won in top-class international company outside Japan.

The few Japanese horses to venture into top-class competition overseas have returned empty-handed. The victory of Hakuchikara in the Washington's Birthday Handicap at Santa Anita, California, in 1959 was no more than a hint of promise for the future which was still unfulfilled twenty years later. Takamagahara, the first Japanese runner in the Washington DC International, finished tenth in a field of thirteen in 1962, well behind the two Russian representatives Zabeg and Livan, who were fourth and eighth respectively. The occasional Japanese horses that have run in the Laurel race since then have not distinguished themselves. Only Speed Symboli, who was fifth at Laurel in 1967 and occupied the same place in the King George VI and Queen Elizabeth Stakes at Ascot two years later, gave any grounds for hope that Japanese breeding was making significant progress. Sirius Symboli, the winner of the Japanese Derby in 1986, ran without distinction in the important French races the Group 2 Prix d'Harcourt and the Group 1 Prix Ganay the following year, while Symboli Rudolf, who had been Japanese 'Horse of the Year' twice, broke down in the Grade 1 San Luis Rey Stakes at Santa Anita in March 1986.

Nevertheless the history of the Japan Cup, which was introduced in 1981 as Japan's first international race, tells a different story and reveals the Japanese Thoroughbred in a more favourable light. The race is run over 1½ miles (2400 metres) at Tokyo in late November. Entry is by invitation, and was restricted in the first year of running to horses from Argentina, the USA, Brazil, Canada, India, New Zealand, Australia and Turkey, but was subsequently extended to include European countries. Although most of the foreign runners have been just below the highest class, they have included horses of the supreme quality of All Along, Trillion, Triptych and Tony Bin.

The winners have included Mairsey Doates (1981), Half Iced (1982) and Pay The Butler (1988) from the United States, Stanerra (1983) from Ireland, Jupiter Island (1986) from Great Britain and Le Glorieux (1987) from France; but there have also been two victories for the homeside with Katsunagi Ace, who defeated the talented British gelding Bedtime in 1984, and Symboli Rudolf, so disappointing on his expedition to California, in 1985. In addition to the two winners, seven other Japanese horses finished in the first three in the first eight runnings. Even when due allowance has been made for the facts that the race is run at a time of year when many Northern Hemisphere horses may be jaded at the end of a long season, and that all the foreign horses have long air journeys to reach Tokyo while the Japanese horses are running on their home ground, this is a thoroughly respectable record and suggests that Japanese thoroughbreds have attained a standard of performance not greatly inferior to the world's best. Tamamo Cross, second to Pay The Butler in 1988 and the best four-year-old in Japan, was by the Japanese-bred C. B. Cross, a son of the European sprinter Fortino II.

Perhaps the most obvious cause of the slow progress of the Japanese Thoroughbred is that Japan, in comparison with any other large-scale racehorse-producing country, is a late-comer to thoroughbred racing and breeding. The first thoroughbred mares were not imported from Australia until 1895, and even after that initial inflow further importations and the consequent advance of breeding were spasmodic as the Government blew alternately hot and cold, and at times restrictions were placed on the betting which is the life blood of a prosperous breeding industry. For this reason Japan is generally deficient in the long-established strains, adapted to local climate and environment over many generations, which have given continuity and basic strength to breeding in all other important horse-producing countries.

The still young and immature Japanese breeding industry had an almost fatal setback in the Second World War. Production of thoroughbred and so-called 'half-bred thoroughbred' foals fell to the lowest level, 221, in 1946. It was not until betting restrictions were removed that year, and the Japan Racing Association (JRA) was founded by statute eight years later to take control of racing on the ten principal courses and give financial support to breeding, that the conditions for revival and expansion were created. Japanese foal production did not pass the 1000 mark until 1959; but after that it grew from 1031, at a rate unequalled anywhere else in the world, to reach a peak of 8218 in 1976, an increase of nearly 700 per cent in seventeen years. A growth rate of that magnitude could be attained only by abandoning some of the accepted criteria of selection and by breeding from inferior mares that should have been culled. However, a relatively small reduction in the thoroughbred population in the following decade gave scope for using stricter criteria of selection.

More than 80 per cent of Japanese thoroughbreds are bred in the Hidaka region in the northern island of Hokkaido. The winters are hard, but experience in other countries, notably Canada, has shown that hard winters are not an insuperable bar to the production of world-class racehorses. Thoroughbreds find humidity more debilitating than cold and snow, and the high humidity of the Japanese summers is probably the most unfavourable aspect of the climate.

The best antidote to the baleful effects of too rapid thoroughbred population growth is the importation of high-class breeding stock, and in this respect both the JRA (JRA funds of 150 million yen were allocated to bloodstock investment in 1988 alone) and individual Japanese breeders have been extremely active. Although intermittent purchases of quality mares have been made in the West – for example at the 1978 Newmarket December Sales Higeto Furuoka, a Tokyo publisher of educational books, bought through Heron Bloodstock Services the top-class staying filly Royal Hive, whose price of 224,000 guineas was a short-lived December Sales record, and three of the four highest-priced mares – the main thrust of Japanese buying has been directed at stallions. Between the two World Wars the importation of the Irish Derby deadheater Primero, a brother of the Derby winner Trigo, left a permanent mark on the evolution of the Japanese thoroughbred, and after the Second World War the most profound influence on the rehabilitation of Japanese breeding was the 1949 Irish Derby winner Hindostan, imported after the formation of the JRA. Hindostan headed the list of the sires of winners seven times, and his son Shinzan was one of the few native-bred stallions able to compete successfully with the continuing waves of imported stallions.

The imports included the seven Derby winners Pearl Diver, Nimbus, Galcador, Hard Ridden, Larkspur, Grundy and Empery, and if these had been found wanting in some degree when standing

at stud elsewhere their acquisition conformed to the maxim implemented with such telling effect by Federico Tesio in Italy, which
was that winners of the supreme test of the racehorse, even if failures
in an absolute sense, should sire a few high-class progeny and have
a beneficial impact on the breed.

Other European Classic winners to have gone to Japan include
Crystal Palace, English Prince, Natroun, Recitation, Wollow, Tap
On Wood and Moon Madness, and the Kentucky Derby winners
Chateaugay, Dancer's Image and Kauai King have gone there from
the United States. Many top-class horses who did not win Classic
races like Pas de Seul, Posse, Vitiges, Primera, Ile de Bourbon and
the Prix de l'Arc de Triomphe winners Rheingold and Tony Bin
have also been recruited for Japanese studs. The Ebor Handicap
winner Partholon was very successful in Japan, where his progeny
included the outstanding Symboli Rudolf, as was Never Beat, a half
brother of the St Leger winner Hethersett, who was champion sire
four times; so were the specialist fast horses Tesco Boy, who was
champion sire three times, Faberge II, Fortino II, Yellow God,
Zeddaan and Spanish Express. The majority of these had failed to
realize high expectations at stud elsewhere, but in cases like Tesco
Boy and Ile de Bourbon, who left the Derby winner Kahyasi behind
him in England, their potential for siring progeny of merit had not
been revealed at the time they were sold to Japan. Whatever their
shortcomings may have been, these stallions formed a pool of genetic material from which at least some top-class performers were
likely to spring. Collectively they could only raise the standard of
Japanese bloodstock.

In spite of the prominent showing of Japanese horses in the Japan
Cup, Japanese racing on the whole remained rigidly protectionist.
In the late 1980s the only races open to foreign-based horses were
the Japan Cup itself and its preliminary race the Fuji Stakes. Only
about 15 per cent of the 2900 races run annually on the ten courses
controlled by the JRA were open to foreign-bred horses, and those
horses had to be owned by Japanese nationals who paid a fee for
the privilege. In the circumstances the ninety-four Japanese Pattern
races were unacceptable in any kind of international system, but
they did provide a comprehensive series of races for the best horses
and therefore a framework of criteria for the guidance of Japanese
breeders. In 1988 they were confined to the ten principal courses
(Chukyo, Nakayama, Hanshin, Tokyo, Kyoto, Fukushima, Hakod-

225

ate, Kokura, Niigata and Sapporo). Analysis manifests their basically middle distance orientation. The core of the Japanese Pattern is five Classic races for three-year-olds on the English model, with a preponderance of races for three-year-olds and upwards at 1½ miles and beyond. Opportunities for sprinters and precociously speedy two-year-olds are strictly limited.

One of the most fascinating questions to be answered on the world thoroughbred arena as the twentieth century approaches its close is whether the Japanese breeding industry will be able to build on the fair degree of success indicated by the performances of home-bred horses in the Japan Cup. It is reasonable to suppose that pro-gress will be slow unless the protectionist spirit of Japanese breeders is broken down and replaced by much greater willingness to expose the developing Japanese Thoroughbred to the invigorating winds of foreign competition.

12

The Thoroughbred in
South America and South Africa

The result of the Washington DC International in 1955 caused consternation in most of the principal racing and breeding countries. The finish was fought out by two representatives of Venezuela, El Chama and Prendase, with victory going to the former by a head. Up to that time the class of Venezuelan racing had been considered insignificant. Yet here were two Venezuelan standard-bearers capable of beating decisively the invited representatives of the United States, Canada, Great Britain, Ireland, France and Germany. Preconceived notions of the proper order of things in international racing were shattered.

The four-year-olds El Chama and Prendase had dominated their rivals in Venezuela, where Prendase had beaten El Chama in the richest race, the Clasico Simon Bolivar over 1¼ miles (2000 metres). They were invited to run at Laurel as representatives of Venezuela because they were trained there, but they were natives of Argentina. Their prowess emphasized the fact that Argentina was the Colossus of South American breeding, standing far above the other countries of the continent in respect of the quantity and quality of the thoroughbred population. More than thirty years after El Chama's epoch-making victory Argentina, with annual foal production of nearly 8500, had almot double the thoroughbred population of the second racehorse-producing country of the continent, Brazil; and Argentine-bred horses regularly took most of the honours in the international races run in Argentina and Brazil. Although other South American countries like Chile, Uruguay and Venezuela had considerable thoroughbred populations, they did not challenge the leadership of Argentina and Brazil.

Racing has a long history in Argentina. The English were among the first European settlers in the country, and were not slow to reveal their national love of the Turf. English residents of Buenos Aires were responsible for the first recorded races in the country, which were some matches run on a course to the south of the city in 1826. However, the first thoroughbred stallions from England, Elcho and Bonnie Dundee, did not arrive until 1853, and a further twelve years elapsed before the first contingent of thoroughbred mares arrived and the racehorse-breeding industry was properly launched.

Carlos Pellegrini was the true Father of the Turf in Argentina. This remarkable man studied law, became a journalist and then entered politics and rose to be President of the Republic. Like a great statesman of a later age, Sir Winston Churchill, Pellegrini sought relaxation from public affairs in racing and, on 15 April 1882, became the first president of the newly formed Argentine Jockey Club. Four months later the Jockey Club issued a code of rules, which was promptly adopted by all the racing clubs in the country; at the same time the Jockey Club took control of the Palermo racecourse which was under construction on land owned by the Buenos Aires city council. The first Argentine Derby, the Gran Premio Nacional, was run in 1884, and three years later the Gran Premio Internacional, afterwards called the Gran Premio Carlos Pellegrini, was founded and became the principal international race in South America.

The first volume of the Argentine Stud Book was published in 1893. It contained the names of 224 mares and about 300 stallions, representing a curious disproportion between the sexes and a modest numerical foundation for what was to become one of the world's most powerful breeding industries. Progress was astonishingly rapid. Argentine breeders proved themselves some of the most determined and astute buyers of high-class stallions from England. The famous horses which have been stationed in Argentina for at least part of their stud careers have included the Triple Crown winners Ormonde, Diamond Jubilee and Bahram; other Derby winners in Cameronian, Pont l'Eveque and My Love; Craganour, who was disqualified in favour of Aboyeur after finishing first in the 1913 Derby; the Derby winner Blue Peter's brother Full Sail; and a constellation of good sires whose brightest stars include Cyllene, Jardy, Kendal, Rustom Pasha, British Empire, Gulf Stream, Selim

Hassan, Court Harwell, Advocate, Timor, The Yuvaraj, Claro, Aristophanes, Tracery and his son Copyright.

The large majority of these stallions have been middle distance performers themselves, or at least have possessed middle distance pedigrees. Middle distance stallions are required to sire horses suitable for the Argentine Pattern of Racing, which is based on the European model. The Classic programme for three-year-old colts involves a Quadruple Crown, rather than the Triple Crown of British custom. The Quadruple Crown comprised traditionally the Polla de Potrillos (2000 Guineas) over 1 mile (1600 metres) in August, the Gran Premio Jockey Club over 1¼ miles (2000 metres) in September, the Gran Premio Nacional (the Derby) over 1 mile 4½ furlongs (2500 metres) in October and the Gran Premio Carlos Pellegrini over 1 mile 7 furlongs (3000 metres) in November. The last-named race constituted a particularly severe test for three-year-olds, not only on account of the distance but also because it was open to older horses.

The traditional Classic programme was modified in 1979, when the distance of the Gran Premio Carlos Pellegrini was reduced to 1 mile 4½ furlongs (2500 metres), and in 1984, when the distance was reduced again to 1½ miles (2400 metres).

Severe test though the Gran Premio Carlos Pellegrini undoubtedly was in its traditional form, three-year-olds succeeded in passing it with no little regularity. Indeed Forli in 1966 was the ninth horse to win the Quadruple Crown in the twentieth century. A neat, medium-sized chesnut horse by Aristophanes out of the Advocate mare Trevisa, Forli had many of the physical attributes of his grandsire Hyperion, and was acclaimed one of the greatest performers ever bred in Argentina. He was a relentless galloper who usually led all the way. His performance in the Pollo de Potrillos was brilliant, as he outclassed his opponents to win by twelve lengths in record time. He was less impressive in the subsequent Classic races, but he had problems like red-worm infestation and, in the Gran Premio Nacional, a gale force headwind in the straight at Palermo which must have retarded such a habitual front-runner.

After his crowning triumph in the Gran Premio Carlos Pellegrini, Forli was sold to a United States syndicate headed by A. B. (Bull) Hancock of Claiborne Farm, and won two races at Hollywood Park before he broke down and suffered the only defeat of his career in the Citation Handicap at Arlington Park. At Claiborne Farm he became a leading stallion with a high international reputation. His excellent progeny included the three times American 'Horse of the Year' Forego, Forceten, Intrepid Hero, and Key To Content in the USA and Thatch, Posse and Formidable in Europe.

Forli was by no means the only Argentine-bred horse to distinguish himself as a stallion in the United States. Endeavour II (by British Empire) was exported to the United States as a five-year-old in 1947 and founded a dynasty which lasted through Pretense and Secretariat's plucky Classic rival Sham to Jaazeiro, one of the best milers to run in England and Ireland in 1978. Nigromante sired the descriptively named Candy Spots, whose chesnut coat was splashed with patches of white hairs on the flanks, quarters and legs, and who won the Preakness Stakes, the Santa Anita Derby and the Florida Derby, besides being third in the Kentucky Derby and the Belmont Stakes in 1963. Nigromante's influence was also transmitted through his daughter Perillante, who became the granddam of Bold 'N' Determined, a brilliant American three-year-old filly of 1980. Nigromante sprang from one of the most enduring of Argentine male lines, as he traced back through Embrujo to Congreve, Copyright and Tracery, the 1912 St Leger winner. Embrujo was also the sire of Prendase of Washington DC International fame.

Strains developed in Argentina have also had their impact on Classic form in Europe. The Argentine-bred Petare went to stud in the United States, where his son Sadair was one of the fastest two-year-olds of 1964 and sired the French 1000 Guineas winner Pampered Miss. Meadow Court, winner of the Irish Sweeps Derby and the King George VI and Queen Elizabeth Stakes in 1965, was a grandson of Miss Grillo, who had brought off the splendid double of the Gran Premio Nacional and the Premio Seleccion (Argentine Oaks). Another Argentine-bred mare, Carmosina, was the dam of the 1976 St Leger winner Crow. Carmosina's dam Sixtina was by Aristophanes out of an Advocate mare, so was bred on the same lines as Forli.

Although the male line of Tracery had persisted for several generations, it appeared to be a waning asset in the final quarter of the twentieth century. At the time the most powerful strains in Argentine breeding for the Classic racehorse were probably those of Full Sail through Seductor, Sideral, El Centauro and Cipol: Tourbillon through Timor, Pronto and Practicante: Hyperion through Aristophanes: Arctic Prince through Snow Cat, Snow Crest and Crest Pan: and Gulf Stream through Fresh Air and Good Bloke.

The Argentine breeding industry, which was to have a beneficial influence on the production of the Classic racehorse far beyond the continent of South America in the second half of the twentieth century, had risen swiftly from the foundations so firmly laid in the days of Carlos Pellegrini. Its progress has been assisted by some men of outstanding ability like Miguel Martinez de Hoz, who founded the Chapadmalal Stud on his estate bordering the Atlantic 250 miles south of Buenos Aires. This became such a vast concern that in 1959 his sons Miguel and Jose Alfredo were able to divide the property into two separate studs, Comalal and Malal Hue, and still each be left with a large-scale breeding operation. The Martinez de Hoz studs, and other great studs like Don Santiago, the source of El Chama, and Ocho de Agua, where Forli was bred, have been the backbone of quality breeding in Argentina.

Nevertheless the Argentine breeding industry had acute problems to face in the final quarter of the twentieth century. Overproduction was chronic. Its annual production of thoroughbred foals gave it the third largest output in the world after the USA and Australia, and attempts to find outlets for all but the best quality horses tended to be frustrated by other South American countries concerned to protect their own breeding industries. The magnetic power of the United States market tended to draw off the best of Argentine production and leave the second best to provide the breeding stock for the next thoroughbred generation. Just as Forli had ended up at Claiborne Farm in the 1960s, so the Argentine-bred Lord At War, the winner of the Grade 1 races the San Antonio Handicap and the Santa Anita Handicap in 1985, retired to another Kentucky stud, Walmac International, twenty years later.

At the same time hyper-inflation, import controls and various economic ills have prevented Argentine breeders from taking adequate measures to replenish their resources with high-class stock from abroad. Political and social unrest, the Falklands war, and the tendency of Argentine governments to interfere in the affairs of the Turf, have conspired to create an atmosphere of uncertainty in which it is difficult for breeding to flourish.

Some observers believe that the encouragement of greater precocity by bringing forward the opening date of two-year-old racing from December to October, and the reduction of the distance of

231

important races like the Gran Premio Carlos Pellegrini, will undermine the criteria of selection which have promoted the traditional virtues of the Argentine thoroughbred. Others saw a graver threat to the future of the Classic racehorse in Argentina in diminished imports of high-class stallions and mares. Although the broad expanses of the pampas appear to provide an ideal natural environment for horse breeding, Franco Varola, in his book *The Functional Development of the Thoroughbred* published in 1979, expressed the opinion that the thoroughbred tends to show enlargement of the bones after a few generations in Argentina owing to the high mineral content of the pastures. The English bloodstock agent George Forbes was on the same tack when he reported of one large-scale Argentine breeder after a visit to South America:

He has recently decided to cull some of his older Argentine-bred mares, and to import English stock who show more refinement, because the local Argentine thoroughbred after three or four generations loses the quality which is retained only in the European product.

It is this inevitable coarsening process which is held to account for the gradual decline of the influence of a stallion even as prepotent as Congreve, who was leading sire of winners seven times between 1937 and 1945, and was afterwards leading broodmare sire five times. Writing in the December Sales issue of *The British Racehorse* in 1959, Varola stated that Congreve had transmitted 'a certain rusticity' to his progeny.

The lack of high-class imports allowed native dynasties like those of Full Sail, Timor, Snow Cat and Gulf Stream to persist in the last quarter of the twentieth century. However, the inevitable accompaniment of this persistence appeared to be the gradual deterioration of Argentine bloodstock.

One of the most remarkable performers ever produced in Brazil was Emerson, who ran only as a three-year-old and won all his five races at that age in 1961. His victories were gained over distances ranging from the 7 furlongs (1400 metres) of the Premio de Potros to the 1 mile 4½ furlongs (2500 metres) of the Grande Premio Derby Sulamericano at the international meeting at Sao Paulo, in which he beat the winners of the Derbys of Argentina and Uruguay. His other victories included two Grade 1 races in the Brazilian Pattern, the Grande Premio Cruzeiro do Sul (Brazilian Derby) and the Grande Premio Derby Paulista. He broke down after his fifth race, the Grande Premio Derby Sulamericano.

Although he was bred in Brazil, Emerson was out of the Argentine-bred mare Empenosa, winner of the Polla de Potrancas (Argentine 1000 Guineas) and the Premio Seleccion; and his sire was the French Derby winner Coaraze. At the end of his racing career he was brought by a group of French breeders and spent his stud career at the Haras de Nonant-le-Pin in Normandy. He was a consistent sire of winners, and had his best season in 1972, when his daughter Rescousse won the French Oaks and was second to San San in the Prix de l'Arc de Triomphe, and was mainly instrumental in raising him to second place in the list of sires of winners.

The chief contribution of Chile to the world sum of Classic racehorses was the supremely tough and stout-hearted Cougar II. He raced in his native country at two and three years of age without giving much indication of the excellence he was later to achieve; he was a well-beaten third in the Chilean Derby, and his best win was in the Grade 2 Gran Premio Municipal Vina del Mar over 9½ furlongs (1900 metres) at Valparaiso. He was then exported to the United States, where he raced from four to seven years of age with steadily mounting success to finish with a career total of twenty victories from fifty races. There could be no stronger testimony to his top racing class than the fact that his haul included nine Grade 1 Stakes races. He was voted 'Champion Grass Horse' as a six-year-old in 1972, and had displayed first-rate stamina to win the San Juan Capistrano Handicap, the longest Grade I race in the United States, over 1¾ miles (2800 metres) at Santa Anita. He retired to Stone Farm in Kentucky, where he sired the 1982 Kentucky Derby winner Gato Del Sol.

Repicado II, the best Chilean two-year-old colt of the 1967–68 season, made his mark on North American racing and breeding in unusual fashion. He raced with moderate success in the United States and went to stud in California. His success as a stallion was equally moderate, but he did have the distinction of being sire of Radar Ahead, one of the few top-class racehorses ever bred in the state of Arizona. Radar Ahead won the Grade 1 Swaps Stakes over 1¼ miles (2000 metres) at Hollywood Park as a three-year-old in 1978.

The mare Papila also showed the breeding value of Chilean stock. Foaled in 1943, she was second in the Chilean Oaks and was then exported to the United States, where she won three races before going to stud and becoming the dam of Crimson Satan, the champion North American two-year-old of 1961. Marimbala, whose sire Balconaje was a scion of the Argentine male line founded by Timor, proved another good advertisement for Chilean bloodstock when she won the Grade 1 Santa Margarita Handicap in 1983 after winning the Derby and the Oaks in her native country.

However the South American mare who had the most important influence on the Classic racehorse outside that continent came from Peru, whose thoroughbred products generally have not earned high regard. This was Pamplona II, who was by the leading Peruvian stallion Postin (by Hyperion's half-brother Hunter's Moon) out of the British-bred mare Society's Way, by Kingsway. She was the best Peruvian three-year-old of 1959–60, when she won the Polla de Potrancas (1000 Guineas), the Derby and the Gran Premio Nacional (St Leger), and was the champion older mare the next season. She won fourteen races altogether; but the performance which stamped her as a racemare of the highest class was finishing third to the colts Escorial and Farwell in an international field for the Grade 1 Gran Premio 25 de Mayo over 1 mile 4½ furlongs (2500 metres) in Argentina.

The Texas oil magnate Nelson Bunker Hunt, who bred and raced on a world-wide scale, had the gift of serendipity in respect of bloodstock. He happened to be in Lima on business shortly after Pamplona had broken down and run her last race. He met by chance her owner Juan Magot, who told him that she was the best mare ever bred in Peru and took him to see her in the racecourse stables. Hunt found her a fine quality mare and, after returning home and reflecting for a few days, wired an offer of $50,000 for her which was accepted.

Pamplona proved a bargain at that price, because she bred Pampered Miss (by Sadair), who won the French 1000 Guineas in 1970, and Empery (by Vaguely Noble), who triumphed in the Derby six years later. Her achievements provided a striking illustration of the wide range of backgrounds from which top-class breeding stock may spring.

South Africa

With a history of racing stretching back to the end of the eighteenth century and a substantial thoroughbred population, South Africa looms large among the racing and breeding countries of the world. In the late 1980s South African breeders were producing more than 4000 foals a year, only about 500 less than Great Britain. But South Africa has not matched quantity with quality production; indeed had not Hawaii proved his excellence as performer and stallion in the 1970s and 1980s, South Africa would have had little impact on the breeding of the Classic racehorse in an international context.

The British first began to occupy the Cape of Good Hope in 1795, and were not long in introducing their favourite sport. The first recorded race meeting was held on Green Point Common near Cape Town in September 1797 when the principal race, the Turf Club Purse, was won by Colonel Hope's five-year-old brown horse Zemman Shaw. The foundation of the South African Turf Club, with membership restricted to officers of the army and navy and 'respectable inhabitants of the Colony', is officially dated five years later. However, the chief impetus to the growth of racing and breeding at the Cape in the early part of the nineteenth century came from the despotic British Governor Lord Charles Somerset, who was an enthusiastic supporter of the sport.

Somerset promoted the proper administration of racing by compelling the South African Turf Club to adopt certain rules and regulations; and, more importantly for the future of breeding, imported the thoroughbred stallions Kutusoff, Cottager, Cricketer, Vanguard and Walton. Thoroughbred mares too were imported during Somerset's governorship. One of these was Miss Whipthong, who was a granddaughter of Editha, the ancestress of Galopin, winner of the Derby and the sire of St Simon. Allegations were made that Somerset was not above importing horses and selling them at an exorbitant profit. On the other hand his influence on racing and breeding was undoubtedly beneficial and when Lord Bathurst, the Colonial Secretary in the British Goverment, wrote to him expressing concern at the growth of racing and gambling he replied with a vigorous defence, denying that there was excessive gambling and asserting that racing had 'contributed greatly to the Improvement of Horses in the Colony, which is very peculiarly adapted to the breed of the animal'.

The middle years of the nineteenth century brought rapid expansion of thoroughbred breeding. The *General Stud Book* records that twenty-six stallions were exported from England to the Cape during the 1840s alone. Most of them were of modest class, but a few, like the Cambridgeshire winner Evenus and the Derby second Gorhambury, had first-rate racing performance.

The first South African studs were in the vicinity of Cape Town, but in the second half of the nineteenth century, when the discovery of gold and diamonds at Kimberley brought prosperity to its nearest port, Port Elizabeth, many studs sprang up in the Middleburg, Dordrecht and Colesberg regions in the east of the Cape Province. Port Elizabeth became the headquarters of the Jockey Club of South Africa, who staged the first South African Derby there in October 1885.

The greatest of South African stud operations was founded at Vogelvlei, Dordrecht, by E. V. Birch in 1910. Birch had been breeding draught horses there but, foreseeing that the advent of the internal combustion engine would undermine his business, decided with singular shrewdness to change to breeding racehorses. The venture prospered exceedingly. In the second half of the twentieth century it had evolved into three separate studs owned by different members of the family but selling yearlings collectively under the name of Birch Brothers. Birch Brothers not only monopolized top place in the list of winning breeders, but were often credited with as much as twice the prize money earnings of the second breeder in the list.

Birch Brothers were the breeders of Colorado King and Sea Cottage, two of the three South African-bred horses of world class who raced during the 1960s. Colorado King was by the Italian-bred Grand Rapids II, who was otherwise a sire of little distinction, but his maternal grandsire Fairthorn and his maternal great grandsire Asbestos II were both extremely successful sires in South Africa. Foaled in 1959, he won the Cape of Good Hope Guineas and Derby and the richest South African race, the Rothman's July Handicap at Greyville, Durban, as a three-year-old. He was then exported to the United States, where his seven victories included two races later classified as Grade 1 Stakes, the Hollywood Gold Cup and the Sunset Handicap, at Hollywood Park. He went to stud in California, but left no permanent mark on the breed in spite of siring a number of useful performers like the unimaginatively named Colorado King Jr.

Sea Cottage, foaled three years after Colorado King, was by Fairthorn out of Maritime by Merchant Navy, a superbly bred horse by the Derby winner Hyperion out of the Oaks winner Rose of England. As in the case of Colorado King, his granddam was by Asbestos, so his pedigree combined some of the best strains available in South Africa. Sea Cottage never raced outside South Africa, but he dominated his contemporaries to an extent which left no doubt of his superior class. He was successful in twenty of the twenty-four races he contested in four seasons in training. His victories included the South African Guineas and the Cape of Good Hope Derby, the Champion Stakes twice and the Rothman's July Handicap, in which as a four-year-old he deadheated with Jollify to whom he was conceding 27 lb (12 kilos). He was also a horse of immense courage. Before the Rothman's July Handicap the previous year he had been the victim of a bizarre attempt at nobbling when a sniper fired a bullet into his quarters. It proved impossible to extract the bullet, but Sea Cottage was able to resume his racing career as good and as determined as ever. He retired to his native Vogelvlei Stud and had some success as a sire, though he failed to become one of the leading stallions.

Hawaii, the third of the South African-bred world-class performers, was to have an impact easily surpassing that of either of his two predecessors. He was bred by A. L. Dell at the Platberg Stud, Colesberg, but was brought by the American precious metals king Charles Engelhard for R9030 after having been adjudged champion yearling of the 1965 Rand Show. At that time Engelhard, who won the 1970 Derby with Nijinsky, was one of the most prominent owners on the international scene, but Hawaii was one of the most extraordinary horses ever to carry his colours. Hawaii gave immediate evidence of brilliance by winning his first three races as a two-year-old by distances of seven lengths, eight lengths, and again eight lengths. He won five of his six races as a two-year-old, and ten of his twelve races as a three-year-old and four-year-old in South Africa. His victories included the Cape of Good Hope Guineas and the South African Guineas, but he did not run in the Derby and was beaten in the only two races over distances longer than one mile (1600 metres) which he contested. When Engelhard decided to send him to race in the United States he left South Africa with the reputation of a horse of brilliant speed but limited stamina.

Hawaii corrected the impression that he was a non-stayer when he began to race over longer distances as a five-year-old in the United States. He concluded his racing career by winning the Grade 1 Man o'War Stakes and finishing second to the British representative Karabas in the Washington DC International, both over 1½ miles (2400 metres). He was voted American Champion Grass Horse of 1969.

Hawaii retired to Claiborne Farm in Kentucky. His high quality as a stallion was demonstrated by the progressive placings of his sons in the Derby at Epsom, in which Hunza Dancer was third in 1975, Hawaiian Sound was second in 1978, and Henbit was victorious in 1980. Hawaii had then given South Africa a first degree distinction in the production of the Classic racehorse.

Hawaii, on the other hand, was unique. Numerous attempts have been made to identify the reasons for the failure of the South African thoroughbred generally to influence the evolution of the Classic racehorse. Edmund Nelson made a detailed analysis of the overall programme of races in *The South African Racehorse* covering the 1965–66 season, and diagnosed the principal weakness as an excess of two-year-old and sprint races which put too high a premium on speed and precocity, too many handicaps and too few valuable weight-for-age races. 'The allocation of the big money should be on merit, not the whim of the handicapper,' he wrote. 'Our big handicaps are far too rich in value, and they encourage false values in assessing the offical statistics.'

Nelson was making the logical and classical case against the proliferation of richly endowed handicaps, but it is still true that some other countries, like the United States and New Zealand, have had handicaps as integral parts of their Pattern of Racing without apparent detriment to the processes of selection. However, he was undoubtedly correct in identifying an imbalance in the South African Pattern of racing, which has continued progressively to favour speed at the expense of stamina. The published list of Graded Stakes races in 1980 contained forty-five races for three-year-olds and older horses of which seven, or 15.5 per cent, were at distances less than a mile (1600 metres) and a further 15, or 33.3 per cent, were run at exactly one mile (1600 metres). By 1988 the list contained eighty races for horses of those age groups, of which twenty-six, or 32.5

238

per cent, were run at distances of less than one mile (1600 metres) and a further twenty-one, or 26.25 per cent, were run at exactly one mile (1600 metres). Thus the percentage of races for horses above the age of two run over one mile (1600 metres) or less increased from nearly 49 to 58.75 per cent during the 1980s.

The relative increases in the values of mile and middle distance races tell a similar but even more striking story. Between 1955 and 1988 the value of the Cape of Good Hope (Richelieu) Guineas rose from 8000 to 250,000 rands, and the value of the South African Guineas rose from 4200 to 150,000 rands, giving increases by multiples of 31 and 37 for these two Classic mile races; whereas in the same period the value of the Cape of Good Hope Derby rose from 16,340 to 150,000 rands and the value of the South African Derby rose from 10,000 to 125,000 rands, giving increases by multiples of 9 and 12.5 respectively for these Classic middle distance races.

Moreover the lack of a single national Classic series has hindered the identification of the best horses and their selection for breeding. In 1988, for example, there were four regional Derbys – the Eastern Province, the Cape of Good Hope, the Natal and the South African, the last-named being run at Turffontein in the Transvaal.

Concentration on the imperfections of the Pattern of racing may beg the question whether South African climate and pastures form a favourable environment for breeding Classic racehorses. We have seen that Lord Charles Somerset in the first half of the nineteenth century considered the South African environment excellent for horse breeding. The English bloodstock agent Frank Beale came to the same conclusion during an extensive tour of South African studs in 1975, and expressed the opinion that of all the areas of the world he had visited the Karroo of South Africa came nearest to his ideal for raising horses. Huge paddocks averaging 1000 acres provided the semi-natural conditions appreciated by the horse and, although grass was apt to be sparse in dry weather, there was an abundance of mineral-bearing shrubs which the horse was able to select according to his needs. However, Beale did qualify his approval of the South African environment by stating that thoroughbred stock there tended to lose size and substance after a generation or two, in contrast to some other countries in the Southern Hemisphere where the tendency is to lose quality.

No male dynasty has established itself in South Africa, and the list of sires of winners has been dominated invariably by imported stallions. Utrillo II, the sire of Hawaii, was imported from Italy. He failed to sire another horse of real merit, and the exportation of Hawaii meant that there was no chance for the line to continue. On the other hand Hawaii was a third generation native-bred South African on the dam's side of his pedigree, as his great granddam Armond was imported from England as a two-year-old in 1921. The strength of Hawaii's breeding as a potential stallion was that he was the son of a great broodmare. His dam Ethane bred no fewer than twelve winners and one of them, William Penn, was a top-class performer who actually beat his two-years-younger half brother Hawaii in the Champion Stakes over 1¼ miles (2000 metres) at Greyville. Unfortunately William Penn was a rig and useless for breeding.

Armond was of course not the only imported mare to exert a profound influence on South African breeding in the twentieth century. Another, and probably the most important of all, was Drohsky. A daughter of Polyphontes, Drohsky was imported from England in 1930, and became a peerless broodmare, producing the South African Derby winner Lenin and the South African Oaks winner Murmansk, and other high-class performers in Smolensk, Russia, Growler, Samovar and Moscow. Nevertheless, it is on the regular importation of stallions that South Africa depends to maintain a reasonable standard of racing performance in its thoroughbred population, and in this context it is significant that no stallion has succeeded in founding a lasting dynasty.

Traditionally South African breeders preferred middle distance horses of the type of High Veldt. Bred by Queen Elizabeth II by the Derby and St Leger winner Hyperion out of Open Country by the St Leger winner Fairway, and a creditable second to the world-beater Ribot in the King George VI and Queen Elizabeth Stakes over 1½ miles (2400 metres), High Veldt was a top-class middle distance horse by pedigree and performer and became an outstanding stallion. However, the sustained growth in the numbers and value of races run at a mile or less in the last quarter of the twentieth century has militated ineluctably against the true middle distance horse as prospective stallion. The most successful stallions in the 1980s were the British-bred Royal Prerogative, who had won six races over distances ranging from 7 furlongs (1400 metres) to 1¼ miles (2000 metres), and the American-bred horses Plum Bold and Jungle Cove, who were both by Bold Ruler and were prime influences for speed. Other notable stallions of the 1980s were the 2000 Guineas winner Roland Gardens, high-class milers like Jan Ekels, Sparkler and Gay Fandango, and Northfields, a half brother of the great Habitat who had already made a name for himself at stud in Ireland.

In spite of the increasing isolation of South Africa in the international community on political and racial grounds, the South African breeding industry contrived to recruit stallions from abroad in considerable numbers. However, there was little sign that those stallions were capable of improving the quality or the middle distance capacity of the South African Thoroughbred to a level at which it could compete effectively with the principal thoroughbred-breeding countries in the production of Classic racehorses.

13

The Classic Racehorse and the International Pattern

Classic horses, as we have remarked, are an elite in the thoroughbred population. They earn most of the glory and the lion's share of the prize money, are elected champions in national polls, pampered and immortalized in eponymous races. Gladiateur, Ormonde, Pretty Polly, Solario, Ribot, Brigadier Gerard and Mill Reef are among the Classic winners whose names appear in the titles of European Pattern races; and the names of the American Classic winners Man o'War, Count Fleet, Assault, Gallant Fox, Nashua, Bold Ruler, Secretariat and Affirmed appear among the titles of North American Graded Stakes races. Classic horses of both sexes achieve astronomical capital values and are mated together in an attempt to propagate their kind, though the genetic variability of the breed ordains that this is not a sure method of breeding further Classic winners or creating a hereditary Classic elite.

In 1982 more than half the North American races for horses above the age of two were run at 6 furlongs (1200 metres) or less. Indeed 41 per cent of all the 65,145 races were run over precisely 6 furlongs and were worth an average of $6133, while the shorter races were worth even less. Prize money increased roughly in step with longer distances, and reached its peak at the pure Classic distance of 1¼ to 1½ miles (2000 to 2400 metres) with an average first prize of $37,480 for the 574 races, though they accounted for only 0.9 per cent of all the races run. Prize money for the few races over distances longer than 1½ miles (2400 metres) dropped sharply to an average of $11,880.

Nevertheless, the relationship between Classic prowess and race values is not constant. As the pamphlet *Graded Stakes in North America for 1980*, compiled by the *Blood-Horse* magazine under the auspices of the Thoroughbred Owners and Breeders Association, stated:

The number of good horses in a field, or the lack thereof, reflects an appraisal by racing men of the importance of a stakes [race]. This is a balanced appraisal, often weighing purse value against the value of tradition attached to fixtures.

The same interplay between the monetary value and the traditional importance of races can be observed in Great Britain. Certainly the prestige of the Derby, sanctified by two centuries of history as the premier Classic race, transcends all other means of assessing its importance; and the fact that in 1986 its added money of £150,000 was £25,000 less than the added money for the King George VI and Queen Elizabeth Diamond Stakes for three-year-olds and upwards run over the same distance at Ascot in July did not diminish its standing in the national or the international racing canon.

This contrast between intrinsic and monetary value is liable to cause confusion, particularly among outside observers of a national racing programme, and even more so in an inflationary age when nominal prize money is rising steeply but not always uniformly. The remedy lay in a method of grading races according to their intrinsic importance and this now exists in the form of the International Pattern Race system. The creation of this system is admirably and succinctly described in a prefatory notice in the catalogue of the annual Keeneland July Selected Yearling Sales in Kentucky:

Several years ago representatives from the major European racing countries – England, France, Ireland, Italy and Germany – met and drew up a listing of the leading non-handicap races in each age division in each country. These races were designated as Pattern Races. Similarly, a committee of authorities later selected Pattern Races for the United States. Each country then divided these races into three groups – G1 [Classics], G2 [semiclassics] and G3 [other top races].

The catalogue compilers interpreted the word 'Classic' more broadly than the British usage, but the generally agreed sense of 'championship tests' for Group 1 is clearly implied.

The idea of a planned Pattern of Racing originated in the report of a committee under the chairmanship of the Duke of Norfolk appointed in 1965 to study and make recommendations on the general programme of all races in Britain, with special attention to the needs of top-class horses. The report placed squarely on the

243

shoulders of the Turf authorities the obligation to ensure that a series of races over the right distances and at the right times of year was available to test the best horses of all ages; and it recommended that those races should be endowed with sufficient prize money to ensure that horses remained in training long enough and raced often enough to be tested properly for constitution and soundness. Specifically the committee recommended three categories of races comprising five 'Classic Races', nine 'Prestige Races' and thirty-four 'Feature Races' for this purpose. It is notable that the first two categories jointly foreshadowed the composition of the British Group 1 in the later International Pattern.

The introduction of a formal Pattern of Racing in Britain followed two years later as a result of the work of another committee, this time under the chairmanship of Lord Porchester, appointed to examine the spread of the races specified in the Norfolk report and to make any recommendations about measures needed to rationalize it and rectify any deficiencies and anomalies. The initial Pattern which sprang from the work of the Porchester committee comprised 130 races, but in later years the number was gradually whittled down in the light of experience and was finally stabilized at about 100.

The latter committee was retained by the Jockey Club as a permanent watchdog of the Pattern, and was finally given the title of the Flat Race Pattern Committee to differentiate it from a similar committee formed to look after the interests of the best hurdlers and steeplechasers.

As an addition to the primary function of supervising the conditions and the prize money of the Pattern races, which were heavily subsidized by the Levy Board, and investigating proposals for introducing new or eliminating old races, the Flat Race Pattern committee was given the responsibility of maintaining liaison with foreign racing authorities in all matters concerning the Pattern. This last responsibility was soon to assume crucial importance as the future of international racing in Europe was placed in jeopardy. The cause of the trouble was the sharp discrepancy between higher prize money levels in France on the one hand and other European countries on the other hand which existed in the 1960s. The result was that British and other foreign horses tended to have an unfair advantage against French horses of similar class in important races in which the weights carried were determined by the amounts of prize money already won, while French horses were at a corresponding disadvantage when they raced abroad. So powerful a head of resentment built up in the French racing community that the demand for exclusion of foreign-trained horses from all French races except those devoid of penalty and allowance clauses – virtually the Classic and Prestige races of the Norfolk report – threatened to become irresistible.

The answer to this critical problem, and the salvation of international racing, was found in the introduction of an International Pattern and the Group system of classifying races. The basis of this European Pattern, agreed at first by the racing authorities of France and Great Britain but finding ready assent in Ireland, Italy and Germany, was that extra weight to be carried by runners in Pattern races should be determined not by prize money earned but by the class of the horses as indicated by the standing of the race or races previously won. The composition of the whole European Pattern, and the classification of individual races into three groups, involved lengthy negotiations between the French and British authorities, and a settlement of the issues satisfactory to all parties was greatly assisted by the warm relationship that developed between Lord Porchester on the British and Jean Romanet, the director-general of the Société d'Encouragement, on the French side. The final solution was based on the acceptance of three Groups of Pattern races defined with rather more detailed precision than the version in the Keeneland catalogue:

Group 1. Championship races, including Classic races, in which horses meet on weight-for-age terms with no penalties or allowances.

Group 2. Races just below championship standard in which there may be penalties and/or allowances.

Group 3. Races of mainly domestic interest, including Classic trials, which are required to complete the series of tests for the best horses.

Moreover a bonus for the sake of a rational international programme which sprang from the Franco-British deliberations was a considerable degree of integration of the Patterns of the two principal European racing countries. For example, when the French decided to introduce an autumn championship race for two-year-old fillies in 1971, the year the International Pattern came into being, they gave it a distance of 1 mile (1600 metres) so that it would complement, and not clash with, the long-established Cheveley Park Stakes in Britain. This race began as the Criterium des Pouliches, but was renamed the Prix Marcel Boussac in 1980.

Other benefits of the Pattern race grouping system quickly became apparent. It was seen as the most reliable formula yet devised for indicating the quality of performance of racehorses, and it has the immense advantage of transcending national frontiers. It has great value as a guide to selection by breeders, and has an obvious application in cataloguing for bloodstock sales. Indeed the Keeneland Association conclude their notes on Pattern racing and the grouping system with the sentence: 'We hope that our buyers will find this an additional aid in evaluating pedigrees.'

Breeders and racing authorities in many other countries were not slow to perceive these benefits and have hastened to introduce Patterns of their own. An official Pattern helps to make a racing programme intelligible to outsiders and to enhance the reputation of the principal races and their winners. The propagation of the Pattern gospel can be traced in the pages of the annual Pattern races books published jointly by the British and French authorities. The number of countries or regions represented grew year by year and by 1984, the last year in which countries outside the European Pattern system were included, had reached a total of twenty-three. After that it became impracticable to include them in the book because of the difficulty of obtaining lists from many countries in time for publication. This is not to imply that all Pattern race form is equal. On the contrary, gulfs are set between the form in the leading and the lowliest racing and breeding countries. But Pattern race performances are indicators of class judged by the general standards of each country.

The introduction of a Pattern presents few difficulties in a country like Britain, where the Jockey Club and the Levy Board jointly exert overwhelming influence through their combination of administrative power and financial sanctions; and none in a country like France, where the control of the Société d'Encouragment is absolute. It is not simple at all in countries where centralized control over racecourse executives is loose or, as in the United States, non-existent because ultimate power is vested in State Racing Commissions and executives are at liberty to devise their own programmes. In such countries a published Pattern is a means of disseminating information, not of organizing a series of tests for the best horses. The list of 'Graded Stakes Races', as they are called in the United States, originally was the work of a panel appointed by the Thoroughbred Owners and Breeders Association (TOBA). The panel was expanded in 1988 to form the 'North American Graded Stakes Committee' on which TOBA had three representatives and the New York Jockey Club, Breeders Club Ltd, the Society of International Thoroughbred Auctioneers and the Thoroughbred Racing Association one representative each.

The panel may favour weight-for-age races rather than handicaps, but has not been able to ignore handicaps. In the United States, and some other countries, good horses run in handicaps as a normal part of their racing programmes, and some of the most memorable and significant races involving top-class horses are handicaps. The series of encounters between Ferdinand and Alysheba, the Kentucky Derby winners of 1986 and 1987 respectively, illustrate the complementary roles of weight-for-age races and handicaps in the American Graded Stakes system. They met for the first time in the Breeders Cup Classic in November 1987, when Ferdinand won by a nose on weight-for-age terms. Their next two encounters were in handicaps at Santa Anita the next spring. On the first occasion in the Santa Anita Handicap Alysheba, in receipt of 1 lb, won by half a length; and on the second occasion, when they met at level weights in the San Bernadino Handicap, Alysheba won by a nose after an epic struggle. Of the 420 Graded Stakes programmed in North America in 1988 no fewer than 230 were handicaps, while in Australia and New Zealand approximately one third of the Graded Stakes were handicaps. Nevertheless, some of the purposes of a Pattern must be blurred by the inclusion of handicaps, since a handicap is by definition a race in which the chances of the runners are equalized by adjustment of the weights carried.

Inclusion or exclusion of handicaps is only one of the ways in which the various national Patterns differ. Overall comparison of the Patterns provides some telling evidence about the kinds of performance in which different thoroughbred-producing countries specialize. The most striking contrasts are found in the category of two-year-olds. In Ireland two-year-olds were eligible to run in thirteen (36 per cent) of the thirty-six Pattern races scheduled in 1988; in Great Britain two-year-olds were eligible to run in twenty-seven (26 per cent) of the 104 Pattern races; in France two-year-olds were eligible to run in twenty-two (20.6 per cent) of the 107 Pattern races; in Italy two-year-olds were eligible to run in seven (18.4 per cent) or the thirty-eight Pattern races; and in Germany two-year-olds were eligible to run in one (2.8 per cent) of the thirty-six Pattern races. Thus the emphasis placed on two-year-old racing differed widely in the five countries of the European Pattern. The incidence of two-year-old races in the North American Graded Stakes system was near the lower end of that scale, because two-year-olds were eligible to run in only fifty (11.9 per cent) of the 420 Graded Stakes; and New Zealand, with two-year-olds eligible for ten of the eighty-one Graded Stakes, had a similar percentage of 12.3.

Further comparison reveals that in 1988 sixteen, or 59.2 per cent, of the British Pattern races in which two-year-olds were eligible to run were in the distance bracket 5 to 6½ furlongs. The corresponding percentages in other important racing countries were 53.8 in Ireland, 31.8 in France and 26 in North America. These figures show that the Patterns of Great Britain and Ireland place more emphasis on precocious speed than the Patterns of other important thoroughbred-producing countries do; surprisingly however New Zealand, a country renowned for the stamina and durability of its horses, ran 70 per cent of its two-year-old Graded Stakes over exactly 6 furlongs.

While the International Pattern race system provides a rough and ready system of assessing the class of horses and is therefore a useful tool for breeders to apply to selection of breeding stock, it is necessarily an inexact measure. In order to obtain a more precise tool it was necessary to supplement the Pattern race system with machinery to compare the absolute merits of horses from different thoroughbred generations and from different countries. The senior British handicapper David Swannell took the first step in this direction when he linked the British Free Handicap, the official assessment of the top echelon of each age group, to a norm of 100 lbs, the notional rating of a horse capable of dominating its contemporaries. The norm was introduced in 1973, and within four years had exposed some striking contrasts in the quality of individual Derby winners; for example, the best Derby winner of the period, Grundy, was rated 101, whereas the worst, Empery, was rated only 90, so that Swannell's device indicated that Grundy was superior by 11 lbs (5 kilos), or the equivalent of 5 or 6 lengths, to another Derby winner of the same short period.

The next step was to project the concept of the norm into the international arena. An international conference of racing authorities in Dublin in July 1977 agreed that a European Free Handicap should be compiled, and four months later the senior handicappers of France, Britain and Ireland met in Paris to implement that decision. As a result of their deliberations the first European Free Handicaps, embracing the best horses that had run in the three countries during the past season, were issued at the end of the year. They were entitled 'International Classifications'.

The International Classifications were divided into two age groups, three-year-olds and four-year-olds and upwards; and each age group was sub-divided into the distance sections of 10 furlongs (2000 metres) plus, 6 furlongs (1200 metres) plus to 10 furlongs (2000 metres), and 5 furlongs (1000 metres) to 6 furlongs (1200 metres). The sections corresponded generally to the categories of middle distance horses and stayers, milers and sprinters respectively, though in 1986 the Classifications were refined and divided into five distance sections of 5 furlongs (1000 metres) plus, 7 furlongs (1400 metres) plus, 9½ furlongs (1900 metres) plus, 11 furlongs (2200 metres) plus and 14 furlongs (2800 metres) plus. The fact that the highest rating given to any horse in the first edition of the International Classifications was the 98 of the Prix de l'Arc de Triomphe winner Alleged – he was promoted to 100 in the 1978 edition after his second 'Arc' victory – showed that the handicapping committee were not prepared to bestow the favour of superlatives lightly. Indeed, the norm accepted for the International Classifications was linked deliberately with the norm previously applied to the English Free Handicaps, so the respectable ancestry of the system was acknowledged and continuity was assured.

A happy coincidence was that 1977 was the year in which the New Zealand horse Balmerino campaigned in Europe and was second in the 'Arc'. Balmerino, who was five years old, was placed equal top of the 10 furlongs (2000 metres) plus section for senior horses with another horse of the same age, Orange Bay, who had been second to the Derby winner The Minstrel in the King George VI and Queen Elizabeth Diamond Stakes. Since Balmerino had run with much distinction in his native country and Australia earlier in his life, his rating of 94 provided the most accurate means yet available of aligning the best European with the best Australian standards of thoroughbred performance. The prowess of Balmerino, as reflected in his rating, was a death blow to lingering notions of permanent European superiority.

The first International Classifications were so well received, and their advantages were so apparent, that in 1978 they were extended to include a single two-year-old section. Pride of place went to the English horse Tromos with a rating of 91. The later career of Tromos was to fade out in disillusion, but Irish River, who had shared second place on 89, moved up to joint top place of the miler section of the three-year-old part of the 1979 Classifications with 91. He was bracketed with the leading English miler of the same age, Kris. Within a few years the scope of the Classifications was extended by taking form shown in Italy and Germany into account in compiling them.

Simon Weatherby, the Secretary of the British Jockey Club at the time, aptly described the International Classifications as 'a logical extension of the International Pattern system'. Numerous benefits could be expected to flow from their introduction. They should help to enhance interest in high-class racing on both domestic and international fronts; they should be accepted as a professional and impartial basis for the assessment and valuation of horses; they should provide breeders with more accurate criteria for selection than any available in the past; and they should be a tool for measuring the improvement or deterioration of thoroughbred performance in the countries concerned over a period of years.

Clearly the next 'logical extension' would be to include other countries besides the original three. The inclusion of the best horses racing each year in North America, where standards of performance were believed to be the highest in the world in the late 1970s, would multiply and enhance all the benefits attributed to the first International Classifications.

Geoffrey Gibbs, Swannell's successor as senior handicapper, became a tireless apostle of the transatlantic spread of the concept of the norm and of Classifications. He gained priceless knowledge of American racing form and its relationship to European form, as well as knowledge of the officials responsible for handicap weights on the principal American tracks, through his membership of the panel of handicappers appointed to select the best horses to make up the limited fields for super-valuable races like the Budweiser Million and the Breeders Cup events. This experience convinced him that races run on both sides of the ocean provided ample evidence for the accurate correlation of American and European form, and his frequent visits to the United States began to partake of the nature of proselytising missions. By the late 1980s he seemed to have established the feasibility of co-ordinated Northern Hemisphere ratings quite firmly, and only a degree of scepticism lingering in the minds of American officials and a failure to match Gibb's enthusiasm and sense of urgency appeared to be delaying their introduction. One minor obstacle had been removed by raising the International Classifications norm for a horse capable of dominating his contemporaries from 100 to 140 so as to bring the Classifications into line with American practice.

The forecast extension of the International Classifications was generally perceived as having beneficial implications for the breeding industry and for cataloguing standards at the principal bloodstock sales. In the meantime rationalization of the structure of the European Pattern was put in hand. It had long been clear that the structure had two basic faults. One was that within the various national Patterns the groupings did not invariably reflect the true relative importance of individual races; and the other was that Pattern race standards differed widely from country to country. The process of rationalization was initiated in Britain, where in 1985 a sub-committee was formed under the chairmanship of the Flat Race Pattern Committee chairman Tim Holland-Martin with the following terms of reference:

To examine the programme of British Pattern races . . . by distance, date and race conditions and, where necessary, to make recommendations to ensure that there are regular opportunities for high-class horses of all ages and both sexes to run over the full range of racing distances throughout the season: to set these races in the context of the European Pattern: to impose limits on opportunities so that the best horses are encouraged to race against each other: and to establish criteria and a method of assessment by which the Pattern . . . races can be kept under annual review.

Using the official ratings drawn from the handicappers' files, the sub-committee assessed every British Pattern race on the basis of the average quality of the first four horses to finish over a five-year period, setting minimum rating standards for each group – 120 for Group 1 (115 for two-year-olds), 115 for Group 2 (111 for two-year-olds) and 110 for Group 3 (108 for two-year-olds). It was found that the British Pattern stood up well to these searching tests, though significant changes which resulted from the implementation of the recommendations of the sub-committee included the upgrading of the mile races the Queen Elizabeth II Stakes, the St James's Palace Stakes and the Coronation Stakes, in addition to the Vernons Sprint Cup, from Group 2 and Group 1, and the downgrading of Royal Ascot's famous traditional sprint the King's Stand Stakes from Group 1 to Group 2.

The British example prompted similar reviews in the other countries of the European Pattern. However, hopes that these reviews would lead to a radical overhaul were not fulfilled because some national racing authorities found the medicine prescribed by the rating figures too drastic to swallow. A compromise, which seriously diminished the value of the whole exercise, was reached when the European Pattern Committee permitted individual countries to use lower rating standards for the various groups than those adopted by the British – and accepted also by the French – on the condition that their rating standards were made public and subsequently maintained; for a rider to the British review laid down that all Pattern races should continue to be assessed annually on the basis of their average ratings for the previous five years, and that any further upgradings or downgradings indicated should be duly implemented. The decision of the Irish to adopt rating standards for each group 5 lbs lower than those of Britain and France laid them open to biting criticism and called in question their claim to be regarded as a front-rank thoroughbred-racing country.

The Italian authorities, on the other hand, showed courageous realism by accepting many of the lessons of their review and reducing their total number of Pattern races from forty-nine in 1987 to thirty-eight in 1988, with the axe falling most heavily on Groups 1 and 2. However, the verdict on the changes made as a result of the reviews could only be that, while substantial improvements had been made to the structure of individual Patterns, the opportunity for sweeping rationalization of the European Pattern as a whole had foundered on the rock of national prejudice.

14

Further International Aspects of the Classic Racehorse

Almost a dozen countries have proved that they are capable of producing top-class racehorses from time to time. Some of those countries have bred racehorses of world class from relatively slender resources and without the aid of investment in the choicest Classic stallions and mares from Great Britain. The assumption of the early editors of the *General Stud Book*, and of English breeders of the same period, that Great Britain enjoyed unique advantages and that the British thoroughbred was destined for eternal supremacy, has required drastic modification.

The breeding industries of most of the successful thoroughbred-producing countries have been sustained by practically continuous importation of stallions from the principal European breeding countries, particularly Great Britain, Ireland and France, and from the United States in recent times. Whether standards could have been maintained by reducing the flow of imports and making more extensive use of locally bred stallions is uncertain, though the changing practices of Australian breeders suggest that in that country at least there was excessive dependence on imported stallions in the past. What is certain is that thoroughbreds can be bred and reared successfully in a wide variety of regions and climatic conditions.

Ideal conditions for breeding thoroughbreds are probably found in the temperate zones, with plentiful rainfall to promote a lush and constant growth of grass, soil providing the minerals and trace elements necessary for strength and quality, and water supplies having a calcium content of 200–300 parts a million. The limestone pastures of Ireland and parts of England, notably the Bedale area of Yorkshire which was the cradle of the thoroughbred, provide exactly these conditions.

253

Probably the least favourable environment for breeding thorough-breds, and that most liable to cause rapid deterioration of the stock, consists of tropical humidity and dearth of the minerals and trace elements essential for proper growth and bone formation. The Indian sub-continent and Malaya are regions in which racing has achieved popularity but the foundation of a viable breeding industry to supply it has proved impossible. The country-breds have shown marked inferiority to second-rate imported thoroughbreds and sub-sequent generations have declined sharply and progressively in respect of vigour, constitution and racing ability.

Between these environmental extremes – the excellence of the temperate zones and the malign effects of tropical humidity – the Thoroughbred has shown a remarkable adaptability. Horses from Canada, like Northern Dancer and his Derby winning sons Nijinsky and The Minstrel, and Anilin and Zabeg from Russia, have proved in international competition that top-class racehorses can be bred in countries which have to endure long and intensely cold winters; horses like Swaps from California have proved that top-class race-horses can be bred in semi-desert areas. Indeed the Thoroughbred appears to have greater powers of adaptation to changes of environ-ment than most other animals that have been subjected to many generations of selective breeding for specific qualities. This charac-teristic of the Thoroughbred is thrown into sharp relief by this passage from an article by Stanley E. Brock in *The Geographical Magazine* of February 1964. With reference to the Spanish Longhorn cattle of the savannahs of Guiana, Brock wrote:

During the last ten years ranchers have been experimenting to try to improve the quality of the well-established Longhorn. In 1954 Santa Ger-trudis bulls and heifers were imported from Texas. This breed, evolved by the famous King Ranch, is considered to be a heat-tolerant animal suitable for relatively poor grazing areas. It is composed of three-eighths Zebu (a strain of humped cattle from India) and five-eighths Shorthorn. The Santa Gertrudis however have not been a complete success. They have only done well when crossed with the local stock, and on a few sections of the Dadanawa Ranch where the grazing is notably better.

Experts felt that the need was probably a purer strain of Zebu. It appeared that the five-eighths Shorthorn in the Santa Gertrudis made it a little too much of a temperate animal to thrive in a year-round shade temperature of 90 degrees F., two or three degrees north of the Equator. As a result, in 1957 ten bulls and ten heifers of the Brahman breed were acquired from

Jamaica, and later a further number were imported from the United States. The Brahman is a variety of the Indian Zebu, now bred in the south and west of the United States to suit conditions existing there.

The Brahman stood the test, and seemed to have solved the problem . . . It can exist under all the conditions which the old Longhorn tolerates so well.

Even in a heavily diluted form the Shorthorn, the end product of generations of selective breeding in a temperate climate and on lush pastures, could not adapt itself to the environment of the savannahs. The Thoroughbred, without benefit of any crosses which must have diminished the pre-eminent asset of speed, has been much more resilient.

If the ancestors of the Thoroughbred were exclusively, as Admiral Rous supposed 'true sons and daughters of the desert', then it is hardly surprising that good racehorses have been bred in the more arid parts of California. But if the Admiral was right, then it is surprising that the thoroughbred attained perfect development in the temperate zones, and astounding that thoroughbreds of the highest class have been bred in Canada and Russia. This is the basic dilemma that confronts the student of thoroughbred evolution.

It is unlikely that a solution can be found if the Thoroughbred's pure descent from the Arabian is insisted on as an article of faith, or even if the existence of other elements in the ancestry of the thoroughbred are admitted but dismissed as of no consequence. Sir Rhys Llewellyn, who made a close study of genetics in relation to the Thoroughbred, has argued in articles on 'Heredity and Environment' and 'The International Outcross' published in *The British Racehorse* that the Thoroughbred's powers of adaptation may be attributed to the original blending of Arab and British bloodlines whose contrast provided the variability and the vitality which were to sustain the new breed in its development.

These British bloodlines which existed in the seventeenth century combined the ancient Galloway strains and miscellaneous strains imported from Italy and Spain at different periods. The crossing of these bloodlines with the Eastern stallions imported in the century following the Stuart restoration created the thoroughbred not only as the embodiment of equine speed but as an animal able to flourish in most parts of the world.

In 'Heredity and Environment', Llewellyn wrote: 'In the early generations of the Thoroughbred close inbreeding, based upon per-

255

formance, must have played an important part in the elimination of unwanted dominant and recessive genes, and resulting in some degree of purity.' This is the process which led to the production of the first great racehorse Flying Childers; but in subsequent generations Flying Childers, his brother Bartlett's Childers and their descendants were so mated as to ensure variability. The breeder of racehorses has a double problem on his hands. He may hope, by means of inbreeding, to project the influence of a brilliant stallion or mare into future generations, as was done so successfully in the case of St Simon; but he must beware lest he continue the process to the stage where, as the geneticists warn, inbreeding is liable to take toll of vigour and fertility.

The strict methods of selection adopted by the early racehorse breeders in Great Britain, and the even stricter standards adopted later by breeders in countries like France and the United States in establishing breeds on the English plan, brought astonishingly rapid progress in racing performance for a number of equine generations. But selection in the end brings diminishing returns, and progress has slowed down gradually to an almost imperceptible crawl since the days of Admiral Rous. Mr Peter Burrell, the Director of the English National Stud, put the point clearly in a paper on the *Principles of Thoroughbred Breeding* read to the British Cattle Breeders Club in 1962:

Nothing is easier than to improve a breed; to, say, increase the average milk yield of a moderate herd by using proved sires of higher yield; but if you ever reach a position where you have nothing better to use for improvement, retrogression is the rule. Having improved the special traits of the racehorse by stringent selection to the limit of speed, the tendency to retrogression is sometimes so great that our utmost efforts may do no more than prevent further retrogression. In other words, selection no longer causes progress.

Professor E. P. Cunningham of the Irish Agricultural Institute expressed a similar opinion in a paper given at the International Symposium on Genetics and Horse-Breeding at the Royal Dublin Society in 1975. Cunningham took the published winning times for the Derby, the Oaks and the St Leger from 1850, and averaged them for each ten year period. He found that they showed a steady improvement, of about 2 per cent per decade, up to 1900, with no evidence of improvement since then. His conclusion was that the thoroughbred population had reached a genetic plateau.

It is depressing for ambitious breeders to be told that they must run as fast as they can even to remain in the same place, as if they were trying to mount a descending escalator. The judgements of Burrell and Cunningham need to be tempered only by the reflection that modern methods of course management may mask some slight but genuine improvement in thoroughbred performance. Grass husbandry and efficient watering systems have made immense strides, and resilient surfaces can be provided on turf courses even in drought conditions in the sophisticated racing countries. The Derby record time of 2 minutes 33.8 seconds set up by Mahmoud in 1936 was achieved on an Epsom course so hard and bare of grass that it would have been considered unfit for racing thirty years later. Mahmoud's record may stand for ever, but it may be wrong to conclude that his performance represented the summit of excellence over the premier Classic course and distance of 1½ miles (2400 metres). Indeed it is reasonable to surmise that the achievement of the 1987 Derby winner Reference Point, who was electronically timed – Mahmoud's record was timed on a hand-held stop-watch – to cover the well-grassed course on going described as good in a time only 0.1 of a second slower than the record, had considerably more real merit than Mahmoud's when allowance is made for the environmental factors.

In the United States, where dirt tracks have provided uniform surfaces over a long period, the repeated lowering of record times has testified to continuous improvement of the thoroughbred, though inevitably at a slower rate than 100 years earlier. This improvement has been attained as a result of aggressive purchasing of the best stock wherever it may be available, and strict selection based on the racecourse test. The eclecticism of wealthy American breeders, which has resulted in the crossing of strains evolved under widely differing conditions of climate and racing pattern, has opened up fresh avenues for thoroughbred progress. As Llewellyn observed in *The British Racehorse:* 'Selective outcrossing between the best bloodlines evolved in widely contrasting environments offers an opportunity for exploiting . . . heredity by establishing new and possibly favourable gene combinations . . .' Llewellyn called this the 'international outcross'.

Bold Ruler may be chosen as a supreme example of the international outcross. Foaled in the United States in 1954, he was by the fiery and brilliant Nasrullah (himself by the Italian-bred Nearco and having The Tetrarch's daughter Mumtaz Mahal as his grand-dam), who was bred in Ireland and raced in England; Bold Ruler has as his dam Miss Disco, who did not have a single imported ancestor nearer than the third generation and was a first-class speci-men of strains developed in the United States, since she won ten races including the Test Stakes which was later classified Grade 1. Bold Ruler won twenty-three of his thirty-three races and more than $750,000, won the Classic Preakness Stakes and was voted 'Horse of the Year' at the age of three. He then became the world's greatest sire of speedy horses, heading the American list of sires of winners eight times, a record for the twentieth century, between 1963 and 1973; and his male line supplied seven of the ten winners of the Kentucky Derby, including the American Triple Crown winners Secretariat and Seattle Slew, in the 1970s.

France has provided a notable exponent of the international out-cross in François Dupré, the Parisian hotel-owner who died in 1966. Dupré took one of the most significant steps to resuscitate decadent European bloodlines when he imported Relic, a fast grandson of Man o'War, to his Haras d'Ouilly in 1950. For Relic's daughter Relance proved one of the greatest broodmares of thoroughbred history and, through matings with Tantième and Tantième's son Tanerko, representatives of pure European strains, produced the Classic winners Match III, Relko and Reliance II. Dupré incorpor-ated elements gleaned from Germany, England, Ireland, Italy and Canada in his breeding plans, and any inbreeding found in the pedigrees of Haras d'Ouilly products was merely accidental. He showed a flair, boldness and defiance of convention in his stud policies that deserved success. Few breeders would have dared to adopt Deux Pour Cent, a plain horse of plebeian pedigree who won the Grand Prix de Paris only on a disqualification, as his foundation sire. Deux Pour Cent was the sire of Tantième, but Dupré did not scruple to sell him at the age of thirteen, as he did not scruple to sell Relic after six seasons at Ouilly, when they were judged to have served their purpose. As 'Maximum' stated in his obituary of Dupré in *Courses et Elevage:* 'It is impossible to say that Dupré had any steadfast principle of breeding except the quest for variety.'

The operation of the international outcross was facilitated after the Second World War by improvements of transport, particularly the conversion of aircraft to horse carrying. In every breeding season hundreds of mares were shuttled between Britain, Ireland and France to be covered, and by the 1970s some of the leading European breeders were keeping mares in Kentucky either at studs of their own or as boarders at public studs. Some mares were flown across the Atlantic to visit stallions. International exchanges of bloodstock proceeded at an ever-increasing rate; and the rapid expansion of the Japanese breeding industry depended heavily on air transport, as the fact that J. A. Peden Ltd, the English bloodstock transport agency, flew 104 stallions and mares to Japan in five Boeing 707 planes in the winter of 1969–70 clearly indicates.

Air transport facilitated not only the operation of the international outcross but the spread of international competition on the race-course. The vision and initiative of John Schapiro, the president of Laurel Racecourse, brought about the foundation of the Washington DC International over 1½ miles (2400 metres) at Laurel, situated between Washington and Baltimore, in 1952. Entry was by invitation only, and the idea was to bring together the best horses from as many countries as possible. By his tact, powers of organization and flair for publicity Schapiro made the race, run annually in late October or early November, an instant and enduring success on the twin levels of public entertainment and international competition. By 1988, when it had been run thirty-seven times, the race had been contested by horses representing twenty-three different countries and had been won by representatives of six different countries. The score showed nineteen successes for the United States, thirteen for France, two for Great Britain and one each for Venezuela, Australia and Ireland.

By that time Schapiro had sold Laurel, the race was sponsored as the Budweiser International and the distance had been reduced to 1¼ miles (2000 metres). The huge cost of staging the race was justified in terms of the interest aroused throughout the racing world. On the other hand the method which Schapiro had adopted of attributing the runners to the countries in which they were trained and not to their countries of origin made it a blunt instrument for comparing the produce of various national breeding industries. Of the thirteen so-called French winners three (Dahlia, Nobiliary and Youth) were bred in the United States, two (Admetus and April Run) were bred in Ireland and one (Le Glorieux) was bred in Great Britain: of the American winners one (Mahan) was bred in France: of the British winners one (Karabas) was bred in Ireland: the Irish winner (Sir Ivor) was bred in the United States: and the Venezuelan winner (El Chama) was bred in Argentina. In so far as they have significance in the context of international breeding the results are a monument to the superiority of American breeding because twenty-one, or 55.3 per cent, of the races in the series were won by American-bred horses. But even this scoring method involves a distortion, because most of the American-bred winners were racing on their own territory, with no problems of travel fatigue and acclimatization, and had the advantage of being selected at a time when they were at the top of their form.

It must be admitted that the Washington DC International has limitations if it is judged as a means of comparing the thoroughbred standards of the principal producing countries. The brochure of the International Racing Bureau issued on its foundation in London in January 1970 claimed: 'International competition is healthy for the breed, providing a yardstick for countries trying to improve their bloodstock. It is also healthy for race track attendances and gives racegoers an opportunity of seeing in action the famous horses and jockeys of other nations.' All this is perfectly true, but it is equally true that the difficulties of bringing all the best horses together in a kind of world championship are insuperable. The differences in the seasons and the age bases of horses in the Northern and Southern Hemispheres, the contrasts of the patterns of racing, the varying reactions of individual horses to long-distance travel and changes of climate, environment and track surface all tend to militate against the staging of true world championship tests and introduce an element of gimmickry into attempts to do so.

That is not to say that the Washington DC International (Budweiser International) or the many other races with international overtones of which it was the forerunner were wanting either in entertainment value or as valid tests of the ability of top-class horses drawn from a wide variety of backgrounds. The example of the Laurel race was fertile soil in which many other comparable races germinated and flowered. By the late 1980s there was a close-packed programme of Turf races with an international flavour in North America beginning with the Arlington Million in late August and continuing with the Turf Classic, the Rothmans International, the Laurel race, the Breeders Cup Turf and the Breeders Cup Mile, plus the E. P. Taylor Stakes and the Yellow Ribbon Stakes for fillies and mares only. Determination to exploit the international dimension found expression in the introduction of four other Turf races, all designed to attract overseas runners, both at Arlington on Million day and Laurel on International day. In Europe the King George VI and Queen Elizabeth Diamond Stakes and the Prix de l'Arc de Triomphe fully maintained their status as regional championships for three-year-olds and upwards in summer and autumn respectively, though neither race attracted American runners regularly. Elsewhere the Japan Cup in Tokyo and the H. E. Tancred Stakes at the Sydney course Rosehill were making an increasing impact on the international scene.

The mainspring of international racing in the 1980s was the annual flow of horses previously trained in Europe to compete for the extremely valuable prizes on offer in North America. It became apparent that many of those horses were capable of reproducing their European form on American Turf tracks with considerable accuracy, and the feasibility of correlating American and European form in a future expanded version of the International Classifications was proclaimed enthusiastically by some of the European handicappers.

At the same time two obstacles to the complete integration of form on the two sides of the Atlantic persisted: the duality of races on dirt and Turf surfaces in North America, and the medication issue. In spite of the increase in the number of international Turf races, the American Classic and many other Grade 1 races continued to be run on dirt, and many of the best American horses were confined to dirt racing. Alysheba, the winner of the Kentucky Derby in 1987 and the best American four-year-old the following year, was able to pursue in the autumn of 1988 a campaign exclusively in Grade 1 dirt races which formed a programme parallel to the big Turf races, and culminating in the $3M Breeders Cup Classic in which his hard-earned victory was seen as clinching his claim to be a true champion. The reservation about accepting that claim must be the abiding difficulty of collating dirt and Turf form, and therefore of comparing Alysheba with the European middle distance champions Mtoto and Tony Bin, the respective winners of the King George VI and Queen Elizabeth Diamond Stakes and the Prix de l'Arc de Triomphe, who of course raced only on grass.

American and European attitudes on the medication issue were impossible to reconcile in the late 1980s. Any kind of medication of racehorses was anathema to European Turf authorities, but the use

261

of Lasix to control bleeding in the nose and lungs and the anti-inflammatory drug Butazolidin (Bute) to alleviate the stresses and strains inseparable from racing and training on dirt was deeply ingrained in American thoroughbred practice. In contrast to Europe, where the rules of racing are the responsibility of the Turf authorities, the rights of rule making in the USA are held by individual State legislatures and racing commissions. Each State has a vested interest in keeping revenue-generating horses on the track, and is therefore predisposed to tolerate the use of Bute and Lasix. Of the principal racing States only New York bans the use of these two drugs for racing purposes, and moves to outlaw them from Grade 1 Stakes, or even the Breeders Cup races, have made very halting progress.

One baleful consequence of the increasingly international orientation of racing and breeding, and the constant exchanges of bloodstock between country and country, has been a serious growth in health risks. During the 1960s and 1970s racing authorities and government agencies in many countries were concerned with the problems of controlling the spread of a number of diseases which included strangles, klebsiella, contagious abortion, equine influenza and equine anaemia, all capable of causing havoc in the breeding industry. In 1977 a grave new threat arose when contagious equine metritis (CEM), a previously unknown disease, was identified. A serious outbreak then occurred at the British National Stud, though it is not thought that Britain was the first country in which the organism causing the disease had appeared. Efforts to prevent the spread of the disease, of which outbreaks were also reported in Ireland, France, Australia, the United States and elsewhere, involved severe restrictions on the import of bloodstock in many countries. The introduction of strict countermeasures, including rigid codes of practice, in Britain and other affected countries swiftly brought the incidence of CEM under control, but relaxation of restrictions on the international movement of breeding stock was slow to follow. In 1985 an outbreak of equine viral arteritis (EVA) occurred on studs in Kentucky and threated disruption of the breeding industry. The outbreak was contained, but the disease was seen as a potential danger to breeding worldwide.

Fortunately the impact of restrictions designed to prevent the spread of disease had only limited adverse effects on international racing. Large scale international racing and breeding enterprises sprang up practically without interruption to exploit the growing opportunities, with the Texas oil magnate Nelson Bunker Hunt and the French art dealer Daniel Wildenstein among the front runners. They represented an intrusion of big business which revolutionized the bloodstock world in the 1960s and 1970s. The operations of Hunt, who pursued his racing interests with an air of boyish enthusiasm, were world-wide, and those of the saturnine Wildenstein spanned the Atlantic. Hunt showed an audacious spirit of enterprise when he bought a half share in Vaguely Noble after the subsequent 'Arc' winner had been sold for the then record sum of 136,000 guineas at the Newmarket December Sales in 1967, and made that horse the cornerstone of his mating plans when he retired to stud in Kentucky. The owner of Bluegrass Farm in the heartland of the American Thoroughbred, Hunt bought and sold horses as yearlings besides racing his own produce. He bred and owned Dahlia, an incomparable international performer among mares, who won Group 1 or Grade 1 races in France, Ireland, Britain, Canada and the United States. He also owned a colt in Exceller who, without possessing Dahlia's exceptional brilliance, had an outstanding international record with Group 1 or Grade 1 victories in four different countries. In addition he won the Derby with Empery, the French Derby with Youth, the French Oaks with Gazala and the Washington DC International with Nobiliary. Dahlia, Exceller, Empery and Nobiliary were all by Vaguely Noble.

Wildenstein owned superb fillies in Allez France, Pawneese and Madelia, who won the French Oaks in three of the five years 1973 to 1977. Allez France also won the French 1000 Guineas and the 'Arc', and Pawneese was the first filly since Fille de l'Air in 1864 to complete the double of the Oaks and the French Oaks. Another of his fillies, Flying Water, showed blinding speed to win the 1000 Guineas and the Champion Stakes, and his colt Crow excellent stamina to win the St Leger and the Coronation Cup. His success continued into the 1980s, when his filly All Along became an international performer of the highest distinction, winning a total of five Group or Grade 1 races including the Prix de l'Arc de Triomphe, the Turf Classic, the Rothmans International Stakes and the Washington DC International. All Along's great year was 1983. After that the Wildenstein racing fortunes entered a comparatively quiet period, though his operations showed little diminution in scale, Hunt, on the other hand, suffered a serious setback as a result of a disastrous intervention in the silver market, and his racing and breeding interests were virtually liquidated in the 1980s.

Nevertheless it was an Englishman, Robert Sangster, who epitomized the incursion of calculating business methods into racing on a grand scale. Sangster, the managing director of Vernons Pools, took his cue from David Robinson who had pioneered the application of business methods to racehorse ownership in Britain. Robinson, whose fortune was derived from TV rentals, won the 2000 Guineas with Our Babu in 1955 and then built up his racing interests until, at their climax in the late 1960s and early 1970s, they comprised two large private stables in Newmarket and more than 100 horses in training. Although he did not win another Classic race, he was leading owner in 1969 with forty-two individual winning horses of ninety-six races and £92,553 in prize money. No owner had won so many races during an English season in the twentieth century, and in each of the following two seasons Robinson passed the century mark with 109 races won in 1970 and 106 races won in 1971. After those peak years ill-health caused him gradually to curtail his ownership of racehorses and finally to withdraw from the Turf altogether.

The revolutionary aspect of Robinson's operations was that he depended for his supply of racehorses not on studs of his own but on purchases by an expert selection team at the yearling sales in Britain and Ireland. The team, whose most prominent members were the Irish breeder Lord Harrington and the retired trainer Jack Colling, inspected all suitably bred yearlings in minute detail before the sales, and Robinson was ready to commit the financial resources necessary to outbid all ringside rivals for the horses of their choice.

Sangster adopted Robinson's principles of selection and heavy investment. But Robinson had concentrated on Irish and British horses bred for precocious speed and promising a substantial return on the initial investment as two-year-olds. Sangster appreciated that this concept was too narrow in the rapidly expanding international world of the thoroughbred, and that the profitability of bloodstock investment could be maximized not through prize money earnings but solely by the capital gains expected from the yearlings with Classic middle distance pretensions and 'stallion pedigrees' – that is, bred to the highest international standards on both sides of their pedigrees. Horses of this kind, the argument ran, could be syndicated for stud at the highest valuation ruling on the international market if their performances matched their pedigrees, and would retain a considerable residual of 'salvage' value as potential stallions even if they failed on the racecourse. It was calculated that the operations of an expert purchasing team acquiring a score or more of the choicest yearlings offered at the American Keeneland and Saratoga Selected Sales, where the quality was the highest in the world, should yield at least one top-class performer every year, and that one champion would ensure the profitability of the whole enterprise.

Although one or more partners were involved in most of the ventures, the cornerstone of Sangster's policy was his alliance with the Irish trainer Vincent O'Brien, whose marvellous eye for the potential excellence of a young horse amounted to genius. O'Brien was backed by a powerful team, but his examination and appreciation of each yearling was decisive in the selection process.

The aims of the Sangster enterprise were realized perfectly when The Minstrel, who had been purchased for $200,000 at Keeneland as a yearling, won the Derby, the Irish Sweeps Derby and the King George VI and Queen Elizabeth Diamond Stakes in 1977 and was syndicated for $9 million to go to stud in Kentucky. The same year Alleged carried Sangster's colours to victory in the Prix de l'Arc de Triomphe and, after winning that race for the second time in 1978, was syndicated for $7.2 million, also for stud in Kentucky.

Robinson's purchasing policy was domestic and had limited aims; Sangster's was international and reached for the sky. Sangster's bloodstock operations also had a dimension which was absent from those of Robinson, which was that he was a breeder on the widest international scale with studs or breeding interests in England, Ireland, France, the United States and Australia. The extent of this international network gave immense flexibility to his investment in thoroughbreds. Sangster himself summed up his bloodstock philosophy in an interview with David Hadert published in *Pacemaker International* in 1977:

Horseflesh is an international currency. It's an asset you can always shift. Unlike having property in England, say, that you can't move. You can shift a horse. If you have the Derby winner you will get bids from America, Australia, Japan . . . It's a very international commodity.

Inevitably the progress of Sangster's venture was watched intently by all eyes in the world of the thoroughbred. Some of the glances were envious, and not all were approving. In the same interview he stated that he was looking for a super stallion, 'not the glory of ownership or winning'. He was expressing a spirit of unrepentant commercialism alien to many of the cherished traditions of the Turf. Although the Arabs often outbid Sangster at the main yearling sales in the 1980s and were active in international racing – Sheikh Mohammed won the Breeders Cup Turf with Pebbles in 1985 – they showed a greater willingness to adhere to those traditions, for their best racehorses were used for the improvement of their own bloodstock at their private studs rather than for direct commercial exploitation. John Hay Whitney, at one time United States Ambassador in Great Britain and an ardent supporter of racing in both countries, had made an eloquent plea for maintaining a balance between the sporting and the commercial aspects of racing in his speech at the annual testimonial dinner of the Thoroughbred Club of America in October 1963, when he said: 'Uncontrolled commercialism can be our enemy. Controlled, it can be our friend.' He argued that the necessary control could be imposed only if all concerned in racing, whether punters, pundits or promotors, learned to appreciate the thoroughbred 'not merely as a gambling device that happens to breathe, but as a horse – a creature of blood and heart and spirit'.

The thoroughbred is indeed a creature of blood and heart and spirit and has proved itself capable, over and over again, of throwing the rules of investment analysis out of the window and turning rational profit projections on their heads. It is necessary only to look at the result of the Prix de l'Arc de Triomphe in 1969, when the first three horses Levmoss (by Le Levanstell), Park Top (by Kalydon) and Grandier (by Tapioca) were all by cheap and unfashionable stallions: or at the Derbys of 1974 and 1975, when the winners Snow Knight and Grundy were by the unfashionable stallions Firestreak and the Great Nephew; or at the Kentucky Derbys of 1976 and 1977, when the winners Bold Forbes and Seattle Slew had been cheaply bought as yearlings at public auction – in order to be convinced of the truth of this assertion.

The thoroughbred itself, with its built-in genetic resistance to total conformity, is the strongest defence against the worst excesses of commercialism. And it is in the United States, where commercialism has taken the longest strides, that the thoroughbred as an animal of unique qualities finds its most devoted advocates. The distinguished American breeder Leslie Combs II expressed the Thoroughbred's distinctive charm in these words at the annual awards banquet of the Agriservices Foundation in 1969:

In this modern day of the jet engine and the paved street, the horse remains with us as a reminder of the graceful and leisurely life from which this country has sprung. Our roots are in the soil, but our hearts and sporting instincts are lifted by the magnificent animal whose utilitarian aspects have passed, but whose beauty and grace remain.

The Thoroughbred in a beautiful and a graceful animal, but his appeal would be limited if he had nothing more than grace and beauty to offer. And if he were to be regarded purely as a gambling counter, he would surely be superseded in a very short space of time by a more efficient, less expensive and less accident-prone counter. The peculiar characteristics of the thoroughbred that have given him a claim to the affections of all classes in nearly fifty countries were expressed most strikingly by no less an authority than Admiral Rous, who wrote in *The Laws and Practice of Horse Racing*:

There are horses which run best apparently lusty, and others are only up to the mark when they carry no flesh, and with very slight muscular developments. There are very few horses which require the same work, the same food, or the same physic. Thickwinded horses with strong constitutions may be sweated every five days during their preparation, and will take three times as much work as some delicate mares and geldings, of which there are many which never want a sweat. One horse cannot gallop when the ground is deep; another, with thin feat, cannot move if the ground is hard; and a heavy fall of rain will often upset scientific calculations. Mares seldom run in their best form before the month of August and geldings are considered to be best in the spring. Taking, therefore, into consideration the differences of opinion respecting individual condition, the effect of weight on the comparative qualifications of the horses engaged, the possible indisposition of some of them, the unequal merits of the jockeys, and the uncertain state of the ground, it is not to be wondered at that some races resolve themselves into problems difficult of solution; and this constitutes the greatest interest in racing, or what is called 'the glorious uncertainty of the Turf'.

The time-honoured truism, that horses are not machines, could hardly be improved upon. The Thoroughbred lives, and will always live in a world of mechanical precision, by his unparalleled combination of beauty, unpredictability and infinite variety.

Glossary

Arabian: Breed of horse raised originally in Arabia and adjacent countries and noted for its beauty, intelligence and graceful movements.

Barb: Breed of horse raised originally in Barbary (Algeria and Morocco).

Bay: Hair colour varying from dull red approaching brown to a yellowish colour approaching chesnut, but distinguishable from chesnut by the fact that a bay horse has a black mane and tail and usually black on the limbs. A horse of this colour.

Broodmare: Female horse used for breeding.

Chesnut: Hair colour of reddish yellow (golden chesnut) or brownish yellow (liver chesnut). Chesnut horses have chesnut and sometimes flaxen manes and tails. A horse of this colour.

Claiming Race: A Claiming Race is a race in which every horse running may be claimed for a sum as prescribed in the conditions of the race.

Colt: A male horse up to four years of age.

Cover: (of stallions). To mate with a mare.

Dam: Female parent of a horse.

Distance: The length of a race; a point 240 yards from the finish of a race (see Heat Race).

Filly: A female horse up to four years of age.

Foal: A horse, colt or filly, in the first year of life; (of mares) to give birth.

Furlong: A unit of distance used in horse racing, equivalent to 220 yards or ⅛ mile or about 200 metres.

Gaskin: Part of the hind leg of a horse, between the stifle and the hock.

Gelding: Castrated male horse.

General Stud Book: The genealogical record of racehorses in Great Britain and Ireland.

Graded Stakes Race: See Pattern Race.

Hand: Linear measure equal to 4 inches, used in determining the height of a horse. Equivalent to 0.1016 metre.

Handicap: A race in which the weights to be carried by the horses are adjusted by an official (the handicapper) for the purpose of equalizing their chances of winning.

Handicapper: An official who makes handicaps; a horse that runs habitually in handicaps.

Heat Race: A race run in parts, or heats. A horse beaten by a distance (240 yards or 219 metres) in a heat was eliminated from later heats. Many

268

early races, particularly in the seventeenth and eighteenth centuries, were run in three heats.

Inbreeding: The mating of closely related individuals (see Outcrossing).

Klebsiella: An equine venereal disease.

Length: The measure from end to end of a horse used as a unit of distance in racing.

Mare: Female horse above the age of four.

Match: A race between two horses, the property of different owners, on terms agreed by them, with no prize added.

Navicular: A small boat-shaped bone in the foot of a horse.

Navicular Disease: Chronic inflammation of the navicular bone causing lameness.

Outcrossing: The mating of less closely related individuals, or unrelated individuals (see Inbreeding). An outcross means a union of this kind, or one of the partners in a union of this kind.

Pattern Race: One of a series of races designated for the purpose of testing the best horses. Also called Graded Stakes races in many countries.

Plate: A race in which a prize of definite value is guaranteed by the race organizer with the entry fees going to the organizer.

Pound: Unit of weight carried by horses in Britain, Ireland and North America. Equivalent to 0.45359 kilograms.

Quarter Horse: A breed of horse developed in the USA for racing over ¼ mile (400 metres).

Roan: A horse with coat of chestnut or bay colour sprinkled with white or grey hairs.

Roarer: A horse affected in the larynx causing it to make a loud noise when galloping.

Selling Plater: A horse running habitually in selling races; often abbreviated as 'Plater'.

Selling Race: A race in which the winner must be offered for sale by auction immediately after the race.

Sire: Male parent of a horse; (of stallions) to beget.

Stakes: Abbreviated form of sweepstakes; also the value of a race or the accumulated value of a number of races.

Stall: Partition between competing horses at the starting line, with gates to each stall which open simultaneously, thus allowing a fair start.

Stallion: Male horse used for breeding.

Stone: Unit of weight, equivalent to 14 lb (6.25 kilos).

Strangles: Acute contagious fever of horses, caused by *streptococcus equi*, and characterized by catarrhal inflammation of the mucous membranes of the nasal passages.

Sweepstakes: A race in which the entry fees are added to the prize money; the sum so added to the prize money.

Tap-root: A mare from which one or more enduring strains have sprung.

Turf: The surface of land matted with the roots of grass on which all flat races and steeplechases in Europe are run.

Turf (The): Racecourses considered collectively; the whole system of racecourses and racing institutions.

Yearling: A colt, filly or gelding between one and two years of age.

Index